Fragile States and the Crisis of Regionalism in West Africa

Gbara Awanen

Publisher: The New Gong, Lagos, Nigeria

DEDICATION

I dedicate this work to Janet, my dear wife, and Tonte, Dumdisi, and Dornubari for sharing this journey with me.

ACKNOWLEDGEMENTS

This book is the offshoot of an academic study while on diplomatic posting in Geneva, Switzerland, from 2007 to 2011. When this study began in the winter of 2007, like every exploratory journey, it was driven by hope; hope to learn, to discover and, hopefully, to understand. While I can now testify that the learning process was profoundly liberating, I am reluctant to lay claim to any startling discovery. Because learning can challenge deeply held beliefs and assumptions, it can be incredibly humbling. Such has been my experience on this journey.

This has not been a solitary journey. I therefore must express my deepest appreciation to Dr. Martin I. Uhomoibhi, formerly Permanent Secretary of the Ministry of Foreign Affairs, Abuja, Nigeria and, before that, Ambassador of Nigeria to Switzerland and Permanent Representative of Nigeria to the United Nations Office in Geneva, for supporting me when it mattered most. Thank you, sir, for the empathy and encouragement, and for being a mentor, brother and friend.

I am equally grateful to my friends and colleagues Mrs. Iyabo Niniola, Miss Mariate Umaru, and Gabriel Teso for their excellent work on the manuscript. I owe you all a debt of gratitude. I also must thank Professor Alexandre Lambert, my doctoral dissertation supervisor at the Geneva School of Diplomacy and International Relations, for his helpful comments and conceptual clarity, which benefited this study tremendously. The errors in this book, in whatever form or shape, are entirely mine.

Finally, to my dear wife, Janet, and our lovely children Tonte, Dumdisi and Dornubari, I remain eternally grateful for the support and encouragement and for enduring, without losing hope, all the hardships and deprivations. In a way, this was a family journey, with all five of us pulling in one direction. I am lucky and immensely proud to belong to this family.

CONTENTS

List of Acronyms

AFRICOM	United States African Command
AOPIG	African Oil Policy Initiative Group
APC	All People's Congress of Sierra Leone
APRM	African Peer Review Mechanism
AU	African Union
CAP	European Common Agricultural Policy
CEAO	Commuaute Economigue de l' Afrique de L'Ouest
CFA	Commuaute Financiere Africaine
ECA	Economic Commission for Africa
EEC	European Economic Community
ECOMOG	ECOWAS Cease-Fire Monitoring Group
ECPF	ECOWAS Conflict Prevention Framework
ECSC	European Coal and Steel Community
EU	European Union
ECOWAS	Economic Community of West African States
ESS	European Security Strategy
LDC	Least Developed Countries
MDGs	Millennium Development Goals
NATO	North Atlantic Treaty Organization
NEPAD	New Partnership for Africa's Development
NPFL	National Patriotic Front of Liberia
OAU	Organization of African Unity
OECD	Organization of Economic Cooperation and Development
PAIGC	Partido Africano da Independence da Guinea Cabo Verde
RUF	Revolutionary United Front of Sierra Leone
SAP	Structural Adjustment Programme
SLPP	Sierra Leone People's Party
TNC	Transnational Corporation

UEMOA	Union Monetaire Ouest Africaine
UNDP	United Nations Development Programme
UN	United Nations
WAEMU	West African Economic and Monetary Union
WAUA	West African Unit of Accounts

PREFACE

When ECOWAS was created in 1975, its overarching ambition was to be the vehicle for the economic integration of West Africa. Nearly five decades on, that ambitious goal remains work-in-progress, in part because of internal strife and civil wars in some member states, notably Liberia and Sierra Leone, beginning in the late 1970s and onwards. Conflicts of varying complexities in several other countries at about the same period also distracted political leaders of the region and, inevitably, slowed down the process of regional integration.

Even as integration stalled, regionalism was being boosted by the very forces responsible for the slow pace of economic integration. Challenged by widespread insecurity across the region in its first decade of existence, ECOWAS quickly adapted and soon transformed into a regional security provider. This evolution is intuitive, since the essential work of regional economic integration can only commence in a stable security environment. However, if the strategic goal had been to remake West Africa into a security community, by which we mean a group of stable and peaceful states among which war and internal civil insurrection have become inconceivable, that has not happened, in part because countries of the region are too poor, too weak, and too dependent on outside powers and interests as to be able to shape a distinct and locally-owned regional agenda, including the capacity to deliver cooperative security and development outcomes.

The national context in which the regional integration project is taking place in West Africa also presents a major challenge, not least because governance at the national level can generate positive or negative impacts within national and regional spaces. Because state infirmities can undermine security, obstruct development, and imperil economic integration, it is a legitimate enquiry to examine the "state of health" of individual ECOWAS Member States and their capacities to contribute effectively to the regional integration project.

Across West Africa, flawed colonial legacies and poor governance continue to create significant social cleavages, poor economic performance, insecurity and instability. The political and cultural antagonisms caused by poor governance also endanger inclusive economic development and the Treaty goal of regional economic integration. Furthermore, the governance deficit at the national level creates political and cultural incoherence among regional elites who drive the regional integration project. Consequently, the challenge of national integration may be as compelling and urgent as the regional integration project itself.

Against this backdrop, it is looking increasingly conceivable that a major challenge for West Africa may be how to create an integrated region from states, some of which have attained advanced levels of disintegration. Overcoming this daunting challenge necessarily calls for swapping West Africa's largely poor, weak, and dysfunctional states with democratic, efficient, and developmental states capable of turning the region's vicious cycle of poverty and conflict into a virtuous cycle of security and development. Regionalism may be deployed as a vehicle for this process of political and social engineering, but regionalism can play a facilitating role only when West African states are themselves fully integrated, democratic, and efficiently and equitably administered.

Among other objectives, this book seeks to evaluate the economic (developmental) and security dimensions of regional integration or regionalism in West Africa. The principal aim is to understand the dynamic evolution of ECOWAS from being a purely economic integration scheme at its formation to an increasingly robust regional collective security provider. Some of the questions worthy of careful study include whether ECOWAS increasing preoccupation with security matters reflects a fundamental shift in priorities, or whether this evolution is merely a pragmatic rebalancing act in aid of the Organization's overarching Treaty goal of economic integration.

This book is divided into six sections. Chapter One reviews the political and theoretical foundations of West Africa's integration, a project that is arguably driven by powerful sentiments and desire for Africa unity as a basis for continental renaissance. Chapter Two provides an overview of the integration process in West Africa, the politics of the creation of ECOWAS, as well as significant challenges associated with the economic integration process in the region.

An attempt is made in Chapter Three to explore the Security-Development Nexus and its relevance in the context of West Africa's integration experience. This approach reflects the logic of the West African socio political environment, where poverty and insecurity are mutually reinforcing, requiring that policy makers strike the right balance between security and development in order to achieve economic progress and social stability. This section also examines the historical foundation of democratic governance in West Africa, the aim being to understand the historical origins of much of the region's modern day governance pathologies.

In Chapter Four, we examine the geopolitics of the West Africa's strategic environment, the aim being to highlight the forces shaping political and economic outcomes in the region. This theme is expanded in Chapter Five to cover the vexatious question of security governance in West Africa. In addition to a review of the region's security challenges, this chapter also provides a case study of legacy conflicts in five ECOWAS Member States, from the late 1970s onwards, all of which have impacted, in various degrees, on the trajectory of the regional integration process. The objective is not only to understand the forces that ignited those conflicts, but also to illustrate their essential similarities to current crises in several ECOWAS Member States. The Concluding Chapter assesses the future of the integration process in West Africa against the backdrop of a growing number of states struggling against forces of disintegration and instability, a dangerous conundrum inimical to the regional integration project.

Dr. Gbara Awanen, mni
Abuja, Nigeria.
November 3, 2020.

Chapter One

THEORETICAL AND POLITICAL IMPERATIVES OF INTEGRATION IN WEST AFRICA

Integration as a Model for African Unity

The importance of regional integration as a means for accelerating economic and social development of African countries has long been recognized across the continent. Indeed, the unity, cooperation and integration of Africa were the primary motivations of the early African nationalists and post-independence leaders, all of whom saw political independence as a springboard to the unity and economic emancipation of the continent. Integration is, therefore, rooted in Africa's contemporary history, even if the original aim had been to forge unity and gain greater political clout and voice in the international arena.

For instance, even before the challenge of globalization and economic interdependence made integration compelling for developing economies, African leaders had established the Organization of African Unity (OAU), now defunct, "to coordinate and intensify cooperation and efforts to achieve a better life for the people of Africa."[1] In what may well be Africa's first formal acknowledgement of an intrinsic link between security and development, the OAU had, in the preamble to its Charter, expressed a conviction that in order to translate its goals of unity, solidarity and progress of the African continent and its peoples, conditions for peace and security must be established and maintained across the continent.[2]

Even before the euphoria that necessarily accompanied the achievement of political independence across Africa in the early 1960s had faded, it was recognised that for the newly independent nations to fully and effectively address the challenges of nationhood, they would have to forge deeper cooperation among themselves, in particular through the integration of national economies. Among the new political elites, it was widely accepted that regional integration could play a crucial role in launching development and economic growth, and also in improving the living conditions of citizens who had just emerged from the exploitation and deprivations of colonial rule. In short, economic integration was seen as a mechanism through which citizens of the newly independent nations of Africa could enjoy the benefits of political independence. This expectation was captured in the popular homily by nationalist leaders for colonized Africans to seek first the political kingdom and every other thing, including improved living conditions, would accrue as bonus.[3]

While the political logic of integration was substantially sound, the economic arguments were equally irresistible. From the economic perspective, the advantages derived from regional complementarity of goods and services, economies of scale, comparative advantage and the promise of industrialization made integration particularly attractive as a strategy for development among African countries. In general, economic integration in West Africa has been pursued for at least two reasons. The first was to foster economic growth and development, while the second was to enhance political unity at the regional level.

In both cases, the overarching motivation was to address the region's structural and institutional pathologies, including the disruptive legacies of colonialism. Colonialism, for instance, not only fragmented West African States into small and economically unviable entities, it also polarized the region in no small way, as epitomized in the lingering Francophone- Anglophone dissonance. The predatory nature of colonial rule, which pitted the state against citizens, has also reproduced itself in the philosophy of governance by which political elites appropriate the institutions and resources of the state for private use.

The theoretical argument suggests that reducing barriers to intra-African trade will create larger regional markets, promote economies of scale and sustain efficient production systems and markets, as well as enhance Africa's competiveness.[5] In other words, regional and sub-regional integration constitute the principal mechanism for restructuring the fragmented African continent into more coherent and stronger regional economic entities. On the whole, regional economic schemes across Africa have yet to deliver sustainable economic growth and prosperity to citizens. After decades of regional integration arrangements, intraregional trade as a proportion of total
trade remains much lower in African regional integration schemes in comparison with other regions of the world.[6] Some of the reasons that have been suggested for the slow

pace of integration in Africa relate to initial conditions, the problem of implementation, and basic design deficiency.[7] Initial conditions relate, for instance, to the absence of complementarities in goods and factors of production among regional partners.

Without exception, all the regional integration arrangements in Africa were established without strong private sector involvement. Many of the schemes also lack viable mechanisms for redistributing benefits from the net gainers to the more disadvantaged partners. Poor implementation of agreements and other membership obligations also stands out as a common feature of regional integration schemes across Africa. In addition to over-ambitious agendas, overlapping memberships and mandates, there remains formidable economic and institutional challenges hindering the prospects of successful integration in Africa. The economic obstacles include the high dependence of most African countries on export of primary commodities and poor quality of infrastructure. Institutional challenges include bureaucratic and administrative hindrances, such as prohibitive road charges, transit fees and administrative delays at borders and ports. These hindrances raise transport costs and constitute disincentives to intraregional trade.

Other challenges relate to the lack of coordination and harmonization of policies and regulations at the regional level8 despite these challenges, the imperative for regional integration are stronger now than ever before, given the multiple socio-economic and political impacts of globalization on African countries. While Africa may not yet be at the epicentre of the global economy, globalization has integrated markets elsewhere and made movements of factors of production easier. These developments continue to have profound economic, political and social implications on the African continent.

Although the development bias of ECOWAS is well captured in its Treaty, it is quite obvious that the framers of the Treaty also sought to promote unity among Member States of the Organization. For instance, Article 3 of the Treaty, which declares the principal aims of the Organization as being to "promote cooperation and integration," also includes the related objective of seeking to "foster relations among Member States and contribute to the progress and development of the African continent."9 One way ECOWAS has sought to promote unity and foster relations among its members is, of course, through the integration process of linking national economies and the harmonization of economic and fiscal policies among countries of the region. There has also been a gradual movement towards political convergence, as reflected in the Organization's increasing emphasis on democratic governance in Member States. In practice, ECOWAS has demonstrated its zero-tolerance for unconstitutional change of government by applying a variety of sanctions, including suspension of the offending state from participating in its activities. Mali, whose elected leaders were forcefully removed from office following a mutiny by the military in August 2020, is the latest example of ECOWAS's zero-tolerance for unconstitutional change of government in Member States.

Some of the states that had been so sanctioned included Mauritania, Niger and Guinea Conakry, all of which suffered democratic reverses in the past decades. Mauritania elected to withdraw from the Organization rather than comply with its directives on the restoration of constitutional order. In the latest case of Cote d'Ivoire, where two candidates in a run-off election had both claimed the presidency, ECOWAS even went a step further by recognizing Alassane Quattara, then opposition candidate, who was adjudged duly elected by the country's election commission. In a bold and unprecedented move, the Organization had called on the incumbent President, Laurent Gbagbo, who had tried to use the power of incumbency to steal the vote, to hand over power to the opposition candidate or face military action.

To be sure, while success in the area of political convergence and common values is mixed, the Organization's record in conflict prevention and resolution has been impressive. Functionalists like David Mitrany have argued that the provision of common needs through functional strategies across national borders could potentially create an identity of common citizenship. In West Africa's recent tragic history, conflict prevention and resolution, and poverty eradication – a core objective of ECOWAS – are common needs to all countries of the region. As we would argue in subsequent sections of this study, conflict and poverty generate regional externalities that affect all countries of the region. This is why integration is particularly relevant to West Africa, not least because it could facilitate the provision of common needs, or what some have referred to as regional public goods. Additionally, integration could help create what David Mitrany has referred to as "identity of common citizenship," a traditional objective of all integration schemes but one which countries of West Africa need badly to overcome colonially imposed divisions.

Bjorn Hettne has suggested that in the contemporary world of globalization, the political ambition of creating territorial identity, political convergence, collective security and regional coherence are the primary goals of regional integration schemes.[11] Hettne calls this phenomenon 'new regionalism,' to differentiate it from the 'old regionalism', which focussed exclusively on economic integration. The new regionalism which Hettne speaks about goes well beyond notions of free trade and market integration, that is, the linking of several national markets into one functional economic unit. By new regionalism, Hettne means a process of regional integration comprising economic, political, security, social and cultural aspects of life. All of these issues have lately dominated ECOWAS's integration agenda in West Africa. While this study adopts Hettne's definition of regionalism, it is concerned only with the security and economic (developmental) dimensions of regionalism in West Africa.

Integration as a Strategy for Regional Security and Development

European integration in the post war period provides one of the few successful examples of the merging of security and development in the context of regionalism. According to David J. Francis, the primary motivation of European integration was to prevent inter-state wars on a continent that had fought two destructive wars in one generation, create a conducive environment for regional peace and security, and build cooperation and communication among the states and communities in ways that would promote interdependence.[12] The difficult transition from post war recovery to development, including the need to address Europe's perennial security problems were therefore instrumental to the creation of the European Coal and Steel Community (ECSC) in 1951, and the European Economic Community (EEC) in 1957. These bodies were constructed on the principle that regionalinterdependence could promote collective security and therefore spare Europe from the prospects of another war.

Since then, the EEC has evolved into the 27 member European Union (EU), with a common "European Community identity", such supranational institutions like the European Commission, Parliament, the European Court of Justice, and a common currency, the "Euro". The established EU governmental structures, including the governing principles of inter-governmental relations, are based on the notions of liberal economics and democratic politics.[13]

In an effort to respond to diverse regional challenges, the EU has implemented constructive development and security programmes, including but not limited to the European Common Agricultural Policy (CAP), a common market with a customs union, free movement of persons and factors of production, a common foreign and defence policy. All these common policies and programmes have led to the intensification of economic, social, political and security interdependence. In the security sphere, for instance, the success of European policies on regime and security convergence has led to political stability and democratic governance in former military and authoritarian states as Greece, Spain and Portugal, including the new member states from Eastern Europe. Even more importantly, traditional "enemies" like France and Germany are now firmly locked into a robust and beneficial partnership involving economic, political and security relations.[14]

While the success of the EU integration model might have served as an incentive to the various integration schemes in the developing world, the European experience has limited applicability to regional economic integration in a developing area as West Africa. Amitai Etzioni has argued that "limited horizons, lack of administrative and political skills, and preoccupation with problems of domestic modernization all present major barriers to successful integration efforts in the developing world."[15] In the West African experience, there are the additional challenges of poor physical infrastructures, and the persistence of colonial ties and external dependencies, amongst others.

Furthermore, because European nations started integration from a relatively strong industrial base, they could well afford to treat their economic integration project as a matter of welfare politics. On the contrary, the situation is the exact opposite in the developing regions like West Africa where, as Joseph Nye has pointed out, integration seems to produce not gradual politicization, but over-politicization. Such premature politicization of economic issues, Nye has warned, could greatly reduce the scope for bureaucratic initiatives and quietly arranged packaged deals.[16]

Just as the so-called requisite conditions for successful economic integration in the developed countries may not necessarily apply to developing countries facing different challenges, the criteria for judging the success or failure of an integration process cannot be applied uniformly to efforts in both developed and developing areas, the simple reason being that the integration processes in the two cases are different.[17] The two processes are different because, whereas in the former the overarching objective is to enhance economic growth through trade and increased competition, in the latter, integration is intended to serve primarily as a means of accelerating economic development. In other words, for developing countries, integration is approached as a strategy for development.

Linking the phenomenon of economic integration to development has become crucially important to developing countries, such that S. B. K. Asante, the Ghanaian integration theorist, would rather use the term "developmental regionalism" in place of economic integration because, as he contends, the latter is imprecise, static and irrelevant to the developmental objectives of the developing countries.[18] Regardless of the terminology used, there can be no doubt that, for the developing world, the process of regional economic integration, or regionalism, is now inextricably linked to development.

On the other hand, linking economic integration to security is relatively new, a development that became more urgent following the end of the Cold War and the implosion of intra and inter-state conflicts across much of Africa and also in the Balkans. The evolution of ECOWAS from being a vehicle for the economic transformation of West Africa to a regional security provider over the course of the last two decades represents this paradigm shift. In response to West Africa's security and governance challenges, ECOWAS has elaborated an impressive array of protocols and mechanisms in the area of conflict prevention and resolution, including on the issue of democratic governance. Some of these include the ECOWAS Mechanism for Conflict Prevention, Management, Resolution, Peacekeeping and Security; the ECOWAS Conflict Prevention Framework; and the Protocol Relating to the

Mechanism for Conflict Prevention, Management, Resolution, Peacekeeping and Security. Others are the ECOWAS Convention on Small Arms and Light Weapons and Their Ammunition, and the Protocol on Democracy and Good Governance, among others.

Over the last two decades, ECOWAS has not only established one of the best known regional security mechanisms in Africa, but has been largely effective in regional peacekeeping. For instance, through the instrumentality of the ECOWAS Ceasefire Monitoring Group (ECOMOG), the regional organization successfully intervened in the brutal wars in Liberia and Sierra Leone from the late 1980s to early 2000. Regional actors also took the lead in efforts to manage conflicts in Guinea Bissau and Cape Verde during the same period. Partly on account of its success in regional peace keeping, but also because of its efforts to create a regional normative framework on conflict prevention and resolution, including democratic governance and good governance of the security sector, ECOWAS has rightly acquired the reputation as the most ambitious attempt yet to link peace, security and development in Africa.

Yet, when ECOWAS was created in 1975, its ambitions were modest, and these were limited to the economic integration of countries in the West African region. A central concern of this study is to understand why an organization that was created specifically to integrate the economies of its member states would increasingly focus on security issues, even as its core objectives remain largely unfulfilled. It is quite revealing that in the midst of an underwhelming performance in its core objective of economic integration, ECOWAS is redirecting its priorities away from being a vehicle for the economic transformation of West Africa into a regional security provider.

There is little doubt ECOWAS's functional evolution might have been propelled by the violence and turmoil which swept across the sub-region from the late 1980s through the early 2000s and beyond. For instance, beginning from the late 1980s, Liberia, Sierra Leone, Guinea Conakry, Cote d'Ivoire, Guinea Bissau and Senegal were embroiled in an interconnected web of conflicts and wars which led to massive movements of armed insurgents and refugees across national borders. Nigeria, Mali and Niger were also plagued by internal conflicts of varying intensities which have weakened the capacities of these countries to provide security to their citizens.[19] In the same period, democratic efforts suffered setbacks in Burkina Faso, the Gambia, Guinea and Togo. Indeed, Adekeye Adebajo has assessed the West African sub-region as the most coup-prone in Africa, with more than half of the successful military coups in Africa since the 1960 (forty-one of seventy-five) having occurred in West Africa, a sub-region comprising less than a third of the continent's states.[20]

Another plausible explanation to account for ECOWAS strategic re-direction into security matters may well be the recognition by political leaders in the region that the organization's core mandate, namely the economic transformation of the sub-region, may be difficult to achieve so long as the sub-region continues to be ravaged by violent conflicts. By paying attention to the burgeoning security challenges that have afflicted countries across the region, West African leaders have demonstrated a profound sensitivity to new thinking linking development with security.

Against the backdrop of evidence suggesting that poverty, poor governance and conflict feed each other and may be at the root of much of Africa's recent conflicts, creating a zone of peace to allow for sustainable development is a legitimate endeavour for a regional organization like ECOWAS. Such a goal is also consistent with neo-functional integration theory which perceives regional integration as a peace builder. According to this school, the motivation for forming regional bodies is simple: neighbours are better off if they are friendly and do not fight wars.[21] In this kind of relationship, diplomacy, economic and cultural exchanges, or soft power, rather than military or coercive power, are the currency of interactions.

Overall, organizations like ECOWAS should have an interest in the prevention and mitigation of conflicts because of their disastrous humanitarian and developmental effects on an entire region. The externalization of conflicts in West Africa, in which arms, fighters and refugees spill easily across national borders, means that a regional approach to conflict prevention and resolution, rather than individual national responses, holds the best prospect for success. Partly because of the externalities associated with conflicts in West Africa, but also because these conflicts generate huge costs in terms of missed development opportunities, organizations like ECOWAS are obliged to integrate conflict prevention and mitigation into their policy agendas. It also means that issues like governance must be scaled up on the regional agenda, since there is a high development price to be paid for poor governance. What emerges from the new thinking merging development with security is that, in addition to its traditional tasks of generating economic growth and prosperity, development is now being charged with the responsibility for enhancing security in society.

At the same time as development was being "securitized", the notion of security was also undergoing changes, resulting in particular in a broadening of the concept to include referents other than states.[22] Applying the notion of human security, for instance, security has been "developmentalized" in the sense that the absence of a number of basic human needs, such as food, shelter and health and housing could jeopardise security of the state. Unlike the traditional notion of national security, the human security agenda focuses on the safety and well-being of citizens, rather than states, and on a concept of sovereignty that is conditioned by the state's respect for the rights of citizens.[23]

The unmistakable link between Africa's insecurity and development challenges was aptly summed up by Robert McNamara, a former World Bank President and US Secretary of Defence in the administration of John F. Kennedy. According to McNamara, "In a modernizing society, security means development. Security is not military hardware, though it may include it, security is not traditional military activity, though it may encompass it. Security is development, and without development, there can be no security." [24]

What is particularly revealing about the McNamara perspective of security is not only that it was proposed by a former US Secretary of Defence, but precisely because it frames underdevelopment as the greatest threat to state or national security, a threat against which guns are impotent. Framing underdevelopment as the greatest threat to national security, as McNamara has done, presents difficult policy choices for ECOWAS. It is therefore a legitimate question of interest to this study to seek to understand why, in the midst of growing poverty and economic regression of West African states, the regional vehicle for the economic transformation of the region is increasingly being deployed in the service of regional security. Does this shift in focus represent a shift in priority? If so, is this an indication that it is more profitable to send in armies and security personnel to quell riots, undertake peacekeeping and impose order, rather than concentrate on tackling root causes of conflict, such as endemic poverty, poor governance and economic and political marginalization of sections of society? For a region steeped in poverty, what should be the right balance in the pursuit of economic development and security?

A characteristic feature of West Africa's security environment is that most countries of the region have been involved or are involved in an "interconnected web of conflicts that have seen refugees, rebels, and arms spill across porous borders."[25] An important question we seek to unravel is whether there is a significant and demonstrable link between pervasive poverty in West

Africa and the region's various insecurities, such as violent conflicts, civil wars, drug, and armed trafficking. A related concern of this study is to enquire whether ECOWAS's rather robust foray into security matters has transformed West Africa into a security community. Given the extensiveness of ECOWAS Security and governance mechanisms, including practical successes in the area of regional peacekeeping, could it be said that the West African sub-region is tending towards a security community?

In the late 1950s, Karl Deutsch and his colleagues had explored the concept of security communities and found a nascent security community in the North Atlantic Area.[26]

Empirically, Deutsch and his colleagues were analysing the Western European developments after the Second World War. Such a community was one in which the component states had come to reject the use or threat of use of force as a mechanism for resolving disputes. In contemporary international relations, the European Union and United States-Canada relations are two of such political arrangements.

What is relevant to this study is that Deutsch and his colleagues had argued that economic and cultural cooperation was a far better route toward the formation of such a community than was common membership in a traditional military alliance, such as the North Atlantic Treaty Organization (NATO), arguably the best known and most effective security community in the World. Thus, on the economic and cultural score card alone, ECOWAS integration model would appear as a necessary building block for the organization to progress toward a security community.

A security community was defined as a group of people who had become integrated – that is, a group which had achieved a sense of community and of institutions and practices strong enough and sufficiently widespread to convince people that necessary social, economic, and political changes could be brought about peacefully. According to Deutsch, a security community is one "where there is a real reassurance that the members of the community will not fight each other physically, but will settle their disputes in some other way.[27]

Deutsch and his colleagues sought to identify the factors that helped particular groups of countries to move toward the status of pluralistic security communities. Pluralistic security communities are those where the various states or sovereignties retain their independence and political autonomy, but voluntarily cooperate and behave toward each other in a manner that precludes the resort to war as a means of resolving conflicts. The first of these factors was pluralism itself, which was described as a policy that "concentrates upon increasing the machinery and traditions of mutual consultation, communication and cooperation.[28]

In promoting integration, it was considered essential that there be a stress on pluralism and the preservation of national sovereignty, including emphasis on domestic priorities in each country, because ordinary citizens would measure the success of integration in relation to achieving domestic objectives. In the context of the North Atlantic Area, for instance, Deutsch and his colleagues found that apart from the desire to remove the danger of war, what the citizens within the security community sought were political institutions, whether separate or common, that would provide them with a better quality of life in peacetime.[29] In the long term, security would have to be more than merely the absence of war. According to Deutch, the deligitimisation of war needed to be underpinned by domestic political changes, including political plurality. Values reflecting criteria of legitimacy, such as democratic governance, would be crucial in the evolution and development of community-wide standards and behaviour, helping to determine what was deemed acceptable behaviour and practices[30]

Another finding that was important, also in the context of European integration, was that military alliances appeared to be poor vehicles for promoting the development of security communities. While they may provide an effective shield behind which positive community-building processes could take place, they were not in themselves the fundamental institutional requirement. To be effective, military arrangements needed to be associated with non -military steps, which would provide the main dynamic in the security and community-building processes.[30]

Similarly, while the existence of external military threats could be helpful to the process of integration, it was found not to be absolutely essential. On the other hand, communication was seen as the crucial mechanism through which political communities were built, communication being a set of transaction flows that cumulatively built a social fabric.[31] For instance, communication allowed individuals and groups within the community to develop shared identity and values, and the "we" feeling that was the bedrock of a security community.

In general, the key factors Deutsch and his colleagues identified in a successful integration, also for building security communities, were a high correlation of values, which for Deutsch's North Atlantic Community, were democracy, the rule of law and social market economies.[32] The second factor was a growing level of mutual responsiveness among political communities or states, that is, among member states constituting the community. Finally, there was the requirement of the existence of a distinctive way of life characterized by growth of welfare, and governmental (states's) rejection of war as an instrument of policy. Fundamentally, therefore, it was the increasing unattractiveness and improbability of war that was seen as being essential to the development and consolidation of pluralistic security communities.[33]

With its increasing focus on security matters, could it be said that ECOWAS has evolved into a security community, or at least that it is tending in that direction? Unlike Karl Deutsch's North Atlantic community, the West African sub-region is too fragmented and too divided. The sub-region is also heavily dependent on external actors, both for its security and developmental needs. As well as being one of the poorest regions of the world, it is also one of the most unstable. Most countries of the region are faced with problems of an existential nature, such as identity politics, violent conflicts, and even problems of political succession. In other words, the sub region is still way far off from achieving convergence on basic political values. In several of the countries of the region, even the basic issue of citizenship remains hotly contested.

The legacies of colonialism have also fostered deep-seated cleavages among countries of West Africa, as epitomized in the Francophone-Anglophone divide. Perhaps of greater significance is the fact that one external actor – France – is the dominant regional security provider with elaborate security agreements with all Francophone Members States of ECOWAS. This has naturally fuelled fear and mistrust among the non-Francophone members of ECOWAS, notably, Nigeria, which is, arguably, the region's hegemon. To its credit, Nigeria spearheaded the formation of ECOWAS. By any objective standards of measurement, such as population, military power, economic strength, Nigeria is a natural leader of West Africa. While it has taken leading roles in security and stability operations in the sub-region on several occasions, as in Liberia and Sierra Leone, its potentials remain largely unfulfilled by its own internal contradictions. The countervailing pressures are not so much a function of outside forces as are the result of

Nigeria's internal pathologies – sectarian crises, corruption and mismanagement of national resources, amongst others.

Regardless of pejorative connotations associated with hegemony, ECOWAS needs a pivotal state to articulate the rules and norms for the region, and to drive and manage the integration process. For ECOWAS, such a state is Nigeria. However, despite its huge potentials Nigeria, as we have argued here, is bedevilled with significant internal problems of its own. Because hegemony is not just bullying dominance, a hegemon needs to set standards to convince others to follow its lead. Hegemony therefore involves leadership and influence, attributes of soft power that only a well-run state can project. Sadly, this has not been the case with West Africa's hegemon. If a country like Nigeria is badly run, how can ECOWAS hope to achieve the economic transformation of the region or spread the norms of good governance and democratic politics among Member States?

Given that weak states 'drive' the regionalism project in West Africa, could it be inferred that regionalism is doomed to fail in West Africa, since states of the sub-region involved in the integration project lack Deutsch's 'favourable' background conditions that nurtured the successful European integration experience? In view of the fact that ECOWAS's huge investment in regional security has yet to turn the region into an island of peace, critics have derided the organization's elaborate security and governance mechanisms as a sham. There have been suggestions that the whole security and governance mechanisms of the organization are like a mutual aid society, by which political leaderships in the various states of West Africa support one another in times of domestic turmoil in the expectation that the favour would be returned or redeemed in the future should the wheels of political misfortune turn in one's direction. In the case of West Africa, such political misfortune has included coups, rebel insurrection, and widespread violent public discontent.

There is, therefore, a sense in which it could be argued that subscription to these mechanisms and protocols represent a subtle warning to internal political forces that rebellion would invite the wrath of the collective might of all ECOWAS Member States. Such a threat of overwhelming force, of course, raises the cost of rebellion and, more importantly, guarantees the political survival of leaders, several of who are autocratic and unpopular in their own countries. However, given ECOWAS robust and principled response to recent crises of political succession in some member states, it may be premature to write off the organization's commitment to democracy and good governance. Ironically, ECOWAS Protocol on Good Governance and Democracy, either by design or default, reinforces the perception of ambivalence towards democracy in member states. Whereas this celebrated document brashly proclaims a zero-tolerance for unconstitutional change of government in Member States, it is notoriously silent on what might be the fate of incumbent governments that subvert democratic principles – the very condition that, in many cases, have precipitated violent and unconstitutional change of government across the sub region in the first place.[34] The pessimists could be right to infer that ECOWAS seeming ambivalence towards democratic governance in member states is to promote regime security at the expense of participatory democracy by community citizens.

Despite the shortcomings of ECOWAS's security and governance frameworks, their promotion at least implies the recognition that sustainable development in the region cannot be achieved in a climate of insecurity and instability. There is also a sense in which ECOWAS growing interest in democratic governance could be said to reflect a regional consensus that democratic governance constitutes, at least in principle if not in practice, an important element in the security- development nexus. As the EU success story does illustrate, viable, strong and modern states anchored on democratic principles are crucial to the success of security and developmental regionalism; indeed, to the success of the security-development nexus in the context of West Africa's integration process.

Notes

1.   African Union, Charter of OAU, available online at www.africa.union.org/root/au/Documents/Treaties/text /OAU_Charter 1963.pdf.

2.   Ibid.

3.   Anecdote generally attributed to Kwame Nkrumah, Ghana's first post-independence President and leading proponent of Pan Africanism. Pan-Africanism provides the organising ideology underpinning the notions of African unity and integration. Although Pan Africanism predated the independence movement across Africa, the idea was that the achievement of independence would be turned into the political project of uniting Africa and combining efforts to achieve economic prosperity for all Africans living on the continent.

4.   Olayode, Kehinde, "Reinventing the African State: Issues and Challenges for Building a Developmental State", Paper presented at the 11th General Assembly of the Council for the Development of Social Science in Africa, Maputo, Mozambique, 6 – 19 December, 2005.

5.   Asante, S. K. B. Regionalism and Africa's Development, Macmillan Press, London, 1977, P.26.

6.   Ibid.

7.   Gambari, Ibrahim, Political and Comparative Dimension of Regional Integration: The Case of ECOWAS, Humanities Press International, Inc. New Jersey, 1991, P.18.

8.   Ibid.

9.   ECOWAS, Treaty of ECOWAS, ECOWAS Commission, Abuja, Nigeria, 1993.

10.   David Mitrany, A Working Peace System, Quadrangle Books, Chicago, 1966, p.24.

11.	B. Hettne, "Introduction" in B. Hettne, and A. Inotai, eds; The New Regionalism: Implications for Global Development and International Security, UNU/WIDER, Helsinki, 1994, pp.4-6.

12.	David Francis, J. "Linking peace, Security and Developmental Regionalism. Regional Economic and Security Integration in Africa, "Journal of Peace-Building and Development, Vol.2, No. 3, 2006.

13.	Ibid.

14.	Ibid.

15.	Anitai Etzioni, Political Unification: A Comparative Study of Leaders and Forces, Oxford University Press, New York, 1964, pp.318-321.

16.	Joseph S. Nye, "Comparing Markets: A Revised Neo-Functionalist Model," International Organisation, Vol. 24, No. 4 (Autumn 1970), pp. 831-832.

17.	S.K.B. Asante, Regionalism and Africa's Development, Macmillan Press, London,1997, p.25.

18.	Ibid.

19.	Adekeye Adebajo, "Introduction", in Adekeye Adebajo, and Ismail Rashid, eds.; West Africa's Security Challenges: Building Peace in a Troubled Region, Lynne Rienner, Boulder, 2004, p.1.

20.	Ibid.

21.	See David Mitrany, A Working Peace System, 1966, p.26

22.	Lars Burr, Steffen Jensen, and Finn Stepputat, The Security-Development Nexus: Expressions of Sovereignty and Securitisation in Southern Africa, HSRC Press, Cape Town, South Africa, 2007, p.9.

23.	Ibid.

24.	Robert McNamara, "Security in the Contemporary World," Address to the American Society of Newspapers Editors, Montreal, Canada, 18 May 1968.

25.	See Adekeye Adebajo, "Introduction". P.1

26.	Karl Deutsch, et al, Political Community and the North Atlantic Area: International Organisation in the Light of Historical Experience, Princeton University Press, Princeton, N.J., 1968.

27.	Ibid.

28.	Ibid.

29.	Ibid.

30.	Ibid.

31.	Michael Sheehan, International Security: An Analytical Survey, Lynne Reiner, Boulder and London, 2005, p.30.

32.	Ibid.

33.	Ibid.

34.	Protocol A/SPI/12/01 on Democracy and Good Governance Supplementary to the Protocol relating to the Mechanism for Conflict Prevention, Management, Resolution, Peace-Keeping and Security, ECOWAS Executive Secretariat, Dakar, December, 2001.

Chapter Two

OVERVIEW OF THE INTEGRATION PROCESS IN WEST AFRICA

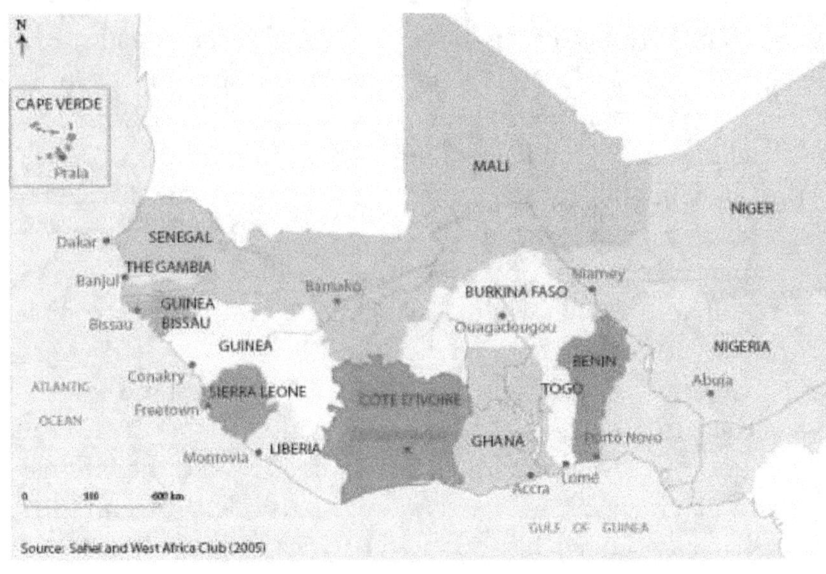

Source: Sahel and West Africa Club (2005)

ECOWAS member countries

West Africa: The Region

In geographical terms, West Africa comprises the sixteen (16) states pictured in Table I above. These states make up the westernmost region of West Africa. Whereas fifteen of these states are members of ECOWAS, the exception is Mauritania which, though a founding member of the organisation, elected to withdraw from the regional body in 2000, in reaction to its suspension by the regional organisation following a military take-over of government in the country. The region is composed of Francophone, Anglophone and Lusophone States. The organisation thus has the special feature of transcending the linguistic, political and cultural divisions bequeathed West Africa by its former colonial masters – Britain, France and Portugal.

The West African States of ECOWAS constitute a geographical area larger than Western Europe. It is the most heavily populated of all of Africa's sub-regions, with 236 million people, and a total gross domestic product (GDP) of US$82 billion in 2000. Per capita income for 2000 averaged an estimated US$322. Cape Verde, with a per capita income of US$1,300, was the "richest" ECOWAS country in 2000, while Sierra Leone, with a per capital income of US$132, was the poorest.[1]

The West African sub-region is the most diverse in Africa in terms of the size of countries, the degree of economic development, linguistic diversity and the internal and external links of its economies. As S.K.B. Asante, the Ghanaian scholar has noted, "if Africa as a whole is badly fragmented, West Africa must be the most fragmented sub-region in Africa.[2] West Africa not only represents the most heterogeneous conglomeration of states in Africa, it has the largest number of mini states, some with populations too small in size to be viable political entities. At the extreme is Nigeria – the region's giant with a population of 150 million people, while Cape Verde, with a population of 520,000 is the smallest. In general, only Nigeria, Ghana, Cote d'Ivoire have populations of more than 15 million people.

With a land area of 6,415,401 square kilometres and its large population, West Africa is an important world sub-region. It produces a wide range of commercial crops, including tropical oils, groundnuts and coffee. The region also produces over 60% of the world's cocoa. Other important income-earning activities include rubber, livestock and fishing. The region is also endowed with vast energy resources, such as coal, hydroelectricity and petroleum. Other mineral resources include high quality iron ore, bauxite, copper, tin, gold and manganese.[3]

Another important feature of West Africa's socioeconomic landscape is the artificiality of national borders. Again, Asante has argued that "if most of Africa's borders are artificial and arbitrary, West Africa's are absurd and capricious."[4] For Adebayo Adedeji, a leading Nigerian economist, the artificiality of West Africa's borders "constitutes the greatest obstacle to the achievement of more stable and dynamic statehood."[5]

Two other significant characteristics of West Africa are the sub-region's abysmally high levels of poverty and the generally low living standards of people of the region, arguably among the poorest in the world. For instance, in 2001, fourteen West African countries were ranked in the lowest category of the United Nations Development Programme's Human Development Index scale.[6] Only two of West Africa's states – Cape Verde and Ghana –
were ranked as middle income countries. Life expectancy at birth in the sub-region varies considerably, from 37.9 years in Sierra Leone to 69.4 in Cape Verde. Only in eight

of West Africa's countries is the average life expectancy above 50 years. Furthermore, of the 15 members of ECOWAS, three (Niger, Burkina Faso and Mali) are landlocked, and all except four (Nigeria, Cote d'Ivoire, Ghana and Cape Verde) have been classified among the Least Developed countries.[7]

Table I - West Africa: Selected Human Development Indicators

Country	Human Development Index (HDI) Rank (vs 173)	Life Expectancy at Birth (2000)	Adult Literacy Rate (2000)	GDP Per capita (PPP US $) 2000
Cape Verde	100	69.7	73.8	4,863
Ghana	129	56.8	71.5	1,964
Togo	141	51.8	57.1	1,442
Nigeria	148	51.7	63.9	896
Senegal	154	53.3	37.3	1,510
Cote d'Ivoire	156	47.8	46.8	1,630
Benin	158	53.8	37.4	990
Guinea (Conakry)	159	47.5	41.0	1,982
Gambia	160	46.2	36.6	1,649
Mali	164	51.5	41.5	797
Chad	166	45.7	42.6	871
Guinea-Bissau	167	44.8	38.5	755
Burkina Faso	169	46.7	23.9	976
Niger	172	45.2	15.9	746
Sierra Leone	173	38.9	36.0	490

Source: United Nations Development Programme, Human Development Report, 2002

West Africa is also among the world's most politically unstable sub-regions. The internal security of several West African countries has been undermined by the epidemic of military coups, counter coups and insurrections. A recent study by Adekeye Adebajo ranks West Africa as "among the world's most unstable sub-regions, accounting for 37 out of 62 successful military coups in Africa between 1960 and 1990."[8]

West Africa's many socio-political challenges are further compounded by poor infrastructures, low industrial base, fragile borders and economies that are highly vulnerable to fluctuating world prices for imports, even as prices of the export of their cash crops continue to decline. All of these factors make West Africa arguably one of the most compelling cases for regional economic integration.

Relevance of Traditional Integration Theories to West Africa

The institutional origins of integration schemes lie in the developed Western world. With the establishment of the ECSC and, later, the Treaty of Rome establishing the EEC, some of the theories of integration were put into practice. The apparent success of the EEC did influence Third World countries to attempt economic integration schemes of their own. Inevitably, the traditional Western theories of integration have been used to explain integration arrangements in the developing world. Given the different circumstances of the two worlds, that is, the developed versus the developing world, there is a compelling need to evaluate the relevance of these received theories to the integration efforts of developing countries.

We would examine only two of such theories here, and also indicate an appropriate approach towards evaluating integration efforts in developing countries. However, before we consider the substantial issue of integration theory, we would propose a definition of the concept of integration itself and how this relates to regionalism, the preferred concept used in this study to describe the wider dimensions of integration taking place in West Africa at the moment. This is necessary because all through this study regional integration and regionalism are used interchangeably.

The main objective of all economic activities is an increase in welfare.[9] The approach towards this goal deals with the organization of the human community, because different actors often have conflicting interests and priorities. Economic integration is one of the means to achieve increase in general welfare, because integration can increase the welfare of the integrated group, or of some countries within the group, or of the world as a whole.[10]

Economic integration does not have a clear-cut meaning for all economists. In economics, the term "integration" was first employed in relation to industrial organizations to refer to "combinations of business firms through agreements, cartels, concerns, trusts and mergers.[11]

Traditionally, regional integration is generally seen as the harmonization of trade policies leading to deeper economic cooperation and with political integration as a possible future result, the so-called 'spill-over' effect. Bela Belassa goes on to define economic integration as being both a process and a state of affairs. As a process (dynamic concept), integration means the removal of discrimination between countries, while as a state of affairs (static concept), it means the absence of different forms of discrimination.[12]

John Pinder in his definition refers to the Oxford Dictionary, which describes integration as the combination of parts into a whole. Union is the outcome of the combination of these parts or members. He conceptualizes integration as a process towards union, and hence defines economic integration as the removal of discrimination between the economic agents of the member states, as well as the creation and implementation of common policies.[13] On its part, the European Commission defines economic (market) integration as "a state where the outcomes of economic decisions are independent of national frontiers."[14] For Machlup, one of the most obvious signs of integration is the non-existence of customs posts between integrated countries.[15]

What these different perspectives reveal is that integration is a complex concept, denoting different things to different persons at different times. In the developed market economies, integration is taken to be a way of introducing the most profitable technologies, allocating these in the most efficient way, and to foster free and fair competition, while in the developing countries, it is often a tool for economic development. Despite the definitional uncertainty, the notion of economic integration has evolved to describe a state of affairs or a process involving

the combination of separate economies into a larger economic unit.[16] Defined as a process, it includes all measures that aim to abolish discrimination among economic units from different countries or jurisdictions. It can also be considered as a state of affairs, which is characterized by the absence of various forms of discrimination among member countries of the integrating group.

While there are considerable divergences in perspectives among integration scholars, in general a fair amount of consensus exists on three basic elements of economic integration:

(i)   That economic integration refers basically to division of labour;

(ii)   That it involves mobility of goods, or factors or both; and

(iii)   That it is related to discrimination or non-discrimination in the treatment of goods and factors, as for example, with regard to origin or destination.[17]

From these definitions, one can reasonably draw the conclusion that economic integration is both a process and means by which a group of countries strive to increase its level of welfare. It involves the recognition that even a weak partnership among countries can achieve this goal in a more efficient way than through unilateral and independent pursuit of policy in each country. Integration requires at least some division of labour and freedom of movement for goods and services within the group. Relatively higher levels of integration arrangements also require a free mobility of factors of production within the integrated area, as well as certain restrictions on these movements between the integrated area and countries outside of it.

The essential point is that the countries that integrate adopt a kind of inward-looking approach and take more care about what happens in the group than about what happens outside of it. In addition, at least some consultation, if not coordination of monetary, fiscal and regional development policies are necessary for the success and durability of the integration process.

Economic integration between at least two countries can be of the following seven theoretical types: [18]

•   A preferential tariff agreement, which assumes that the tariffs on trade among the signatory countries are lower in relation to tariffs charged on trade with third countries.

•   A partial customs union, which is formed when the participating countries retain their initial tariffs on their mutual trade but introduce a common tariff on trade with third countries.

•   A free trade area, which is an agreement among countries relating to the elimination of all tariff and quantitative restrictions on mutual trade. Every country in the free trade area retains its own tariff and other regulation of trade with third countries but is bound by the rules of origin, which seeks to prevent import of cheap goods from a third country for re-export to countries in the free trade area.

•   A customs union, where participating countries not only remove tariff and quantitative restrictions on their intra-group trade, but also introduce a common external tariff on trade with third countries. Here, the participating countries take part in international negotiations about trade and tariffs as a single entity.

•   The common market, where in addition to the full operations of a customs union, there is free mobility of factors of production, including common regulations on the movement of factors with third countries.

•   An economic union, which assumes not only a common market, but also the harmonization of fiscal, monetary, industrial, regional, transport and other economic policies; and

•   A total economic union, which assumes union with a single economic policy and a supranational government with great economic authority. Here, there are no administrative barriers to the movements of goods, services and factors.

It must be understood that the process of integration does not necessarily have to be gradual from one type to another. The establishment of any of these types depends primarily on the agreement among the participating countries. It is also necessary to underscore the fact that the decision about entering into a customs union or any other type of integration arrangement has always been primarily political, even if economic consideration usually plays a very important role. For instance, the question to cede aspects of national sovereignty to a supranational body is generally made by politicians. The EU, which is the best known example of a successful economic integration scheme globally owns its early origins to politics more than economics. The EU was, after all, not established in 1957 in order to liberalize trade, but rather to exclude the possibility of war between France and Germany.[19] For the EU, economic integration was just a means for the achievement of that political objective.

In contrast to the narrow concept of economic integration, regionalism is a heterogeneous, comprehensive and multi-dimensional phenomenon, taking place in several sectors, and often pushed or rather constructed by a variety of actors – states, market and society at large. The general view is that regionalism implies a change of a particular region from relative heterogeneity to increasing homogeneity with regard to a number of dimensions, the most critical being economic, political and security relations. This phenomenon best describes the whole range of economic, political, security and cultural interactions taking place in West Africa at this time. In other words, what is happening in West Africa at the moment is much more than economic integration in the traditional meaning of the concept. Regionalism best describes this process.

This process could be analysed from the point of view of its potential to change the mainstream pattern of development. As Hettne has argued, the new regionalism is taking place in a global environment that is characterized by multi-polarity, but an asymmetrical form of multi-polarity.[20] This being the case, a rough distinction can be made between the core and peripheral regions in the same way that countries were analysed by the Neo-Marxist and dependency traditions in development theory. The core regions are thus politically stable and economically dynamic and organize or integrate in order to be better able to control the world. On the other hand, the peripheral regions like West Africa are characterized by political turbulence and economic stagnation.

Consequently, they organize or integrate in order to arrest their condition of marginalization. At the same time, their regional arrangements are fragile and ineffective. The overall weak position of the peripheral regions like West Africa makes 'security regionalism' and 'developmental regionalism' more important than the mere creation of free trade regimes. For scholars like Hettne, developmental regionalism and security regionalism constitute a package which, with varying contents, is particularly relevant to all marginalized areas in the international system.

Take the case of security as an example. Regional organizations are supposed to have an immediate interest in promoting peace since inter-state and intra-state wars normally affect the entire region through spill-over and other regional externalities. However, the role of regional organizations in security and developmental regionalism contains an in-built tension, not least because regionalization challenges the narrow concept of national sovereignty since the regional body is supposed to take over certain state functions – in same cases more, in others less. At the same time, while the member states anxiously guard their sovereignty, they continue to create more and more elaborate regional institutions with expanding responsibilities.

To be successful, therefore, regional schemes in the developing world necessarily require of their members to cede aspects of national sovereignty, a daunting prospect given the fragility of most of these states. As regards developmental regionalism, there are substantial benefits that countries in poor regions can maximize from cooperation and collaboration. While the question of size has undoubtedly lost some of its importance in an increasingly interdependent world, regional cooperation is nevertheless an imperative in the case of micro-states, which have to either cooperate to solve common problems, or to remain client states of the developed or 'core countries'.

Second, while self-reliance as a development goal has rarely proved viable at the national level, it may be a feasible development strategy at the regional level if integration focuses on the coordination of production, improvement of infrastructures, and the use of complementarities in order to strengthen the position   of the region in the world economy.

Third, economic policies may be more stable and consistent if they are underpinned by regional arrangements which cannot be broken by a particular country without some kind of sanction from the others. Finally, regional conflict resolution, if successful and durable, does help to eliminate distorted investment patterns as the 'security fund'(military expenditures) can be tapped for more productive use. This is the peace dividend argument in favour of regionalism.

From a normative point of view, therefore, regionalism can be viewed as positive and beneficial. In practice, however, this is by no means necessarily the case. For instance, increased regional interaction or integration may be conflictual, exploitative, and may reinforce a particular power relation, or create other negative effects. Some countries may undoubtedly lose from regionalism, while others will benefit. However, this is not to imply that regionalism is a zero-sum game; rather it is to stress that among the various countries or actors involved in a regional integration project, some will gain and some more than others, while at the same time, some will lose, and some more than others.[21]

The functionalist approach to international cooperation is premised on the proposition that one can isolate "non-political" problems, such as economic, social, technical and humanitarian matters, and then concentrate on solving these common problems. In the words of David Mitrany, "the problem of our time is not how to keep the nations peacefully apart but how to bring them actively together."[22] This can be achieved by indirectly seeking out areas of mutual interests and "building together those interests which are common, where they are common, to the extent to which they are common."[23] The emphasis is on pragmatic approach to solving practical problems common to all countries in the region.

Functionalists also seek an escape from the vertical divisions of the world (nation states) by focusing instead on a horizontal approach to solving common problems. The functionalists also entertain the hope that cooperation in economic and social fields may spill over into the political arena.

Functionalists reason that the habit of cooperation and the accumulated agenda of collaborative work may well bring about federalism by instalments or peace by pieces.[24]

The main focus of the functionalist approach to integration is the utility of functional cooperation in relation to the avoidance of war and violent conflict. Functionalists attribute war to the inadequacy of the institutionalized nation-state system to deal with human problems, such as poverty, ill-health, illiteracy and social justice. While it is by no means certain that functional cooperation among states would eliminate war, the underlying arguments come close to Immanuel Kant's notion of "perpetual peace" through a pacific union of liberal republics.

Despite the usefulness of the functionalist theory in analysing contemporary international integration, considerable scepticism exits among third world scholars as to its applicability to integration efforts in developing countries. For instance, Ibrahim Gambari, a Nigerian scholar and former Foreign Minister, has not only questioned the suggestion of a spill-over effect, but also the feasibility of separating and isolating economic and social problems from the political.

According to Gambari, "the attempt to subvert sovereignty through functional cooperation may prove unviable in the developing world where the sovereign state remains the dominant force in all integration schemes."[25] In any event, functional economic cooperation, as epitomized in traditional economic integration arrangement, can ever hardly be established strictly for economic reasons alone. On the contrary, economic cooperation can only be pursued within a political context, however vaguely defined or understood by those involved.

According to the Customs Union theory, the principal objective of integration arrangements is to remove, in stages, such discriminations that may exist in trade and general economic relationships across national boundaries. Before Jacob Viner's celebrated work on customs unions, the general view was that because customs unions bring about free trade, they tend to increase world welfare. This "free trade – world welfare" focus, however, neglects issues concerning unfair distribution of world income and the privileged positions of the developed capitalist economies in the international system.

As with all conventional integration theories, the main focus of both the functionalist and customs union approaches to regional integration is on economic prerequisites. These theories try to identify and possibly quantify the gains of economic integration. Most of the studies privilege economic factors which promote more efficient use of resources. Importantly, such use of resources is predicated on the free movement of goods and of factors of production, following the elimination of discrimination and discriminatory policies among member states.

In general, the process of removing discrimination has been conceptualized as a linear movement from a Free Trade Area through Customs Union, a Common Market, an Economic Union, and ending in a total Economic Integration Arrangement. In the last stage, not only do members enjoy free factor flows and operate common external tariffs, members also harmonise economic and fiscal policies and promote common political institutions.

It must be understood that this classification is rather arbitrary, and there is no automaticity in the process of moving from one to the other forms of integration. Moreover, members of an integration arrangement may prefer to label their scheme a common market or economic community, without actually reflecting the general characteristics associated with that form of arrangement.

In general, conventional theories tend to be pre-occupied with production effects and the most efficient utilization of productive resources. However, this focus on production and efficient resource use assumes three conditions that are often not all present in developing countries.

(i)   Potential partners in a customs union conduct a significant proportion of trade with one another,

(ii)   The economies of partners in the union are at least potentially complementary; and

(iii)   Foreign trade is a relatively low percentage of the GNP of member states.

The West African sub region's low rating on each of these criteria says much about the challenge of economic integration in the area. For example, intra-trade among ECOWAS countries is a minor proportion of the total trade between Member States and the rest of the world. Secondly, ECOWAS Member States are not only primary producers; their products are competitive, rather than complementary. Moreover, these countries are heavily dependent on the export of their primary products, while they import intermediate manufactures. This means that foreign trade occupies a rather large proportion of the GNP and general economic activities of these countries.

In general, export of primary products or minerals constitutes the major source of foreign exchange earnings. Consequently, therefore, the application of the criterion of gain through orthodox customs union theory to integration arrangements among less developed countries appears to be of little or no relevance.

For developing countries, the reason for pursuing integration arrangements lies neither in the potential benefits to be derived from changes in existing patterns of trade nor in existing patterns of production, but in the impact of proposed regional markets on their fundamental socio economic and even political problems.[26] For these countries, integration is therefore a strategy for development, because it unleashes opportunities for profitable domestic and foreign investments, which in turn could assist in the mobilization of unemployed or underemployed resources.

Given the rather grim economic situation of countries in the West African sub region, conventional static analysis privileging trade creation (good) over trade diversion (bad) are clearly of little relevance to these countries. John Renninger is rather blunt, stressing that the "ultimate goal of integration schemes in developing countries is to escape from poverty caused by dependence on foreign colonial powers who organized the structure of their economies to suit the needs and convenience of the metropolitan economies."[27] Against this backdrop, regional integration is seen as a mechanism which could turn members of the developing world from being mere suppliers of raw materials and consumers of manufactured goods from the industrialized world. In this context, integration arrangements are expected to drive development goals and aspirations.

This is why industrialization occupies a prominent place in the integration efforts in developing countries. The industrialization project may be aimed at import substitution, or at export markets within or outside the region. Given that the economic size of nearly all countries in West Africa inhibits the achievement of industrialization in individual countries through import substitution or export promotion, it is only through the creation of larger economic units in the form of regional integration that the process of accelerated industrialization can be advanced.

A further motivation driving economic integration among developing countries relates to the perception that these efforts could enhance their collective ability to bargain with the economic giants of the world. The reason for this optimism is not far-fetched. It is virtually impossible for a small or medium-sized Third World country to negotiate favourable trade agreements for the export of its manufactures. Collectively, a group of developing countries may be in a stronger position to negotiate and conclude more favourable agreements concerning trade, aid and capital investments.

Furthermore, collective self-reliance has also been a driver in the coming together of developing countries to form economic communities. As the early promise of external development aid is becoming more and more illusory, the logic of self-reliant development becomes ever more compelling. Regional integration schemes are attractive because they can be viable vehicles for self-reliant growth and development.

If integration efforts in developing countries are to be evaluated from the totality of motivations and objectives of member states, it becomes clear that the conventional integration theories are inadequate tools for analysing the value and efforts of Third World integration. The poverty of conventional integration theory in explaining the attraction of integration to developing countries reinforces the perspective of integration as a development strategy for these countries.

It must be understood that regionalism in the African context is not only or mainly about formal and states-driven regional economic frameworks. Regionalism in Africa is more dynamic and turbulent, and therefore should not be analysed solely through the lenses of Euro-centric integration theory. Applying the European model to the African experience means that the same underlying assumptions and conceptualizations that stem from the European experience necessarily influences the description, expectation and prescriptions of regionalism in the rest of the world, including West Africa. This can be misleading.

The Origins of ECOWAS

Efforts aimed at integrating the West African sub-region go back into the colonial period, when the metropolitan powers tried to amalgamate the colonies to intensify their economic exploitation and to minimise administrative costs. The British, for instance, set up the West African Currency Board for The Gambia, Nigeria, Ghana and Sierra Leone, and the West African Airways Cooperation, among others, in Anglophone West Africa. For the French, the most notable move was the integration of all the French territories into one monetary union, with the CFA as common legal tender.

Several colonial schemes or common services did not survive the early period of independence, especially in Anglophone West Africa, where the most notable surviving colonial integration project remains the West African Examination Council (WAEC), a pre-university examination board for The Gambia, Ghana, Nigeria and Sierra Leone. Liberia joined the council in 1980. Several spirited attempts were, however, made to promote regional integration in West Africa after independence in the 1960s. A number of important factors were responsible for the post-independence integration wave. First, the nationalist leaders saw it as a means of consolidating their hard-won political independence. Second, there was the belief that successful economic integration would lead to prosperity and a better life for the citizens of the newly independent nations – a fulfilment of the nationalist dream. This belief, no doubt, was driven by the desire for self-reliant development and the recognition that individual markets were rather too small and unviable to support rapid economic transformation of the new nations. Third, there was the demonstration effect of the successful EEC, which consolidated unity and cooperation among the European states and ushered unprecedented prosperity to their citizens.

The fact that some of the key actors in the European integration project were also former colonial powers in West Africa not only sensitised the newly independent states about the exciting developments in Europe, but also brought home to their leaders some of the gains and possibilities inherent in a successful integration scheme. In short, West African leaders, like their counterparts in other regions of the developing world, believed that the pooling of their economic and human resources could provide the impetus for rapid economic advancement of their countries.[28]

Beyond nationalist aspirations and the apparent attraction of the European model of economic cooperation, West Africa's political economy provides a strong economic justification for integration of the sub-region. First, because almost all countries in the sub-region rely on the export of primary products for their foreign exchange, they suffer huge financial losses and serious disruptions in economic planning when the world market prices for commodities fluctuate widely, as they tend to do. Integration would be beneficial to counties in the region because it would allow for coordination and rationalisation of commercial and cash crop production in the sub-region. This would necessarily strengthen the income-earning capacity of West Africa as a whole, since the region provides a wide range of crops, including cocoa, groundnut, cotton, coffee, rubber and others.

Second, integration will also allow for the cooperative exploitation, use and export of the abundant mineral resources that abound in the sub-region. Whereas oil accounts for over 90% of Nigeria's export, high quality iron ore is located in Guinea, Sierra Leone and Liberia. Guinea also produces bauxite, while diamond deposits are located in Sierra Leone, Guinea, Ghana and Cote d'Ivoire. Ghana also produces gold and manganese. Joint investments in the exploitation and export of these minerals could raise the income levels of the countries involved.

Third, integration will allow for new transportation and communication networks to be established in place of the old road and railway systems that were designed to facilitate colonial powers' exploitation of the region's resources. These systems generally stretch from the coast to the interior of individual countries without any cross- regional links. To promote expanded regional trade and investments, new transportation and communication systems would have to be established not only to link countries, but also to link different parts of national territories.

Fourth, although the resources and population of West Africa give it a potentially strong base for industrial development, this will not become a reality until there is rationalisation and specialisation through a system of regional industries. While the region provides the possibilities of economies of scale in the production of industrial goods, these will not materialise unless there is a deliberate encouragement of region-wide investment in industries and community policy on the location of industries.

Fifth, only through integration could West Africa be able to redirect is external trade, which historically has been conducted with former colonial powers, although increasingly with other industrialised partners, in favour of more intra-regional trade. Finally, given that many West African countries are landlocked, integration will undoubtedly provide these countries access to the sea in a way that is not possible under bilateral or ad-hoc arrangements.

Politics of the Creation of ECOWAS

The very first idea of a West African free trade area dates back to 1964 when President William Tubman of Liberia, in his inaugural address, floated the notion of a West African free trade area. At the urging of President Tubman, a series of bilateral and multilateral talks with West African governments led to a meeting of four West African states of Cote d'Ivoire, Guinea, Liberia and Sierra Leone, which sought to consider the possibility of creating a free trade zone. The meeting was convened in Monrovia on 24 August 1964.

At a subsequent meeting between 15-17 February, 1965

the ministers of the four participating countries drew up an agreement to create an interim organisation to be superseded by a more permanent organisation for West African Economic Cooperation. An agreement which followed in 1965 charged the interim organisation with, among other things, the responsibility of planning for the establishment of a multilateral system of economic cooperation of a regional character, with a view to removing trade barriers and encouraging the harmonious development of the cooperating states in every field.

Although the success of the Liberian initiative was limited, it led the United Nations Economic Commission for Africa (ECA) to undertake a delineation of West Africa for purposes of promoting and enhancing economic cooperation.[29] The ECA had come to the conclusion in the 1960s that the most viable approach to regional integration was one that, as a first step, embraced more geographical areas, as opposed to an all-embracing continental organisation. Accordingly, the ECA divided the African continent into four sub-regions, namely, eastern, southern, central and western. Following this division, the ECA had proceeded to arrange a ministerial council meeting in Dakar, Senegal, in November 1967 to prepare grounds for a summit meeting of Heads of State for the take-off of a West African regional economic grouping. As with previous attempts, the ECA initiative failed to prosper.

The slow progress towards regional integration in West Africa up to this point has been attributed to several political and practical problems. These included vested interests on the part of the political leadership in the preservation of the status quo, such as the maintenance of colonial ties with the former colonial powers, the different commercial and financial policies inherited from the past colonial administrations, different currencies and payments arrangements and an overwhelming dependence on revenue from import duties. Above all, there was a general lack of political will to surrender national decision-making powers to a supra-national authority.[30]

Following these early setbacks, the initiative that finally culminated in the establishment of ECOWAS was launched by Nigeria and Togo in April 1972. At the end of a state visit to Togo in April 1972, General Yakubu Gowon, Nigeria's Head of State and his Togolese counterpart, President Gnassingbe Eyadema, issued a communiqué announcing their decision to create an "embryonic West African Economic Community," between their two countries. The two leaders proceeded to set up a commission of experts to study and make recommendations on the shape and content of the proposed grouping. The experts agreed to work out broad areas of cooperation in such matters as transport and communications, trade, industry, money payments, and movement of factors between Nigeria and Togo. They also recommended the abolition of transit tax, which had constituted an impediment to the development of trade in the sub-region. Most importantly, the experts proposed that General Yakubu Gowon, the Nigerian leader, calls a summit meeting of West Africa's leaders to discuss and carry forward their proposal for a regional economic community.

Within the short span of one and a half years of their first meeting, the Nigeria-Togo Commission of Experts had produced a draft treaty. With a combination of persuasive power, extension of financial assistance and some arm-twisting, General Gowon was able to get ministers in West

African states to meet in Lome, Togo, in December 1973 to consider the Nigeria-Togo draft treaty, and to adopt basic principles for the establishment of ECOWAS.

Following subsequent meetings in Accra, Ghana, in February 1974 and Monrovia in January 1975, the treaty establishing ECOWAS was adopted by ministers. It was formally signed by the original fifteen member states in Lagos, Nigeria, on 28 May 1975, and it formally came into effect on 23 June 1975, when the mandatory minimum seven member states ratified it.[31] The signing of the first five protocols annexed to the treaty at Lome on 5 November 1976 completed the birth of ECOWAS.

The creation of ECOWAS represented the culmination of many years of efforts by West African states to increase the economic means and bargaining base of their economies. Through a pooling of economic sovereignty, West African leaders sought to transform the region's economy and to improve the living standards of community citizens. In a sense, economic integration of the sub-region aimed to extend the struggle for political decolonization into economic decolonization.[32] The creation of ECOWAS was also a response to the recognition by West African leaders that the fragmentation of the sub-region – the consequence of colonial balkanisation – renders a shift in the pattern of production designed to reduce dependence both difficult and costly. That being the case, the inauguration of ECOWAS was seen by West African leaders as an attempt to enhance economic opportunity across the sub-region and to reduce external dependence. By pooling their resources, the leaders hoped countries in the sub-region could overcome the existing structures of neo-colonisation and underdevelopment.

It would appear from the preceding narrative that the creation of ECOWAS was smooth sailing from start to finish. This is far from the truth, because the processes leading to the establishment of the regional organization were littered with intrigues, mutual distrust and counter-moves by several states and interest groups in the sub-region. The early ambivalence that dogged the formation of ECOWAS relates to legitimate fears of domination by several states, all of which harbour misgivings about a regional economic bloc which would necessarily be dominated by Nigeria – the region's economic giant. These fears which predated the formation of ECOWAS persist to this day. Whereas ECOWAS was considered by its promoters as a vehicle for promoting collective self-reliance of its members, geopolitical intrigues saw to it that from its very beginning these economic aims were attenuated by considerations which decisively shaped the community's treaty.

To be sure, while regional economic integration was played up as the prime objective of ECOWAS, the organisation's emergence reflected Nigeria's pervasive concern with stabilising and controlling its external environment.[33] Almost simultaneously, the creation of the Communaute Economique de l'Afrique de l'Ouest (CEAO) in April 1973, which later transformed into the Union Monetaire Ouest Africaine (UEMOA) in 1994, was an attempt by six Francophone countries – Cote d'Ivoire, Senegal, Niger, Burkina Faso, Mali and Mauritania, with the active support of France – to counterbalance Nigeria's influence within West Africa.

The CEAO and its successor UEMOA were, ostensibly, created as means of strengthening the cooperation of West

Africa's Francophone countries ahead of the establishment of ECOWAS. Whereas there were considerable policy differences even among future member states of the proposed CEAO, a common concern that Nigeria's political and economic influence in the sub-region must be checked proved strong enough to propel the leaders of these countries to reach early agreement on a treaty establishing the CEAO. This project was openly encouraged by President Georges Pompidou of France, who went so far as to declare that Francophone states should coordinate their efforts in order to counterbalance the heavy weight of Nigeria.[34]

Following the end of the Nigerian civil war in 1970, the country immediately initiated moves aimed at the formation of a West Africa grouping, ostensibly to heal the rift between the Francophone and Anglophone states, but in reality to achieve its economic, political and strategic objectives. Nigeria had good reason to seek a rapprochement with its Francophone neighbours since France's support for the Biafra succession bid had constituted a major threat to it. The logic behind Nigeria's policy of good neighbourliness was basically sound, since France exerted considerable influence over all of Nigeria's neighbours – all of which are French-speaking.

Meanwhile, lobbying for the competing exclusive Francophone CEAO and a wider grouping of all West African states reached a climax in 1972, when President Gnassingbe Eyadema invited his Nigerian counterpart to attend Togo's independence celebrations so that the Nigeria leader could be able to hold informal discussions with Francophone leaders who were to meet in Lome on the margins of Togo's independence anniversary. While the

Nigerian leader failed to win any new support for his project, both he and Eyadema spectacularly announced the formation of a union, which they hoped would form the nucleus of an inclusive West African economic community.

Perhaps jolted by the Nigeria-Togo move, or by a conviction that the formation of CEAO was an absolute necessity to curb Nigeria's influence within the sub-region, the CEAO Charter was quickly finalised. Consequently, on 17 April 1973, the CEAO Charter was signed by six Francophone countries, with Benin Republic opting for an observer status. The official reason given by Benin Republic for not signing the CEAO Charter was that "it could not become a member of a community from which Nigeria would be absent."[35] Benin Republic's pitching of its tent with Nigeria was particularly instructive and reflected the country's increasing awareness of its economic dependence on Nigeria.

Following the establishment of CEAO, two key areas of disagreement emerged between Nigeria and members of CEAO. These concerned the nature of the economic outlook of the proposed ECOWAS, and a concern by Francophone states that the corporate identity of their new grouping (CEAO) be preserved and endorsed in the wider ECOWAS treaty. Although Nigeria's calculation had been that the creation of ECOWAS would weaken Francophone West Africa's links with France, this attitude was not really derived from any conviction that the reduction of trade links with Europe and the intensification of inter-African trade were preconditions for the success of economic integration in the region. Certainly, Nigeria was particularly critical of the relations of direct dependence which existed between France and Francophone West

Africa, but its (Nigeria's) economic policies never sought to challenge the robust economic and trade links that had existed between Europe and West African countries.

Against this backdrop, the French scholar, David Bach, has attributed Nigeria's opposition to relations between Francophone West Africa and France to a concern that its industrial sector – arguably the most sophisticated in the region – might have to compete within ECOWAS on unfavourable terms with manufactured products from French companies that proliferate across Francophone West Africa.[36] Bach's conclusion was entirely consistent with sentiments among policy elites in Francophone West Africa, who had supported the creation of CEAO in the belief that it would promote the growth of a wider market, which would attract foreign investors into the group.

Another major source of dissension between CEAO member states and Nigeria had to do with the possibility of an economic agreement between West Africa and the European Economic Community (EEC), as it was then, a project Nigeria had initially opposed. While Nigeria's criticism of an economic and trade agreement with Europe was framed as a rejection of 'neo-colonisation' and dependency, the probable reason might had been due to the fact that its major export to Europe was crude petroleum, which would, anyway, be excluded from a preferential tariff regime under a trade deal with Europe.

A major policy shift by Nigeria in May 1973, however, paved the way for the conclusion of a partnership agreement with Europe, an agreement that was keenly desired by Francophone West Africa. The adoption of the Lome Convention in February 1975, therefore, proved a decisive step towards the formation of ECOWAS, since it unified the legal framework within which all the member states of the proposed organisation would maintain their extra-Africa economic relations.[37] For the Francophone states, ECOWAS no longer represented a challenge to their ties with France. With their relationship with France now secured, the only stumbling block to the creation of ECOWAS remained the insistence by Francophone states that the personality of CEAO be preserved within the framework of any new association which would embrace all of West Africa.

Following consultations and negotiations between the CEAO group and Nigeria, this request was granted, paving the way for the signing of the ECOWAS Treaty by all 15 member states in Lagos, Nigeria, on 28 May 1975. Article 59 of the Treaty of the Constitutive Treaty and Article 84 of the Revised Treaty reflected the accommodation of the wishes of CEAO members by stipulating that Member States of ECOWAS could belong to "other regional or sub-regional associations, as long as this did not detract from the provisions of ECOWAS."[38] The Treaty also went as far as proclaiming the validity of rights and obligations "arising from agreements concluded before the definitive entry into force of this Treaty."[39]

Those states that this provision referred to were merely asked to "take all appropriate steps to eliminate the incompatibilities established by such dual memberships."[40] Frequently described as a dramatic move which overcame the Francophone-Anglophone divide in West Africa, the 1975 ECOWAS Treaty bridged historical differences and fears only superficially, if at all, as it formally acknowledged the parallel existence of CEAO, a grouping whose very foundation had been prompted by fear of a wider economic community dominated by Nigeria.

The acceptance of the corporate identity of CEAO within ECOWAS might have made possible the creation of ECOWAS, but it also compromised the orientation of the original ECOWAS Treaty, also called the Lagos Treaty. Since 1994, the CEAO had been replaced by UEMOA. The continued parallel existence of UEMOA and ECOWAS poses a number of challenging questions about the future prospects of constructing a viable integration arrangement in West Africa. To what extent, for instance, does the parallel existence of the two economic groupings create a competitive rather than complementary mode of integration in West Africa?

It must be understood that UEMOA, and CEAO before it, was created as a means of strengthening the cooperation of West Africa's Francophone States even before ECOWAS was established. However, the similarities between the two organisations are striking; both UEMOA and ECOWAS aim to become customs unions. The treaties of both groupings also provide for free trade and free movement of persons, as well as a common external tariff. In other words, the objectives of UEMOA are not only identical with those of ECOWAS, but all the integration schemes of UEMOA are similar to those of both the Original and revised ECOWAS treaties of 1975 and 1993, respectively. Since all UEMOA members are also members of ECOWAS, the critical question relates to which of the two treaties UEMOA members would have to implement. Will the UEMOA common external tariff also apply to other non-UEMOA members of ECOWAS? These are troubling questions which point to underlying politico-cultural tensions in West Africa's integration project.

The parallel existence of UEMOA continues to fuel suspicion among Anglophone West Africans, many of who see the exclusive Francophone organisation as France's Trojan horse within ECOWAS.41 In a sign of growing frustration and impatience with UEMOA, non-UEMOA members of ECOWAS view the former as a major challenge not only to the 1990 decision of ECOWAS Heads of State reaffirming the wider regional body's commitment to the establishment of a single economic community, but also to the highly significant July 1991 decision designating ECOWAS the sole organisation to promote integration in West Africa.[42]

Institutional Structure, Aims and Objectives of ECOWAS

The revised ECOWAS Treaty annexed to this study, makes extensive provisions for institutions charged with administering and directing the affairs of the community. The revised treaty reflects commitment by political leaders in West Africa to broaden and deepen the regional integration process. For instance, in order to strengthen ECOWAS and its institutions, the regional organisation was invested with supra-nationality, by which member states agreed to a partial surrender of national sovereignty in order to make possible the creation of a regional economic identity. ECOWAS was thus strengthened institutionally, including the establishment of the Community Court of Justice, the West African Parliament, and the Economic and Social Council. Another important new provision was the introduction of financial autonomy, through the instrumentality of the community levy.

The broadening of the ECOWAS mandate also extended to active regional cooperation in the political and defence fields. Under Article 4, four principal organs were established through which the community accomplishes its purposes. These are: the Authority of Heads of State and Government; the Council of Ministers; the Executive Secretariat; and the Tribunal of the Community. Also provided for are several technical and specialised commissions, including a Fund for Cooperation, Compensation and Development.

The Authority of Heads of State and Government

It is provided in Article 5 that the principal governing institution of the community is the Authority of Head of State and Government, or simply the Authority. One of its main functions is to direct and control the "performance of the executive functions of the community for the progressive development of the community and the achievement of its aims.[43] The decisions and directions of the Authority are binding on all institutions of the Community.

As its name signifies, the Authority is composed of the Heads of State and Government, or their accredited representatives. It meets at least once a year in ordinary sessions, and its chairmanship is rotated among the members. Under the 1993 revised Treaty, the Authority of Heads of State and Government have had its powers enhanced; its decisions are now immediately enforceable in member states.

Council of Ministers

The Council of Ministers is next in the hierarchical order of the Community's institutions. Established under Article 6, it consists of two representatives from each member state. It is required to meet twice a year in ordinary session, and extraordinary meetings are convened as and when necessary.

The major functions of the Council, as stipulated in Article 6 (2) include monitoring the functioning of the community; making recommendations to the Authority on the efficient and harmonious development of ECOWAS, and directing and supervising all subordinate institutions.

The Executive Secretariat

Article 8 provides for the Executive Secretariat, which is headed by the Executive Secretary. The Secretariat performs the main administrative and executive functions of ECOWAS, and services all the other institutions. It also initiates and proposes policy measures and programmes to the technical commissions and is required to submit a report of activities to all sessions of the Council, and all meetings of the Authority.

The Treaty expressly specifies that all officers of the Secretariat, in the discharge of their duties, own their loyalty entirely to the community and, as such, are expected to function as uninstructed bureaucratic and technical experts whose positions are insulated from the politics and diplomacy of their states of origin.

The Tribunal of the Community

The Treaty makes provision for the Tribunal of the Community, whose composition, competence and other matters are decided by the Authority. The Tribunal interprets the provisions of the Treaty, settles disputes referred to it and "ensures the observance of law and justice." It is not clear how the Tribunal will ensure the observance of law and justice and make interpretation binding on member states in the absence of supranational authority with enforcement powers.

In addition to the Authority, Council, Secretariat and the Tribunal, ECOWAS institutional structure has five specialised and technical commissions. These are Trade, Customs, Immigration, Monetary and Payments Commission; the Industry, Agriculture and Natural Resources Commission; the Transport, Telecommunications and Energy Commission; the Social and Cultural Affairs Commission and the Fund for Cooperation, Compensation and Development. All these Commissions are made up of experts from ECOWAS Member States. Their primary function is to draw up integration programmes in their respective fields of competence, and to the implementation of these programmes.

In relation to its aims and objectives, Article 3 of the Revised ECOWAS Treaty elaborates these broadly as:
"the promotion of cooperation and integration, leading to the establishment of an economic union in West Africa in order to raise the living standards of its peoples, and to maintain and enhance economic stability, foster relations among member states and contribute to the progress and development of the African continent."[44]

The Challenge of Integration in West Africa

From the point of view of the development needs of West African States, the central purpose of ECOWAS is lofty one. It is also ambitious, given the economic, social and political challenges in the region. For instance, the community's main aims are to ensure in stages:
(i)   The elimination between member states of customs duties and other charges of equivalent effect regarding the

import and export of goods;
(ii)   The abolition of quantitative and administrative restriction on trade among member states;
(iii)   The establishment of a common customs tariff and a common commercial policy toward other countries; and
(iv)   The abolition of the obstacles to the free movement of persons, services and capital among member states.

In Chapter III of the ECOWAS Treaty, provisions provide for the progressive creation of a custom union among member states. For example, within the first two years of the coming into force of the treaty, new duties or the raising of existing duties were to be frozen with respect to community goods. This was to be followed by the progressive reduction and ultimate elimination of all import duties on community goods within eight years. Furthermore, a common external tariff was to be established over another five-year period during which internal tariffs were to be eliminated.[45]

These are lofty goals ECOWAS set for itself. More than four decades on, ECOWAS progression in the context of its stated goals and objectives has largely been sluggish. For instance, the goal of transforming West Africa into a custom union remains precisely that – a goal unmet after well over 35 years since the creation of ECOWAS. ECOWAS shares several problems with other regional integration efforts in the developing world, but in addition to these, there are region-specific challenges that it has had to contend with.

At the general level, the problems afflicting regional integration efforts in the Third world could be categorised into socio-economic and political constraints. The socio-economic constraints derive from the uneven levels of development among member states, which inevitably leads to polarised growth whereby economic activities are concentrated in the more developed parts of the community. In the same vein, the reduction and elimination of tariffs, taxes and duties on intra-community goods and the pursuit of common external tariffs toward third countries often lead to reduced national earnings with some states badly hurt than others.

The unequal balance of trade and payments in the interactions among member states, especially in foreign exchange transactions, would be another challenge, as would the negative effects of trade diversion as a result of higher prices being paid for imports from non-member states in preference to imports from community members. Additionally, free movement of people could precipitate negative social consequences even in states of the community that were seen as poles of growth by exacerbating unemployment problems.[46] On the other hand, the political constraints often involved reluctance by member states to surrender national sovereignties even when all are agreed on the necessity of integration. Differences in political ideologies and models of economic development also have divisive consequences for the smooth running of community institutions and, by implication, the pace of integration itself.

In reality, the dynamic interaction between the socio-economic and political challenges reinforce one another, creating a vicious cycle of conflict and mistrust, both of which can and, often, does subvert the process of intergration in the developing world. In the case of ECOWAS, the obstacles to a smooth progression of the community's central aims and objectives could be unpacked under three broad headings namely, structural problems related to the distribution of costs and benefits, political-diplomacy problems, and finally, the role of Nigeria and France – two key actors in West Africa's affairs – one indigenous, the other external but having real local impact.

Structural Challenges

There are at least five main dimensions to the structural challenges facing ECOWAS. In the first place, the region's infrastructure is inadequate for providing effective economic and cultural links among member states. The inherited transport network, especially the railway system, is not only grossly insufficient for national needs but incapable of facilitating horizontal trade and other intra-regional economic activities. Because the colonial model of development concentrated development in the coastal areas, these areas are relatively better served with infrastructural facilities. Such development model has proved detrimental to the hinterland and has contributed to the widening disparity in the levels of economic activities within member states, and between coastal and land-locked states. The ECOWAS treaty recognized this problem and provided for joint development of transport, communication, energy and other infrastructural facilities, as well as the evolution of a common policy in these fields.[47]

Second, the multiplicity of monetary zones and low level of monetary cooperation within West Africa constitute serious drawbacks to effective regional integration. The persistence of the inherited colonial monetary systems has not only created divisions in the region, but has discouraged intra-regional trade. One example is the continued use of the CFA Franc, once tied to the French Franc but now to the Euro under a special arrangement brokered by France. Efforts to redress this unsatisfactory situation led to the establishment of the West African Clearing House in 1975. Though a modest achievement, the mechanism of the West African Unit of Account (WAUA) falls way short of the monetary integration that could drive the economic integration of the region, in the same way that the Euro has done in the European Union.

The third level of the structural problems within ECOWAS is the low level of trade among member states. Within ECOWAS, the level of intra-regional trade remains low, accounting for a paltry 11 per cent of total trade with third countries.[48] This poor record is the consequence of growing vertical ties with the rich industrialized West in general, but particularly with the former colonial powers. Although ECOWAS trade liberalization scheme is up and running, it is fraught with formidable challenges. For instance, goods continue to be subject to undue control at national borders, and this creates a serious non-tariff barrier which increases the cost of transaction across the sub-region. The slow progress in liberalizing trade in the sub-region must be of concern, since trade liberalization is the first major step towards the formation of a free trade area, customs union and common market, all of which are goals prescribed in the ECOWAS Treaty.

Besides market integration, ECOWAS has not made much progress in policy integration, even though the harmonization of the economic policies of countries engaged in an integration scheme is an essential ingredient of success. Whereas the ECOWAS Treaty explicitly identifies as an objective policy harmonization in such sectors as agriculture, industry, transport, energy, among others, as a goal, progress towards this objective has been slow. This is not surprising, since the degree of policy harmonization reflects the willingness of members of an integrating group to cede certain aspects of national power to a supranational authority.

To be sure, while the integration process may have been slow, ECOWAS could well point to some significant successes. One of these is the empowerment of citizens of member countries through the protocol on Free Movement of Persons, Rights of Residence and Establishment, adopted in May 1979. Although the Protocol may never be able to achieve the goal of creating an all-embracing "community citizenship", it has nevertheless made it possible for peoples across national borders to live, work, trade and forge socio-cultural ties with one another in ways that could never have been possible without ECOWAS. Though arguably the flagship of ECOWAS, member states have often undermined the Protocol on the Free Movement of Persons, Goods and Capital through the imposition of different forms of barriers, such as road blocks, customs and police posts, and tedious paper work.[49]

Despite the fact that ECOWAS has adopted several decisions and protocols, very few substantive changes have taken place by way of enhancing the quality of life of ordinary citizens of member states – a key objective of ECOWAS. Disappointment with the poor performance of ECOWAS is as widespread as the belief in the immense possibilities and virtues of the integration project in West Africa. To attribute ECOWAS's poor performance to the region's lack of initial conditions, as some commentators have tended to do, remains largely unconvincing. Even if one has to accept the argument that the prerequisites for integration are lacking in the case of West Africa's integration, it is still reasonable to expect that the integration project must start from the premise that these pre-conditions have to be created. This is a fair and legitimate expectation after over four decades of ECOWAS existence. There is little purpose in liberalizing trade when the participating states in an integrative scheme have nothing to exchange. For West Africa, therefore, regional integration, among other goals, must create the basis for trade. In other words, it must be a strategy for development. The objective situation on the ground in West Africa suggests ECOWAS's record in this area has been less than impressive.

A characteristic feature of the political economy of ECOWAS Member States is that a substantial portion of their revenue is derived from indirect tax – mainly from import and export taxes. Consequently, a great deal of importance is attached to customs duties, hence the seeming reluctance by the various governments to abolish tariff, a necessary condition for market integration in the sub-region. When confronted by the institutional obligation to abolish trade barriers, governments try to get around relevant treaty provisions by levying other charges that have equivalent effect. The situation is compounded by the inability of the ECOWAS compensatory arrangement to compensate member countries for revenue loss as a result of the abolition of tariffs.[50]

Although regional integration should result in substantial economic benefits, there is legitimate concern among ECOWAS Member States that the gains from market integration would accrue mainly to the lager or more industrially developed countries which are better placed to capture the additional income benefits from an open regional market. Perceptions that partner countries have gained or will gain a disproportionate share of the benefits from integration usually lead to moves that could generate consequences, whether intended or not, of restricting the scope of regional cooperation. Arthur Hazelwood made this point forcefully in a recent study when he observed that: "the case for integration, for a particular country's participation in an integration scheme, rests on the benefits that country itself will obtain from integration. The case of integration is not a case for helping others; it is a case for helping yourselves. It must be appreciated that integration will not benefit one country, or at any rate not for long, unless it also benefits the others; the case for integration arises from self-interest, but the pursuit of self-interest requires the interest of others to be simultaneously served. Integration will not succeed unless every partner benefits, because any who think they will not benefit will not participate, and there will then be no integration. The benefit is for everyone or no one."[51]

The issue of balanced and equitable distribution of the benefits of integration is even more compelling in a poor region like West Africa, where the mere allocation of industrial production could make a big difference in local employment and enhance the quality of life of impoverished citizens. For the less developed members, especially the landlocked countries, it is crucial to have fiscal incentives and a programme of differentials in their favour. Specific measures would also be required for agricultural and industrial development, investment in infra-structures, among others. Given ECOWAS financial difficulties, it is doubtful if such corrective measures could be undertaken by the organization anytime soon.

At another level, those countries that enjoy relatively high levels of development within ECOWAS have had to pay high prices for being the "poles of growth and employment" in the sub-region. Notable among these are Nigeria, Cote d'Ivoire, and lately, Ghana. Whenever their economies are on the upturn, these countries have tended to shoulder heavy responsibilities on behalf of the community. However, whenever these countries encounter serious economic difficulties, the nationalist reflex tends to generate anti-community sentiments and policies, including the expulsion of citizens from other ECOWAS Member States. A related problem of uneven distribution of costs relates to the disproportionate share of ECOWAS budget that is bore by the affluent members. With Nigeria paying 32 per cent, Ghana and Cote d'Ivoire paying 13 per cent respectively, these three countries account for almost 60 per cent of the cost of running the secretariat, and also for the capitalization of the ECOWAS Fund. Naturally, these countries can expect a share of the benefits proportionate to the costs which they bear. Such expectations may cause resentment and acrimony among other member states to the detriment of the integration project. There is no doubt that the key to the viability and success of ECOWAS will be its capacity to balance the benefits of integration in a manner acceptable to all member states.

A second challenge for ECOWAS relates to the absence of strong political will among national political leaders in the region to drive the integration project. Development scholars like Stockwell and Laidlaw have stressed that the role of government in development has grown to the point that successful growth is impossible without the active support of government.[52] John Lewis has gone even further to argue that there is "no substitute for the continuing lead that governments must supply to development-promotion efforts.[53] The various intervention policies and stimulus packages which the US and other developed countries, including China, have used to breathe life into their economies in the wake of the global economic and financial crises provide sufficient proof of the leading role of government in generating economic growth, even in developed economies.

While some scholars have stressed the importance of the informal sector to the success of integration schemes, that of government remains crucial, not least because responsibility for the implementation of regional policies rests with national governments. Lack of political will among ECOWAS Member States manifests in at least two ways. First, there is the historical Francophone and Anglophone divide which has trailed ECOWAS even before it was created. The inability of ECOWAS leaders to transcend this political and cultural divide continues to slow down the pace of integration in West Africa. One important practical manifestation of the Francophone – Anglophone antipathy, as we have observed previously in this study, is the continuing parallel existence of the exclusive Francophone UEMOA, whose objective is to speed up market and monetary integration of Francophone West Africa only.

The lack of commitment to regionalism in West Africa has also led political leaderships in the various countries to pursue independent national strategies and priorities to the neglect of community objectives. The lack of commitment is also reflected in tardy payment of budgetary contributions, low level participation in meetings, as well as slow ratification and implementation of protocols and decisions of the community.[54]

The poor performance of ECOWAS has also been attributed to lack of viable institutions at the national level to manage the integration process. One important consequence of this situation is that decisions that have been taken at the regional level are often not implemented at the national level in the form of legislation and regulations. In other cases, national policies are taken without reference to regional decisions and policies. One aspect of this problem is that senior officials who participate in regional meetings not only generally come to meetings ill-prepared, but also without a firm negotiating mandate. Apart from poor culture of consultation among officials, some other institutional constraints include representation in regional meetings by officials who lack expertise of issues to be discussed, or who have only an indirect relationship with matters under discussion, including lack of involvement of sectorial ministries in the follow-up of decisions taken at the regional meetings.[55]

At another level, while consultation and coordination at the governmental level is generally poor, those between the government and the private sector and other stakeholders are weak and ineffective. In much of West Africa, there is no relevant institutional machinery in place to enable citizens and the business community to find appropriate channels of participation in integration activities at the regional level. Unless these issues are addressed, the objective of regional integration will remain a mirage. In other words, unless national institutions and administrative processes are adapted to ensure that regional policies and programmes are integrated into national policies and plans, little or no progress can be achieved in integrating the West African region. If national institutions are deficient, the situation at the regional or community level is no better. Here, the problems range from poor staffing, resource constraints and an apparent inability on the part of staff of the secretariat to reconcile national and community interests in the conception and implementation of programmes.

One other significant factor that may help explain the slow process of integration in West Africa is the lack of a forum or space for civil society, business and trade associations and ordinary citizens, all of who are directly affected by the formal integrative policies of the community. Theoretically, the importance of the role of interest groups in promoting integration has been stressed by Ernst Haas and others in the neo-functionalist school. According to Haas, by participating in the policy making process, interest groups are likely to develop a stake in promoting further integration, in order to acquire economic pay offs and additional benefits from maintaining the organization through which certain demands can be articulated and goals attained.[56]

This implies that in the integration process, civil societies and interest groups can and does play an instrumental role in the maintenance of the integration system. Through their involvement in the policy making process of an integrating community, these groups get to learn about the rewards of such involvement, and this necessarily leads them to work Toward the perpetuation of the system. Unlike the EU which has a sophisticated mechanism for the formal involvement of economic and social groups in the policy making process, no viable structure of that nature exist in

West Africa. This has led to criticisms that ECOWAS has no popular roots, and that the personalities and institutions of the community are de-linked from the ordinary man in the street. Not a few commentators have, therefore, attributed the ineffectiveness of ECOWAS to the apparent lack of popular participation in the community's decision-making process.

Against the backdrop of the consistently poor performance of official integration efforts across much of Africa, informal regional networks of traders, civil society and other social forces are increasingly being seen as agents of a more viable and authentic "regional integration from below."[57] It is certainly not by coincidence that some of the most successful of ECOWAS decisions relate to the empowerment of citizens of member states through the adoption, in May 1979, of the Protocol on Free Movement of Persons, Rights of Residence and Establishment.

As most of the itinerant traders along the West African coast know too well, there are still several nauseating difficulties constraining the movement of persons and transportation of goods across borders – roadblocks, custom and police posts, time-consuming paper works, including physical dangers to persons as a result of the activities of criminal bandits. All of these have to be addressed to allow community citizens to enjoy the benefits of integration.

ECOWAS top-down approach to cooperation and integration and its over-centralized and over-politicized bureaucracy, perhaps is responsible for the organization's failure to promote a broad-based and integrated development that is people-friendly, both in terms of cultivating the active involvement and participation of ordinary citizens, and in making them the ultimate beneficiaries of the integration process. If the abysmal level of citizen participation in the affairs of ECOWAS is anything to go by, it is doubtful if any reasonable degree of support could be mustered at the grassroots level in support of the community's activities. The failure by ECOWAS to bridge the gap between it and ordinary community citizens has led Charles Ukeje to suggest that "in many countries, people only know of ECOWAS vaguely, most especially during major summits of the organization.[58] This is as strong an indictment as any on the slow progress of integration in West Africa.

Political Problems

At the core of the problems slowing down the ECOWAS integration process is the lack of political enthusiasm, or what is generally referred to as absence of political will among members of the community. Lack of political will is reflected, first, in member states' generally low commitment to implementing community decisions and agreements collectively negotiated at the highest political level of authority.

Generally, lack of political also manifests in slow ratification of protocols and poor discharge of members' financial obligations to the ECOWAS secretariat. Furthermore, the multiplicities of organizations to which Member States belong; as we have seen in West Africa, constitute another problem of poor political response. For instance, the more than forty inter-governmental organizations operating in West Africa compete with one another and with ECOWAS for policy attention, financial contributions and political support. Among the most prominent of these organizations are UEMOA, the Mano River Union, the Cape Verde-Guinea Bissau Free Trade Area, the West African River Development Authority, the River Niger Basin Authority, and the Chad Basin Authority.[59]

Finally, there is the set of political problems that relate to the decision-making process within ECOWAS. Apart from the fact that the supreme authority of the community is vested in the bi-annual summit of Heads of State and Government, all members must agree before decisions are adopted at the community level, even though such decisions are still subject to ratification by each member state. This not only makes for a slow pace in decision-making, but also affects the pace of the integration process.

Key Actors in West Africa's Integration Process

By virtue of its humongous population, the diversity and richness of its resources, the level of education and entrepreneurship of its people, Nigeria is a dominant power in West Africa. Together with Togo, Nigeria started the nucleus of ECOWAS, and drove the diplomatic offensive that led to the establishment of the Organisation. The country has also been the principal financier of ECOWAS, contributing 32 percent of its budget. Despite all these, Nigeria's policy towards ECOWAS has been ambivalent, even incoherent, at times.

Some have suggested that Nigeria bullied ECOWAS Member States to cede the Executive Secretariat to Lagos, instead of Lome, Togo. However, as tangible gains failed to materialize for the country, Nigeria's enthusiasm for the integration project began to cool. In respect of Nigeria's policy ambivalence, the French scholar, Daniel Bach, has pointed out that the geopolitical objectives which informed the Nigerian Government's enthusiasm in promoting the establishment of ECOWAS were beginning to be realized through other means, in particular through burgeoning bilateral links with Francophone West Africa, and changes in France's African policy.[60]

Although all the administrations in Nigeria, from the late 1970 to the mid-1980s, had continued with the policy of providing subsidized oil to a number of West African countries, all of them did only what was absolutely necessary for ECOWAS and no more. No new initiatives were undertaken by Nigeria during this period to push forward the integration process which it had struggled to construct. On the other hand, the decision to expel more than one million community citizens from Nigeria in 1983 under the pretext that they violated their immigration status, derogated from the spirit of ECOWAS.[61]

In 1985, Nigeria not only closed its land borders for reasons of national security, but once again expelled millions of ECOWAS citizens who were declared illegal aliens. These actions, however justifiable they might have been from the point of view of national security, had the effect of portraying Nigeria as a regional leader who was becoming less committed to the community it had created. These actions also generated mistrust and antipathy to the regional integration process.

France

Although not a member of ECOWAS, and nowhere mentioned in the treaty establishing the community, France has played a significant, and not always positive, role in the regional integration process in West Africa. For historical reasons, and as a result of a continuing network of political, cultural, economic and military ties, France remains extremely close to its former colonies to a degree that Britain has not been able to match in its relations with her former colonies across Africa.

The seeming paternalistic relationship between France and Francophone West Africa has often been regarded with great suspicion and worry by Nigeria. The latter's bitter experience with Francophone West Africa during its tragic civil war (1967-1970) could only confirm this feeling. Two contradictory impulses flowed from this situation. On the one hand, Nigeria considered it necessary to break or at least weaken the ties between France and her former colonies in West Africa. On its part, France felt compelled to encourage the Francophone countries to institute an exclusive economic community among themselves in order to counterbalance the heavy weight of Nigeria.[62]

France however failed to frustrate Nigeria's push for a regional economic community in West Africa for at least two reasons. First, the growing dependence of Niger and Benin Republic on Nigeria's economy ensured that these countries broke ranks with their fellow Francophone. Second, Nigeria's expanded oil wealth also allowed the country to dispense favours to several needy countries in the region such that it could draw on political goodwill even among those that resent its influence in the region.

Beyond the Nigerian factor, the conclusion of the Lome Convention which legitimized extra-African economic relations with France by the Francophone West African States did more to convince France that ECOWAS would not undermine its strategic interests in West Africa.[63] Following the Lome Convention, Francophone countries agreed to participate in ECOWAS as long as the new community would respect the continued existence of their exclusive organization. This position was strongly encouraged by France. Nevertheless, UEMOA's competitive relationship with ECOWAS has not helped the process of integration in West Africa.

Indeed, it is generally believed, at least among Anglophone countries, that the true hearts of the Francophone states lie in their own exclusive economic community - UEMOA - and with France, rather than with ECOWAS. It is this divided loyalty that has led some critics of French policy in West Africa to regard the UEMOA as the French Trojan horse inside ECOWAS.

Notes
1.   ECOWAS: Annual Report 2001, ECOWAS Executive Secretariat, Abuja, 2001, p.10.
2.   S.K.B. Asante, "The Travails of Integration," in Adekeye Adebajo and Ismail Rashid, eds.; West Africa's Security Challenges: Building Peace in a Troubled Region, Lynne Rienner, Boulder and London, 2009. p. 53.
3.   Regine Chi-Bonnardel, The Atlas of Africa, The Free Press, New York, 1973, pp. 111-113
4.   See S.K.B. Asante, 2009. p. 53.
5.   Adebayo Adedeji, "ECOWAS: A Retrospect Journey," in Adekeye Adebajo and Ismail Rashid, eds.; West Africa's Security Challenges: Building Peace in a Troubled Region, Lynne Rienner, Boulder, 2004. P. 23.
6.   UNDP, Human Development Report 2002, Deepening Democracy in a Fragmented World, Oxford University Press, Oxford and New York, 2002. pp. 149-145.
7.   Ibid.
8.   See Adekeye Adebajo, "Introduction". p.2.
9.   Miroslav N. Jonanovic, The Economics of International Integration, Edward Elgar Publishers, Cheltenham, UK, 2006, p.49.
10.   Ibid.
11.   Bela Balassa, The Theory of Economic Integration, George Allen Unwin, London, 1973, p.21.
12.   Ibid.
13.   J. Pinder, "Problems of European Integration," in G. Denton, ed. Economic Integration in Europe, Weidenfeld and Nicolson, London, 1969, pp.143-170.
14.   EU,The Single Market Review, Impact on Competition, Kogan Page, London, 1997, p.23.
15.   F. Machlup, A history of Thought on Economic Integration, Macmillan, London, 1979, p.24.

16.   See S.K.B. Asante, Regionalism and Africa's Development, 1997, p.8.

17.   Ibid.

18.   See Miroslaw N. Jonanovic, p.22.

19.   Ibid.

20.   Bjorn Hettne, "Development, Security and World Order: A Regionalist Approach," in Sheila Page, ed. Regions and Development: Politics, Security and Economics, Frank Cass, London, 2000, p.52.

21.   Morten Boas, and Helge Hveem, "Regionalism Compared: The African and Southeast Asian Experience," in Bjorn Hettne, Andras Inotai, and Osvaldo Sunkel, eds.; Comparing Regionalism: Implications for global Development, Macmillan Press, London, 2001, pp.93-131

22.   See David Mitrary, 1966, p.7.

23.   Ibid.

24.   Ibid.

25.   See Ibrahim A. Gambari, 1991, p.3.

26.   Ibid.

27.   John Renninger, Towards Collective Self-Reliance: The Quest for Unity in West Africa, UNITAR, New York, 1977, p.79.

28.   Amadu Sesay, "Can ECOWAS Re-invent the Nationalists' Dream?" in W. Alade Fawole and Charles Ukeje, eds.; The Crises of the State and Regionalism in West Africa, CODESRIA, Dakar, 2005, p.192.

29.   Julius Emeka Okolo, "ECOWAS Regional Cooperation Regime," in German Year book of International Law, Vol. 32, 1989, p.112.

30.   Adebayo Adedeji, "Economic Community of West African States: Ideals and Realities," Public lecture delivered at the Nigerian Institute of International Affairs, Lagos, 30 April, 1975.

31.   Cape Verde became the 16th member upon its accession to the treaty in 1978.

32.   See S.K.B. Asante, The Travails of Integration, 2004, p.54.

33.   David C. Bach, "The Politics of West Africa's Economic Cooperation: CEAO and ECOWAS," The Journal of Modern African Study, Vol.21, No.4, 1983, p.605.

34.   Statement in Jeune Afrique, 12 February 1972, p.23.

35.   Daily Express, Cotonou, Benin Republic, 19 April 1973.

36.   See Daniel Bach, 1983, p.610.

37.   Ibid.

38.   ECOWAS: Treaty of ECOWAS, Chapter XXI, Article 84.

39.   Ibid.

40.   Ibid.

41.   Adebayo Adedeji, "Problems and Prospects of Regional Cooperation in West Africa," in African Association for Public Administration and Management, Problems and Prospects of Regional Cooperation in Africa, English Press, Nairobi, 1969, p.67.

42.   See S.K.B. Asante, "The Travails of Integration," 2004, p.55.

43.   Revised ECOWAS Treaty, 1993.

44.   Revised ECOWAS Treaty, 1993.

45.   ECOWAS Treaty, Articles 12, 13, 14.

46.   See I. A. Gambari, 1991, p.33.

47.   ECOWAS Treaty, Article 2 (2) (f).

48.   See S.K.B. Asante, 1997, p.50.

49.   Charles Ukeje, "From Economic Cooperation to Collective Security: ECOWAS and the Changing Imperatives of Sub-Regionalism in West Africa," in W. Alade Fawole and Charles Ukeje, eds.; The Crisis of the State and Regionalism in West Africa, CODESRIA, 2005, pp.148-149.

50.   S.K.B. Asante, 1977, p.67.

51.   Arthur D. Hazelwood, "Economic Integration: Lessons for African Recovery and Development," in O. Teriba and P. Bugembe, eds; The Challenge of African Recovery and Development, Frank Cass, London, 1990, p. 601.

52.   Edward G. Stockwell and K.A. Laidlaw,Third World Development: Problems and Prospects, Nelson-Hall, Chicago, 1981, pp.251-296.

53.   John P. Lewis, "Overview: Development Promotion: A time for re-grouping," in John P. Lewis and V. Kallab, eds; Development Strategies Reconsidered, Transaction Books, Oxford, 1986, p.29.

54.   See S.K.B. Asante, 1997, p.79.

55.   See S.K.B. Asante, 2004, p.29.

56.   Ernest B. Haas, The Uniting of Europe: Political, Social and Economic Forces, Stanford University Press, Stanford, 1958, pp. 50-57.

57.   Kate Meagher, "New regionalism or lose cannon?", Nigeria's role in informal economic networks and integration in West Africa," in Adekeye Adebajo and Abdul Raufu Mustapha, eds.; Gulliver's Troubles, Nigeria's Foreign Policy after the Cold War, UKZN Press, Cape Town, 2008, p.161.

58.   See Charles Ukeje, 2005, p.149.

59.   See I.A. Gambari, 1991, p.44.

60.   Daniel Bach, "The Politics of West African Economic Cooperation: CEAO and ECOWAS," Journal of Modern African Studies, 21.4, 1983, p.63.

61.   See I.A. Gambari, 1991, p.47.

62.   President Georges Pompidou's Statement, cited in Daniel Bach, 1983, p.606.

63.   See I.A. Gambari, 1991, p.48.

Chapter Three

THE SECURITY-DEVELOPMENT NEXUS AND WEST AFRICA'S INTEGRATION

Defining Security

Elsewhere in this study, we had referred to regionalism as a comprehensive process that implies a change of a particular region from relative heterogeneity to increasing homogeneity with regard to a number of dimensions, the most important being economic, political and security relations. We had argued that, in the context of International Political Economy (IPE), peripheral regions like West Africa are defined by political turbulence and economic stagnation. As a solution to their objective conditions of poverty and political instability, these regions are compelled to embrace integration in order to arrest the spectre of their marginalization. At the same time, their regional arrangements are fragile and largely ineffective, not least because the conditions of endemic poverty and political instability are anathema to a successful process of integration. Thus, the overall weak position of the peripheral regions like West Africa makes "security regionalism" and "developmental regionalism" more important than the mere creation of free trade regimes, the traditional aim of conventional regional economic integration project.

A characteristic feature of the West African political landscape is that most countries in the region have been involved, or are involved, in various kinds of intra-state conflicts of varying intensities and brutality. A useful question to reflect upon relates to whether there is a significant and demonstrable link between pervasive poverty in the West Africa sub-region (a developmental challenge), and the region's various insecurities, such as civil war, insurrections, violence, drug and armed trafficking, political instability (a security challenge). This is the concern of the present chapter.

To fully grasp the significance of the security-development nexus, and how this relates to the dual track of security and developmental regionalism in West Africa, it is useful to start with a clear understanding of the concepts of security and development, particularly as they relate to the situation in a developing region like West Africa. For this reason, we would attempt to differentiate between the traditional notion of security, that is, the security of the state and human security. This differentiation is useful because the challenge in West Africa is not, strictly speaking, how to secure the territorial integrity of states, but how to secure and protect citizens from conflicts within states – conflicts that might well have resulted from the actions of national governments in the first place.

Security is ambiguous and elastic in meaning. In the most fundamental sense, to be secured is to feel safe from threats, anxiety, or danger. This condition applies to individuals as well as nation states. Understood in this way, a state believes itself secure when it feels that nothing adverse can be done to it by other states, or by other foreign non-state actors.

To view security in this fashion is to accept that it is a subjective state of mind, not an objective condition of being. It describes how people feel, not whether they are justified in feeling the way they do. In this sense, security depends on the perceptions people have of their position or situation in their environment, not an objective view of their environment. This subjectivity explains why security encompasses so many things: what makes one individual or state to feel secure may not be sufficient to make another individual or state feel the same way. Indeed, one person's (state's) security may well be another's insecurity, not least because individuals, and also states, differ in their tolerance for uncertainty, their ability to live with anxiety, and their capacity to cope with pressure.

Traditional notions of security, shaped largely by the Cold War, were concerned mainly with a state's ability to counter external threats. In other words, "security" was the security of the state: the state was threatened by the military power of another state and was defended by the military power of the state itself. The preoccupation with the threat and use of force gave rise to the notion of national security, which was thought to be synonymous with security. Traditional approaches to security, therefore, necessarily emphasize order, predictability and stability. This largely military conception of security has, accordingly, focused on the state as the primary referent object of security.

With the end of the Cold War, a fundamental rethink

of what security means, or should mean, gave rise to new ideas and a major paradigm shift in the conception of security. One of the most prominent voices in this direction was perhaps Bary Buzan who, in his *People, States and Fear* identified five impactful security spheres, namely military, political, economic, societal, and environmental.[1]

Generally speaking, military security concerns the two-level interplay of the armed offensive and defensive capabilities of states, and states' perception of each other's intentions. Political security concerns the organizational stability of states, systems of government and the ideologies that give them legitimacy. Economic security concerns access to the resources, finance and markets necessary to sustain acceptable levels of welfare and state power. Societal security concerns the sustainability, within acceptable conditions for evolution, of traditional patterns of language, culture and religions and national identity and customs. Environmental security concerns the maintenance of the level and the planetary biospheres as the essential support system on which all other human enterprises depend. These five sectors do not operate in isolation from each other. Each defines a focal point within the security conundrum and a way of ordering priorities, but all are woven together in a strong web of linkages.

Buzan's sectoral approach to security was a direct attack against conventional thinking that privilege military security over everything else. Buzan's new conceptualization expanded the threats a state could face to five. His suggestion that security could be considered in sectoral terms, and that military security should no longer be considered the exclusive form of security in the contemporary world, provided the intellectual underpinning for much of the rethinking about security.

The second element of the traditional consensus on security with which Buzan took issue with was its universal focus on the state as the referent object of security. The referent object is the thing to be secured. For instance, if the referent objects of security is considered to be the state, military threats to states are privileged as the principal source of insecurity, and military preparations become the primary means of achieving security. In traditional security, the state was the referent object, presumably because the security of the state matters the most. Buzan rejected this argument, and suggested that the relationship between the state and citizens was rather problematic in a paradoxical way, because while citizens rely on their states to protect them from harm, the state can be a source of threat to citizens as a result of its interactions with other states in the international system.

The insight we gain from Buzan's analysis is that, whereas the state remains the fundamental purveyor of security, yet it not only often fails to fulfil its security obligations to citizens, but can be at times a source of threat to its own citizens. Of particular relevance to West Africa is Buzan's division of states in the international system into weak and strong, in relation to their capacity to respond to threats. Weak states are those, as we have in West Africa, in which the institutions and political coherence are weak, whereas strong states have strong institutions and firm political foundation. For weak states, a good part of their security problem relates to protecting the state against internal threats.[2] Protecting the state against internal threats constitutes the major security challenge confronting countries in the West African sub- egion. These threats may include civil insurrection, ethnic and identity issues, religious crises, and civil war, including poor governance and political and economic marginalization of sections of society.

The critical question for this study relates to what security means to citizens of West Africa. The objective situation in West Africa supports a fundamental rethink about security. To do this, questions concerning security as a goal, the means of pursuing security and, in particular, the relationship between security and development, including domestic governance, need to be addressed in an honest and objective manner. While much of the analysis in the past had elevated the primacy of security, defined as security of the state, is it plausible, even useful, to make such a claim in West Africa? To be sure, security is important, but how much security is needed or is sufficient, and are there other "national interests" that are equally important at the very basic level? What good, for instance, is security if there is no food, no electricity or drinkable water, as is the fate of millions of citizens across West Africa?

In the context of West Africa, there are substantial military and non-military sources of insecurity. In a region of depressing social and development indicators, security must mean more than order and stability of political regimes. In West Africa, as much as in Africa, security is about survival and the conditions of human existence; it is about peace, development, social, political and economic justice, because the absence of these values creates and fertilizes the conditions for conflict and armed violence. Ken Booth may have had the people of West Africa in mind when he emphasized the absolute imperative of a holistic approach to security. According to Booth, "for people, states and the global community, there will be no predictable peace without justice, no justice without security, and no permanent security without peace."[3]

It is obvious that those who have called for an expansion of security to embrace new sectors, such as economic, political and social (poverty, disease etc.) are challenging the existing value-hierarchy of society. Thus to "securitize" an issue not previously deemed to be a security threat is to challenge society to promote that particular issue higher in the scale of values, and to commit greater resources to addressing the related problems. In general, the invocation of the word "security" creates priorities for action, and the use of exceptional measures to address the issue in question. To securitize an issue has the capacity to bring increased political attention to certain issue areas. When a government or interest group frames an issue as a security issue, their purpose has often been to cause the particular issue to receive the same political attention and the same access to problem-solving resources that military issues have traditionally received.

Something is designated a security issue because a convincing argument can be made that the particular issue is more important than other issues on the political agenda, and that it should take absolute priority. Buzan and others have argued that an issue becomes a security issue not necessarily because there is a real existential threat to society in an objective sense, but because the issue can be constructed as a threat, and is then accepted as such by the political establishment.[4] Ole Weaver has suggested that power holders can always use the instrument of securitization to gain control over that particular issue, be it a political, economic, social or security challenge. As he argued, "something is a security problem when the elites declare it to be so ... In naming a certain challenge a security problem, the state can claim a special power or a special right, one that will, in the first instance, always be defined by the state and its elites."[5] In the whole business of securitizing an issue, the state has unquestionable authority, reason being that if the state says something is a security problem, then it is almost necessarily so. In a sense, therefore, 'securitization' is simply a stronger instance of the phenomenon of politicization.

The notion of securitization carries obvious implications. As had been argued elsewhere in this section, the mere invocation of security in relationship to an issue, even an ordinary issue, allows the state to take extraordinary measures to combat whatever threat that has been so identified. In many cases, these extraordinary measures would be unacceptable were the issue in question not securitized. For example, most states are permitted to withhold information from their citizens in the name of national security. Most democratic states even reserve the right to suspend civil and political rights, in particular to detain citizens without charge, and to use military forces against their own citizens in the name of national security – actions that, in normal circumstances, would be considered illegal and entirely unacceptable.

The right to suspend civil liberties and also to use military force against citizens in democratic societies remain controversial and contestable. However, the most pervasive of the special powers and rights claimed by states in the name of national security is that on financial resources of the state. For instance, the creation and maintenance of military forces consume large quantities of a state's resources to the detriment of other compelling social needs.

This is why it is important for citizens and civil society to be alert to attempts by governments to call every issue a security challenge.

Given the challenge of development and state building in West Africa, citizens must be particularly alert to attempts by the state to securitize issues of their fancy. As Weaver has warned, there is a danger in militarizing (securitizing) every issue because "the state is privileged in the securitization process." A good example of this is the US so-called "war on terror" and "war on drugs," or any such phantom "wars', which permit the use of exceptional measures, including the use of extra legal means and consume extraordinary state resources in their execution.

Another danger in trying to securitize issues in order to claim access to resources is that the issue in question will become the preserve of the military. In other words, extending the scope of security not only consumes scarce state resources, but also militarizes society. Both of these consequences are damaging to the developmental needs of West African States. Countries of West Africa need all the resources they can muster to drive development and improve the living conditions of their citizens. These countries also need less, and not more, militarization of their societies because experience has showed that the military perhaps constitutes the most important source of instability in countries of the sub-region. The evidence of coups, counter-coups, and violent civil insurrections point to the danger of excessive militarization of countries of the region.

On the other side of the coin, the creative use of the instrument of securitization can have salutary effects in the political economy of West African states, with the proviso that citizens and civil society are actively involved in the process. Precisely because traditional security areas have benefitted from high levels of assured state funding in a way that has not been true for other areas, such as public health, education, poverty eradication, job creation, and so on, most of the new security threats that have been identified by those who have called for the redefinition of security have involved aspects of human welfare and safety, including internal sources of instability, such as ethno-religious conflicts and national identity issues.

The involvement of citizens and civil society in the security debate means that they can reject attempts by power elites to frame special interest issues as security challenges. Involvement in the debate means that citizens and civil society can promote issues such as food security and health that threaten the human security of citizens. For West Africa, if any issue is to be securitized at all, that must be poverty, arguably the most serious threat to security in the sub-region. There is no reason, for instance, why economic and political marginalization cannot be securitized, as also the issue of good governance, particularly democratic governance. We insist that security is a normative concept, and much of security policy is the pursuit of a particular kind of social and political objective. Securitization is seldom an innocent act.

Human Security in West Africa

Several African countries have experienced great upheavals in recent decades, including violent and often brutal conflicts within the borders of many of these states. These situations have helped to expose weaknesses in the state-centric concept of security, to highlight the importance of the interconnections among development, security and governance, and to underscore the need to understand and deal more fully with the variety of issues relevant to the root causes of conflict, conflict prevention and peace building.

For too long, the concept of security has been shaped by the potential for conflict between states. However, the average man or woman in the street instinctively understands what security means: It means safety from the constant threats of hunger, disease, crime and repression; it means protection from sudden and hurtful disruptions in the settled pattern of daily lives, whether in homes, communities, and in the work environment. All these fears and anxieties are captured in the notion of human security, a concept that was first used in a significant way in the 1994 United Nations Development Programme (UNDP) Human Development Report, although arguably its roots are deeper. The UNDP's vision of human security encompasses seven dimensions, namely economic, food, health, environment, personal, community, and political security. The overall goal was to expand the concept of security.

While the concept of national security largely refers to the security of the state against armed attack or insurrection, the referent object of the broader concept of human security, which includes overlapping systems of security at individual, national and international levels, is the security of the individual in his or her personal surroundings and within the community. The Commission on Global Governance, in its 1995 report, had also advocated an expanded concept of human security that included "safety from chronic threats, such as hunger, disease, and repression, as well as protection from sudden and harmful disruptions in the patterns of daily life.[6] In the opinion of the Commission, "the security of people must be regarded as a goal as important as the security of the state.[7]

From the perspective of the Commission on Human Security, an offshoot of the 2000 United Nations Millennium Summit, human security is a "concept that combines human protection and human development, and interconnects peace, security and sustainable development."[9] An important point that was stressed by the Commission is that consideration of human security should not be focused only at the macro or state level, but also at the community and individual levels. Even more importantly, the report of the Commission sought to connect different types of freedom – freedom from want, freedom from fear, and freedom to take action on one's own behalf.

The notion of freedom from want stresses the imperative of ensuring basic human needs in economic, health, food, social and environmental terms. On the other hand, freedom from fear seeks to remove the use of, or threat of use of force and violence from people's everyday lives. The freedom to take action on one's own behalf recognises the critical role of participatory democracy. Additionally, the report offered two general and interlinked strategies to promote human security. The first stressed protection, which sought to shield people from dangers and to systematically address insecurities. The second highlighted empowerment, which aimed to enable people develop their potential and become full participants in decision making, both in economic and political terms.
Given the breadth of its analysis, the report of the Commission on Human Security created a new paradigm

for tackling a number of key social, economic and political concerns, including people in violent conflict, refugees and internally displaced persons, extreme poverty, health care, basic education and human rights, among others.

Recognizing the importance of the human security approach, the UN 2005 World Summit Outcome was sufficiently inspired to declare as follows: "We stress the right of people to live in freedom and dignity, free from poverty and despair. We recognize that all individuals, in particular the vulnerable people, are entitled to freedom from fear and freedom from want, with equal opportunity to enjoy all the rights and fully develop their human potential."[10]

In a related action, the UN Security Council, meeting at the level of Heads of State and Government at the same 2005 World Summit, adopted a resolution on conflict prevention, particularly in Africa. The resolution, which aims to operationalize the concept of human security, addresses some of the core concerns of the concept, namely that security and development are mutually reinforcing, and that a broad strategy is needed to address the root causes of armed conflict and political and social crises in a comprehensive manner, including by promoting sustainable development, poverty eradication, national reconciliation, good governance, democracy, gender equality, the rule of law and respect for and promotion of human rights.[11]

Africa has traditionally followed an expansive approach to the concept of human security. For example, the African Non-Aggression and Common Defence Pact states as follows: "human security means the security of the individual with respect to the satisfaction of the basic needs of life; it also encompasses the creation of the social, political, economic, military, environmental and cultural conditions necessary for the survival, livelihood and freedoms, the respect for human rights, good governance, access to education, health care, and ensuring that each individual has opportunities and choices to fulfil his/her own potential."[12]

Kofi Annan, former UN Secretary-General, had provided what remains one of the most profound and expansive definition of the concept of human security. According to Annan: "Human Security in its broadest sense embraces far more than the absence of violent conflict. It encompasses human rights, good governance, access to education and health care and ensuring that each individual has opportunities and choices to fulfil his or her own potential. Every step in this direction is also a step towards reducing poverty, achieving economic growth and preventing conflict. Freedom from want, freedom from fear and freedom of future generations to inherit a healthy natural environment – these are the interrelated building blocks of human and therefore national security."[13]

The United Nations uses a Human Development Index focusing on levels of economic development, life expectancy, and levels of education as indicators of human insecurity. By this measure, for instance, it has been demonstrated that it is possible to achieve relatively significant increases in human security by way of small increases in economic development. While there is a range of specific issue areas that can be assessed to measure degrees of human security, dominant issues include human rights and democracy, population and demographic change, food and health, including the human costs of war.

Conflict remains one of the basic sources of insecurity,

particularly in Africa. At the turn of the 21st century, most of the world's armed conflicts were taking place in sub-Saharan Africa. During the last two decades of the 20th century, as many as 28 sub-Saharan African countries were engaged in various degrees of violent conflict. Estimates suggest that at the turn of the 21st century, more people were being killed in wars across Africa than in the rest of the world combined.[14] According to the Commission on Human Security, "most of the 24 major armed conflicts recorded worldwide in 2001 were on the African continent, with 11 of those conflicts lasting eight years or more."[15]

Naturally armed conflict has a strong negative correlation to human development. For instance, most of the countries with the lowest human development rankings have been countries in the throes of conflict, or just emerging from it. Even where conflicts have ended, the deprivations that war engenders, such as hunger and malnutrition, lack of basic health care and housing continue to impact on the human security of affected populations. In West Africa, where some of the most brutal conflicts have taken place in the last two decades, the direct and indirect human and social costs of war have been considerable, although these can be difficult to quantify. For example, according to 2003 estimates, two out of three people, or 65% of the entire population of ECOWAS countries, lived in a country severely affected by conflict, the highest incidence in all the regional blocs in Africa.[16]

Human rights have been a major element of the international security agenda since World War II, and were enshrined in the Charter of the United Nations as one of the three pillars of the United Nations system, the others being security and development. There is, however, considerable debate over what human rights are, what degree of rights are sufficient for all people, and the extent to which the exercise of one individual or group rights might impinge on the rights of others. A particularistic conception of human rights, such as the Euro-American perception of individual liberty, might be seen as an infringement on cultural or religious rights of others in some other societies. Furthermore, military intervention to stop human rights abuses, now being referred to as the 'responsibility to protect' or R2P, can often create new sets of humanitarian problems simply by the nature of the use of force.

The expansion of democracy and representative government has become an important measure of human rights and, by extension, human security. Democracy is seen as increasing human security because well-functioning democracies facilitate the peaceful resolution of internal disputes. In democracies, the political and military leadership are held accountable for their actions, and it is therefore harder to pursue policies that violate or undermine human security needs. In other words, democracy is averse to impunity. It must be understood, however, that democratic institutions alone cannot guarantee stability or peace. If anything, the process of democratization in transitional societies can be highly destabilizing if political, ethnic or religious groups seek power through violent means, or pursue narrow, sectional or nativist agendas. Paradoxically, the democratic principle of self-determination can stir separatist or independence agitations, activities that often result in violent conflict or civil war with all their negative consequences on human security. Generally, however, democracies are better at protecting basic political freedoms, particularly minority rights, which accord a higher sensitivity to the cause of human security.[17]

The relationship between democracy, security and development presents Africa with immense challenges, since democracy is difficult to establish amidst pervasive poverty, and almost impossible to sustain in the absence of economic growth. Despite the obvious difficulty in promoting democracy, security and development in poor countries, there is no doubt that democracy; security and development are closely linked in Africa. For instance, Africa's democracy deficit simply increases the continent's insecurity. This is a view that is rhetorically, if not practically shared by African leaders, who declared in 1990 that "… democracy and development should go together, and should be mutually reinforcing.[18]

As regards the social costs of war, the consequences on human security are fairly self-evident. The use of military force can have a major impact on human security, because war often includes the purposeful or accidental targeting of civilians and related critical civilian infrastructures, such as hospitals or electric power grids. War is conducted with weapons which unfortunately do not discriminate between combatants and non-combatants. While it is fairly easy to count the civilian casualties of war, the social and economic costs have long term consequences that are not so easy to calculate. In general, the human and social consequences of war are usually catastrophic and affect the poorest and most vulnerable social groups, mostly children and women, in a disproportionate manner. For example, in 1996, one tenth of the Liberian population was killed, while one-third of the remaining population were refugees, again predominantly children and women.[19] In the Sierra Leonean civil war, children fought for both sides in the conflict, while thousands of women, young and old, were brutalized and raped.

While human security has been promoted as a goal "as important as the security of the state", the fact remains that individual security, or human security, is dependent upon national security. Despite the desire to put "people first", or adopt a "people-centred" approach to security, one central paradox in human security policies is that most of the practical policy measures on the human security agenda actually involve strengthening the role and resources of the state. For instance, programmes to enhance security sector governance, or to reduce armed violence by stemming the proliferation and misuse of small arms, or to improve the criminal justice system, are executed at the national level, and involve strengthening state institutions. This is just as well, because without secure, stable and viable states that are able to regulate social, economic and political interactions, including law enforcement, individual, community, regional and international security will remain elusive.

The paradox of security in Africa is that human security is not threatened by conventional threats of armed attacks by other countries, but by more insidious measures, many of which flow from the very weakness of the state, including absence of effective control over its own territory. The resort to extra-legal measures to gain and retain power, including political and economic exclusion of sections of the population, among other acts of the state, substantially contributes to the insecurity of citizens. The dilemma is that while human security cannot exist without due provision of national security, ipso facto, an outwardly aggressive, or inwardly repressive regime can be a major source of human insecurity. As a matter of fact, internal repression by governments is a greater cause of human suffering and insecurity, at least in the context of West Africa's recent tragic history.

The human security challenge in Africa is not that African states are excessively strong to constitute danger to human security. The real problem is that several of these states are too weak to be able to provide human security to their citizens. Indeed, today, quite a handful of states in Africa are merely shells of the territorial states, incapable of providing for the security and well-being of citizens. The irony is that this weakness has not stopped governing elites from equating national security with regime security, and "governing" in the interests of their own preservation and advancement, with limited or no provision of human security for citizens. Such states have variously been described as weak, quasi-states, failed states or, in extreme situations, as predatory states, in those instances where the regime literally feeds off the state carcass for its own survival, as was the case in Liberia under Charles Taylor.

The crucial role of a viable and accountable state in generating security and stability, and providing for the economic well-being for citizens cannot be overstated. This nexus is critical, because it recognises the mutually reinforcing interactions between human security and national security. For instance, if human development is freedom from want (a process of widening the range of people's choices), human security can best be understood as the ability to pursue those choices in a safe environment, and on an equal basis with others. Seen the other way round, human development contributes to human security by tackling the structural causes of violence and conflict and also by strengthening the capability of society to deal with conflict in a peaceful and predictable manner.[20]

Against this backdrop, the idea of human security necessarily includes an obligation on the state to provide a facilitating environment for equality and individual participation through democracy, adherence to human rights and the rule of law. The state can only do this if it is responsive to its citizens and efficient in the provision of public goods. A governance approach that is predicated upon the provision of a secure environment also implies a commitment to poverty alleviation, conflict prevention and resolution, control of the means of violence, particularly small arms and organized crime.

In a sense, promoting human security is about making states and their rulers keep their side of the basic social contract, namely that states are created and owe their legitimacy to their ability to provide security in order that individuals can pursue their interests in a safe and secure environment. What this means is that states have responsibility not just to provide for the general welfare or well-being of citizens, or representation (inclusive and democratic governance), but first and foremost, to ensure the security of citizens. This is arguably the basic compact or contract that led humanity out of the Hobbesian state of anarchy. In short, the promotion of a strong version of human security would tend to make the legitimacy of states and their governments conditional on how they treat their citizens.[21]

Deriving from this perspective, we would argue that at least five requirements are needed to complete the transition from a simple focus on national security to human security within the African context. The first is the development of an administrative bureaucracy to manage the state along a rational-legal, as opposed to a personal or patrimonial, basis. The mere existence of such a bureaucracy is insufficient if the state is not in control of its entire territory, and does not provide public order. Because neo-patrimonial regimes depend on a system of clientelism, the appropriation and use of state resources for personal purposes, and the award of personal favour in return for political support, these regimes demonstrate very little developmental capacity, and do not provide security. On the other hand, violence is a common feature of patrimonial regimes; not least because only through violence could the various patrimonial networks secure or maintain a slice of the national pie.

The second requirement is the rise of an independent commercial class, or the middle class in popular parlance. This increases the resource base of the state and diffuses power, dividing the sources of patronage between politics and economics.[22] The third is the transformation of subjects into citizens. In Africa, artificial colonial borders have created a sense of national identity, but such identities have yet to be translated into citizenship with its implied reciprocal relationship of duties and rights between the individual (citizen) and the state. This is a relationship that most African governments still have to earn. For instance, in much of Africa, security and basic infrastructures are provided by individuals or communities pooling their resources together. These citizens, long abandoned by their governments, often refuse to pay their taxes, which further impairs the ability of government to provide public goods. Fourth, there is a compelling necessity for the introduction of democracy that institutionalizes the transfer of sovereignty from the ruler to the people. Finally, the very weakness of the African state demands a regional approach to security and development, where both are pursued as collaborative ventures.

In West Africa, under the framework of ECOWAS, there is a discernible trend towards a regional approach to the crises of insecurity and development in a way that reflects the enormity and urgency of these challenges. This approach is most noticeable in measures to counter the proliferation of small arms, a major source of human insecurity in the region; efforts to deal with the fragility of the security sector; combating cross-border movement of weapons, drugs and armed groups; ameliorating the mass movement of refugees, and promoting development. All these cross-cutting challenges transcend national boundaries and, therefore, require an integrated and holistic regional approach to augment national solutions.

The Economics of Human Development in West Africa

A major goal of poor countries is economic development or economic growth. It is useful to differentiate between the two terms, because they are not exactly identical. For instance, economic growth refers to increases in a country's production or per capita output, and is usually measured by gross national product (GNP), or gross national income (GNI).23 Used interchangeably, these refer to an economy's total output of goods and services. On the other hand, economic development refers to economic growth accompanied by changes in output distribution and economic structures. These changes may include an improvement in the material well-being of the poorer half of the population, a decline in agriculture's share of GNP, and a corresponding increase in the GNP share of industry and services, an increase in the education and skills of the labour force, and substantial technical advances originating within the country.[24]

There is a long tradition of theory to explain development processes in both rich and poor countries. Only three of these, namely Walter Rostow's five stages of growth, otherwise called modernization theory, Andre Gunter Frank's dependency theory, and the neo-classical theory, otherwise called the Washington Consensus, would be reviewed here, principally because of their relevance to an understanding of the context and challenges of development in West Africa. Walter W. Rostow's modernization theory sets forth a historical synthesis about the beginnings and progression of modern economic growth. He conceptualizes the economic stages of growth as (i) the traditional society, (ii) the precondition for take-off, (iii) the take-off, (iv) the drive to maturity, and
(v) the age of high mass consumption.[25]

Although considered by many as ground-breaking, modernization theory never gained universal endorsement. Since the early 1960's there has been considerable debate over whether Rostow's path of economic transformation was appropriate, or even possible for developing countries. Some of the weaknesses of the theory relate to insufficient empirical evidence concerning what are needed for take-off, including imprecise definitions. Other critics have pointed to a lack of theoretical ground for a society's movement from one state to another, and the mistaken assumption that economic development in developing countries will necessarily parallel the early stages of development in today's economically advanced countries of Western Europe and North America.

One of the most robust criticisms of the Rostow model was the dependency theory popularized by Andre Gunder Frank. This theory maintains that countries become underdeveloped through integration into the international capitalist system. Writing in the mid 1960's, Frank had criticized the view held by many development scholars that contemporary underdeveloped countries resemble the earlier stages of development in developed countries. The prevailing orthodoxy was to view modernization in Least Developed Countries (LDCs) as simply the adoption of economic and political systems in currency in Western Europe and North America.

For Frank and other dependency theorists, the presently developed countries were never underdeveloped, although they might have been undeveloped. Their basic argument is that underdevelopment does not mean traditional (that is, non -modern) economic, political and social institutions, but the subjection of LDCs to the colonial rule and imperial domination of foreign powers. In effect, the dependency school is arguing that underdevelopment is the effect of the penetration of modern capitalism into the archaic economic structures of the LDC's.[26] Based on this analysis, Frank cites the disruption of African society by the slave trade and subsequent colonialism as examples of the creation of underdevelopment. This is the sense in the assertion that the economic development of the rich countries contributes to the underdevelopment of the poor LDCs. Therefore, development in LDCs is not self-generating or autonomous, but ancillary, because the LDCs are economic satellites of the highly developed regions of North America and Western Europe. This school also argues that, rather than being an invariable progression, the early economic advancement of some countries may already have given them early insuperable advantage over late comers. This early advantage, it is argued, changes the terms on which subsequent development occurs.

This particular kind of argument does explain why development often produces distorted forms of growth and dependence in poor countries, and why the poorest societies face systematic underdevelopment through their subordinate position in international systems of trade and security. According to Frank, a third world country can develop only by withdrawing from the world capitalist system. Dependency theorists often recommend import substitution policies as a way of promoting industrialization and autonomy, but over time these have generally harmed economies more than they have helped. In any case, normal development in the contemporary world must now occur within the international context of the co-existence of rich and poor countries.

While the dependency theory offers a powerful account of development challenges in LDCs, it fails to adequately demonstrate that withdrawal from the capitalist system results in faster development. For instance, policies by some developing countries to cut their dependence have not had the desired result. Beginning in the mid-1970s, Nigeria took several steps that, on the face of it, should have reduced its dependence on the capitalist West. The Nigerian Government cut substantially the share of its trade with Britain, the colonial power, by acquiring majority equity holdings in local petroleum extracting, refining and distribution, including the promulgation of an indigenization decree shifting the majority of ownership in manufacturing from foreign to local hands. These measures, as welcomed as they were when they were introduced, neither greatly reduced dependence on the West, nor inaugurated the anticipated rapid development of Nigeria.

Finally, the neo-classical model, which has its roots in the liberal free market economies of the Western world, contends that slow or negative growth results from poor resource allocation and excessive state intervention by LDCs. They argue that promoting competitive free markets, privatizing public enterprises, supporting exports and free international trade, liberalizing trade and exchange rates, removing barriers to foreign investment,
reducing government's spending and monetary expansion, and removing regulations and price distortions in the financial, resource and commodity markets will spur increased efficiency and economic growth.[27] Neoclassicism policies are reflected in the Washington Consensus, which includes the Bretton Woods Institutions (the World Bank and the International Monetary Fund), the United States, and the high income Organization of Economic Cooperation and Development (OECD) governments.

In general, there is widespread consensus among economists and policy makers favouring more reliance on market mechanisms to improve the efficiency of resource allocation. Although few economists argue with the need for selective deregulation, critics of the Washington Consensus feel they fail to realize the extent to which externalities, public goods, and income distribution limit the scope of deregulation. Additionally, although there is general support for liberalization and improved competition policy for economic activities previously limited to the public sector, there is considerable opposition to the Washington Consensus's emphasis on rampant privatization.

Critics see other problems with the Washington Consensus's prescriptions. For one, cutbacks in government spending may depress the economy, and usually require that spending on education, nutrition and social services be reduced. There is also the charge that the neoclassical prescriptions for liberalization and structural adjustment hurt the disadvantaged portions of the population without providing safety nets for the poor. One famous critic of the Washington Consensus, the Nobel Laureate Joseph Stieglitz has observed that "the net effect of the policies set by the Washington Consensus has all too often been to benefit the few at the expense of the many, the well-off at the expense of the poor."[28]

One of the more sophisticated and modern criticism of the old models of development was given by Amartyn Sen, another Nobel Economics Laureate. Sen has argued that economic growth was an excessively narrow goal, and that development must take into account other factors, such as social equity, economic independence and environmental sustainability. In particular, Sen has argued for the elevation of freedom to the centre of the development debate. In Development As Freedom, Sen conceptualizes development as a "process of expanding the real freedoms that people enjoy."[29] According to Sen, "development consists of the removal of various types of "unfreedoms" that leave people with little choice and little opportunity of exercising their reasoned agency."[30] Thus, Sen would like to see the expansion of freedoms as the primary and principal means of development. The important contribution of Sen to the development debate relates to the notion of freedom, or what he calls "individual agency." Sen would like to see freedom promoted, both as the basic end and as the most effective means of sustaining economic life and countering poverty and insecurity in the contemporary world.

What we learn from this review is that the concept of development is open to different, sometimes, contradictory interpretations. While development means different things to different peoples, in general, the concept is a positive one, connoting "progress" or "change for the better." As such, the definition of development has evolved to embrace not just economic growth as measured by per capita income, but also the satisfaction of basic human needs, such as food, clothing, shelter, education and freedom. This is the essence of human development. Human development is concerned with removing the various hindrances that restrain and restrict human lives, and prevent its blossoming; it is concerned with the quality and richness of human lives. The UNDP uses the Human Development Index (HDI) to measure the quality and richness of human lives as an indicator or barometer of human development in countries of the world.

As indicated elsewhere in this study, the West African sub-region fairs rather poorly in the human development rankings. Poverty is especially endemic in the region. For instance, in his introduction to the 2000 Annual Report of ECOWAS, Lansana Kouyate, Executive Secretary, underlined the widespread poverty in the West African sub region. According to Kouyate, "more than half of the population (of ECOWAS countries) subsists on less than one dollar a day."[31] Such a grim reality, according to Kouyate, means that the current economic growth level cannot bring about any significant reduction of poverty. He went on to blame the crisis of development in the region on the "model of development adopted in the sixties, modified in the eighties under the various structural adjustment programmes, all of which have fallen short of expectations."[32] The solution, according to Kouyate, lies in more and not less regionalism in West Africa.

The Security-Development Nexus

Nowhere in the world are the challenges of security and development more compelling than in Africa, even more so in West Africa. Grinding poverty, multiplicity of wars, armed conflicts from military and non-military sources across Africa and much of the developing world have refocused academic attention and international policy on the security-development nexus. A particular area of concern to policy makers in Africa relates to what role Africa's regional organisations, such as ECOWAS, could and should play in winning the peace and providing an enabling environment for sustainable and inclusive economic growth. These concerns derive from a recognition that it is impossible to achieve the economic growth and development objectives of integration in an environment of wars, armed conflicts, refugee flows – in short, perpetual regional instability.

It is generally accepted that conflict has heavy development and social costs. The force of the security-development nexus rests on the logic that promoting security is instrumental for development, and that inclusive development is an important element in promoting social cohesion and the avoidance of conflict. That being the case, development is held to be instrumental to the achievement of security.[33] Conversely, underdevelopment can often lead to vicious cycles of conflict, which again leads to underdevelopment. The West African sub-region, with its history of conflict, wars, social anomie and poverty, provides a good example of this kind of environment. On the other hand, virtuous cycles should also be possible, ith high levels of security leading to development, which further promotes security and more sustained development. Unfortunately, the virtuous cycle can more easily be broken, not least because it is quite easy to have relatively high levels of security without necessarily experiencing economic growth, or to have high levels of security and economic growth, but not inclusive growth, such that the potential for conflict remains.[34]

The enduring logic driving the security – development debate is simple: security is required for development and development promotes security. This is why the dominant metaphor framing policy discussions on peace building in post-conflict settings is the vicious cycle. The
 logic is compelling. As framed by Ken Menkhaus, endemic insecurity blocks progress in economic rehabilitation and recovery. The lack of economic recovery and employment opportunities in turn impedes demobilisation, and reinforces criminality and armed conflict.[35] The Menkhaus logic suggests that predation breeds poverty, while poverty breeds predation. Likewise, underdevelopment contributes to state failure by depriving governments of necessary tax revenues to be minimally effective, which in turn stymies economic recovery. Thus state failure produces economic collapse, while economic collapse perpetuates state failure.[36] The vicious cycle of insecurity, poverty and state collapse does suggest that poverty and conflict interact in a negative, mutually reinforcing cycle.

Since the end of the Cold War, there has been heightened appreciation of the interplay between security and development as the costs and consequences of violence, conflict and insecurity on development outcomes have become apparent. Conversely, there has been increasing understanding of the role of development processes and strategies in generating insecurity and conflict. Importantly, the strong correlation between low levels of economic development and conflict has been convincingly established.[37] The countries that are at the bottom of the human development index also tend to be the ones that face persistent violence, conflict and human security challenges.

While the end of the Cold War facilitated an activist internationalism, the new agenda of linking security with development gained greater urgency after the 9/11 attacks on targets in the United States, due to heightened awareness of the impact of insecurity in distant lands on the vital interests of the world's major powers. From the UN to the African Union, and from bilateral donors to civil society organisations, all began to embrace the mantra that security and development are interdependent and require integrated approaches. For instance, the final outcome of the 2005 World Summit at the UN was a document that boldly declared, "Without security there is no development, and without development, there is no security."[38]

Contributing to this new thinking was the growing acceptance of the idea of human security. As we had argued elsewhere in this section, proponents of the notion of human security have sought to broaden the definition of security outside its traditional concern with the security of the state and interstate relations to embrace wider dimensions of human welfare, thus incorporating both security and development in a single overarching concept. As a result of this new insight, there is a strong trend towards introducing greater conflict sensitivity to development policies and greater search for integrated security and development policies. Despite substantial efforts in this direction, it is still not fully clear how development and security policies should be integrated to address entrenched socio-economic problems to prevent conflict.

One of the main problems is that the causal connections between security and development are difficult to establish, since they are intermediated through a country's evolving social and political processes and institutions. Indeed, current research does not lead to definitive findings on the role of such factors as poverty, demographic pressures and environmental stress on conflict and insecurity.[39] Crucially, these so-called development "risk-factors" do not provide a necessary or sufficient explanation as to why some countries are more resistant to violence than others, and how certain countries facing grave developmental pressures are able to maintain a relatively steady course while others succumb to violence and conflict. The growing literature on the security-development nexus as well as on conflict prevention and peace building falls way short of offering conclusive answers, hence the need for further examination of the causes of state fragility or resilience to development risk factors.

At the general level, it is at least accepted that there exists considerable evidence of a correlation between levels of underdevelopment and levels of insecurity. For instance, it is incontestable that the higher the level of development, the lower is the likelihood of internal violent political conflict. Indeed, since the end of World War II, developed countries have overwhelmingly been spared the ravages of war and violent conflict.[40] Meanwhile, since the early 1990s,

80 per cent of the world's poorest countries have suffered some form of violent conflict.[41] However, when it comes to unpacking the relationship, the results are far from clear. For instance, it is not easy to determine how developmental 'risk-factors' contribute to conflict. Conversely, it is not obvious to what extent conflict is the source of a country's development challenges, rather than the consequence.

There is no doubt that the difficulty in determining the causal connections between security and development can have consequential policy implications, especially because those who assert the security development nexus want to see the achievement of both in any given context. The big challenge for countries in the West African sub-region concerns how security and development can be pursued complementarily, and how these countries can escape the conflict trap. Therefore, policy planners in these countries have a responsibility to go beyond the often postulated vicious circle of conflict and poverty to identify the critical factors and dynamics that can lead to a virtuous circle of security and development.

For example, some researchers have often cited the absence of democratic processes and rule of law, egregious human rights violations, the repression of basic freedoms and authoritarian rule as crucial sources of conflict. Accordingly, this school of thought holds up democracy as an important instrument for non-violent conflict resolution. However, it should not be overlooked that even as democracy can serve as an instrument for peaceful conflict management, the process of democratization, especially in transitional societies, can trigger conflict.

Furthermore, geostrategic factors have historically been recognised as major explanatory variables for war. Since

9/11, there has been an increasing tendency to view violent internal conflicts in the context of global systemic factors. More recently, the growing reach of globalization has brought about new transnational threats such as terrorism and criminal networks, all of which can cause violence and undermine socio economic development.

Since the mid-1990s, the literature on civil wars and interstate conflict has also been greatly enriched by economic analysis. Economists have not only studied factors such as poverty, inequality, and lack of economic growth as sources of conflict, but also examined the political-economic drivers of conflicts. For instance, the greed thesis emerged from econometric research by Paul Collier, who found a correlation between dependence on natural resources and higher risk of conflict.[42] As a result, resource predation has been seen as providing rebels with the motivation and, or, opportunity to wage war. Thus, private greed rather than social or political grievances has been suggested as an important explanation for conflict. These disparate studies suggest that a range of factors can influence the interplay between security and development in different contexts.

While the relationship between national resource dependence and a country's risk of conflict remains disputed, some researchers have suggested the resource hypothesis as being responsible for the conflicts in Sierra Leone, Angola and the Democratic Republic of the Congo, including the rebellion in the Niger Delta region of Nigeria. In any case, the international effort to criminalize the so-called "blood diamond" provides a tacit recognition that resource rich countries may be at risk of conflict.

The resource-poverty-conflict thesis is important

precisely because it challenges the popular theory that civil conflict in developing countries derives primarily from ethnic, religious or cultural cleavages. Prior research on the causes of civil war had emphasized that socio-economic, political and cultural grievances can lead to widespread discontent and spark rebellion. One of the more popular but controversial argument is the "clash of civilization" thesis by Samuel Huntington, which speculated that the dominant source of conflict in the aftermath of the Cold War would be ethnic differences among peoples with a distinct language, history, religion, customs, institutions and subjective self-identification. In Huntington's words: "In this new word, the most pervasive, important and dangerous conflicts will not be between social classes, rich and poor or other economically defined groups, but between peoples belonging to different cultural entities."[43] Likewise, Robert Kaplan, Daniel Patrick Moynihan and others have also presumed that wars caused by ethnic and cultural divisions would predominate in the post-Cold War era.[44]

The overarching insight that emerges from current research into the causes of conflict is the need to spur economic development and reduce poverty in developing countries, especially in the poorest states which abound in West Africa, in order to reduce conflict risk. While Nicholas Sambanis has argued that economic development on its own may be insufficient to reduce the incidence of civil conflict in poor countries, he nonetheless proposed that "rising levels of economic development, in combination with conflict prevention measures will reduce the overall prevalence of political violence in the world."[45] In this regard, good governance may well be the silver bullet, because it can play a mediating role in the interactions between security and development. Which is why countries challenged by some of the socio-economic challenges that afflict West African countries need to find a development-governance – security nexus that can turn a vicious cycle of conflict into a virtuous cycle of security and development.

It would appear that the world's political leaders are catching on with findings of academic research on the causes of conflict and how to combat it. For instance, at the Millennium World Summit of 2005, World leaders had declared as follows: "We acknowledge that peace and security, development and human rights are the pillars of the United Nations system and the foundation for collective security and well-being. We recognize that development, peace and security and human rights are interlinked and mutually reinforcing."[46]

On the heels of the Millennium Declaration, UN Secretary-General, Kofi Annan, had also asserted as follows: "…. in an increasingly interconnected world, progress in the areas of development, security and human rights must go hand in hand. There will be no development without security and no security without development. And both development and security also depend on respect for human rights and the rule of law."[47]

Both the Millennium World Summit Outcome Declaration and sentiments expressed by Kofi Annan above reflect a growing recognition of linking security and development in peace building in post-conflict societies. These sentiments also point to the instrumental role of governance in stabilizing society and creating the enabling environment for economic growth and societal welfare.

Historical and Theoretical Perspectives on Democratic Governance in West Africa

The governance challenge in West Africa, as indeed in Africa as a whole, cannot be properly understood outside of its historical context. The root of West Africa's governance deficits are deeply entrenched in historical experience that date back to the era of European colonialism. Without exception, modern African States are conglomerations of disparate and often antagonistic groups brought together by European imperialist powers. There is some truth to the claim that the European nation-state model was imposed on Africa, first through colonial rule and then through the process of neo-colonialism governed by a global order in which nation-state status is considered mandatory for becoming a recognised member of the international system.[48]

As an entity brought into being through the instrumentality of foreign military conquest and administered for close to a century by a combination of coercion and co-option, the colonial state in Africa did not represent the sovereignty of the people but rather the abrogation of it. One major and lasting legacy of the colonial governance system in West Africa was the way it prioritised protecting the state and its structures, including state functionaries. Though the various colonial regimes imposed varying administrative systems, all focused on centralised administration and on structures that provided protection to state officials.

In general, the colonial administrations were not constructed to serve the people, neither were they operated under democratic norms and principles. As far as the colonialists were concerned, people of the colonies were subjects who were not entitled to be protected by the state.

Over time, people came to see the state as an adversary which must be opposed, and from which protection could not be expected. The colonial state of Africa was, therefore, a state lacking in natural legitimacy, since it was an external imposition. Given its primary objectives of subjugation and exploitation of conquered subjects and resources, the state relied excessively on force and violence to maintain order in furtherance of the imperialists' agenda. As one Nigerian historian put it, "the colonial state was governed by the principle of amorality since the people did not accept the state in terms of the society's morality."[49] As would be expected in this kind of relationship, a duality in citizenship commitment and consciousness formation was created, the result being that primordial identification became primary over national allegiance.[50]

The attainment of independence did not fundamentally transform the structure of the African state. Out of political expediency, the political class that inherited the post-colonial states in Africa committed themselves to the protection and sustenance of the colonial system and its institutions. Thus, the emerging nationalists who developed their political skills under the colonialists opted to operate the newly independent states with a "bureaucracy trained and tested in the authoritarian habits and practices of the departed colonialists."[51] The post-colonial African state thus retained its forceful and authoritarian character. The distinguishing feature of the post-colonial state in Africa, therefore, is that it originated under repressive colonial rule, nurtured by a political class thoroughly schooled in colonial habits and attitudes, all of which have persisted in various ways in the modern African states despite the political and structural transformations that have taken place since independence.

Instead of transforming the state and making it relevant and responsive to the needs of citizens, the post-colonial leaders in Africa were happy to use the enormous authoritarian structures of the state to appropriate power and to extract economic gains for themselves and their kin groups. The desperation that characterized the competition for the control of state offices more often than not resulted in violent struggles, recriminations, bitterness and polarisation of civil society along ethnic and religious lines. In this kind of environment, politics was approached as a zero-sum contest in which victors lacked magnanimity and relied on brute force and manipulation of the coercive instruments of the state to destroy and enfeeble the opposition.[52]

Furthermore, to facilitate its regulatory and extractive roles, the post-colonial state centralises the production and distribution of national resources, and in the context of state capitalism which was the governing economic model, this encourages the perception of the state as an instrument of accumulation, and patron -client ties as the dominant model of political relations. Thus politics, as a struggle to gain access to the 'national cake', the euphemism for state resources, became a fierce battle in which all means were fair. Overtime, as African economies deteriorated while public expectations of the state were growing, the connections between the state and citizens began to unravel such that the state gradually began to lose its legitimacy as a guarantor of public safety and welfare. The state's reflex response was to assume more authoritarian powers, even at a time its moral authority was being weakened by distributive infirmities.

Political theorists have long argued that neo-patrimonialism is a common feature of politics in the developing world. Robin Theobold, for example, argues that "some of the new states in Africa are, properly speaking, not states at all; rather, they are virtually the private instruments of those powerful enough to rule."[53] Christopher Clapham also maintains that "neo-patrimonialism is the most salient type of authority in the Third World because it corresponds to the normal forms of social organization in pre-colonial societies.[54] Richard Joseph agrees with these analyses, but labels the same phenomenon "prebendalism," by which he means "patterns of political behaviour which rest on the justifying principle that political offices could be competed for and then utilised for the personal benefit of the office holders, as well as their reference or support groups."[55]

All across Africa, political elites extract immediate rents and transfers rather than pursuing inclusive politics and providing incentives for economic growth and development. Wayne Nafzinger, for example, cites "Africa's political milieu, authorisationism and predatory rule and widespread civil war as militating against economic growth."[56] The African development economist, Claude Ake, agrees and clarifies the enormity of the governance challenge in the following words: "With independence, African leaders were in no position to pursue development; they were too engrossed in the struggle for survival... Indeed, instead of being a public force, the state in Africa tends to be privatised, that is, appropriated to the service of private interests by the dominant faction of the elite."[57]

In traditional African societies, chiefs or village heads

were expected to guarantee the livelihood of the community, typically by entreating their spiritual powers to provide adequate rainfall and bountiful harvests. Leaders who persistently failed to satisfy community needs could be removed from office. In patrimonial political systems, such as is characteristic of traditional West African societies, leadership accrues by dint of personal prestige and power. In practice, ordinary citizens are treated as an extension of the 'big man's household, with no rights or privileges other than those bestowed by the ruler.

Consequently, the personal interaction between the 'big man' and his extended retinue of hangers-on defined African politics, from the highest reaches of presidential palaces to the humblest village council. In this kind of relationship, authority is entirely personalised, shaped by the ruler's preferences and whims, rather than by a codified system of law. In return for the loyalty of his subjects, or more appropriately "clients," the ruler provides security and distributes favours and sanctions according to his will. Not even the trappings of electoral democracy can supplant or attenuate this system which co-exists with legal institutions in modern states of Africa because, as Theobold has argued, "under a neo-patrimonial regime, the right to rule is ascribed to a person, rather than to an office, despite the official existence of a written constitution."[58] In this system, the ruler dominates the state apparatus and stands above the law. In general officials occupy bureaucratic positions less to perform public service – their ostensible purpose – but to acquire wealth and status. Although state functionaries receive salaries, they also enjoy unrestricted access to various forms of illicit rents, bribes and petty corruptions, all of which constitute an important entitlement of office.

The fact that the post-colonial states in Africa have been formally constituted on the model of the Western State is not in itself evidence of their institutionalisation. Above and beyond the public display of the attributes of the modern state – such as ministries, security services, among others – the reality is that these are not modern states exhibiting clear distinctions between the public and private spheres. The modern state of Africa has yet to be properly institutionalised because it is not fused with the society, rather it is above it. This has much to do partly with historical factors linked directly to the evolution of the post-colonial state, whose origin lies in the autocratic, arbitrary and poorly bureaucratised colonial state, and partly due to important cultural attributes of rulership in Africa, that is, the personalized nature of power in the traditional African society.

The logic of state service in Africa is, therefore, highly personalised and non-bureaucratic. In this set up, holders of state office, however lowly they may be in the pecking order, are rarely impartial. Either they are using their official position to pursue their personal business interests, that is, the negotiation of their services for a fee, or else they provide the service (favour), which is expected, for clearly understood patrimonial reasons. These "patrimonial reasons" are, indeed, well understood by all in society, precisely because in such a system, appointments to positions of public responsibility, even at fairly low levels, are made largely according to the wishes of the political leaders. The overriding criterion for selection is kin, communal or blood ties and loyalty to the ruling elites, rather than qualification or competence.

Thus the state in Africa is no more than an artificially 'modern' political edifice, its workings deriving from patrimonial dynamics. Within this system, rulers dominate the political system far more than it is possible in a bureaucratic system. Legal niceties or systems of checks and balances are weak and do no restrain power, especially executive power at the highest level. Rulers and their closest cronies are not bound by the law or constitutionalism and, in most cases, they actively try to emasculate or eliminate formal institutional checks on executive power. In particular, the independence of the legislative and judicial branches is severely curtailed because neo-patrimonial rulers are deeply suspicious of any form of institutional pluralism. Overall, under Africa's neo-patrimonial rule, the operation of state apparatus is largely informal, rule of law feebly enforced and the capacity of the state to implement public policy, including security provisions, severely limited.

Around the world, a growing number of people are recognising that governance matters for development - that institutions, rules and political processes play a big role in whether economies grow, whether children go to school, whether development moves forward or back.[59] As argued in the Human Development Report 2002, "promoting human development is not just a social, economic and technological challenge; it is also an institutional and political challenge."[60] This new consensus has given impetus to a growing recognition that many persistent development problems reflect failures of governance. The governance crisis is evident in widespread corruption, inefficient public services, social and political exclusion and a host of other system failures, in several poor countries of the world. The notion of good governance which emerged out of this new thinking essentially aims to correct governance failures in developmental and political dimensions. Indeed, as Kofi Annan, former UN Secretary-General, has observed, "good governance is perhaps the single most important factor in eradicating poverty and promoting development."[61]

While there is little disagreement about what governance means, considerable disagreement exists as to what good governance means, including what it should entail. The reason for this disagreement is not far-fetched. "Good governance" is a normative concept. As such, the values that are assigned to it are those postulated by the defining institutions or actors. While the meaning of the concept continues to evolve, it is generally understood as entailing some combination of participation, transparency of decision-making, accountability, rule of law and predictability. It is also predicated upon mutually supportive and cooperative relationships among government, civil society and the private sector.[62]

There is a growing recognition among scholars, policy makers and civil society activists that persistent "bad" governance is the root cause of much of the social and economic malaise of poor countries of Africa and other parts of the developing world. The quality of governance does matter for development and for a safe and secure society. For instance, the United Nations Millennium Declaration stresses that creating an environment that is conducive to development and to the elimination of poverty depends, among others, on good governance within each country, on good governance at the international level, and on transparency in the global financial, monetary and trading systems.[63]

Given the African experience, it is self-evident that good governance furnishes a potent antidote to the patrimonialism and clientism that infect politics and the social order on the continent. This is so because, politically, good governance is an issue of democracy, accountability, rule of law and transparency. In a democracy, those in power are accountable to ordinary citizens, whose power to elect and to remove non-performing leaders from office is fully institutionalized. It is also an issue of ensuring that the governed have the appropriate institutional means and processes to control and check the activities of their leaders, to ensure that the rights and freedoms of citizens are honoured and respected, and to ensure that governance is conducted in accordance with the laws and not at the whims and fancy of egoistic leaders. In a democracy, people are also keen to ensure that decisions and their implementation are conducted in a transparent and inclusive manner, so that those responsible for these decisions could be held accountable for their performance or lack of it, as the case may be.

Good governance is also an economic issue because citizens are keen to see national resources allocated appropriately as directed by their elected representatives, and efficiently utilized according to best practices. Consequently, from the perspective of economics, good governance provides the assurance that economic decisions would be driven by considerations for efficiency and public good rather than the satisfaction of private interests.

The economic benefits of good governance have long been recognized by the United Nations.[65] Whereas the 1990 Human Development Report had identified investment in education and health and the promotion of equitable economic growth as the two pillars of development, the 2002 report had highlighted promoting participation through democratic governance as a third pillar of 21st century human development strategy. As argued in the report, the importance of democratic participation derives principally from the fact that it promotes individual as well as collective agency, both of which are central to social and political progress. The report reasoned that countries can promote human development for all only when they have governance systems that are fully accountable to all people, and also when all people can participate in the debates and decisions that shape their lives. Because poor people tend to suffer most when institutions function badly, promoting human development requires good governance which can foster fair, inclusive accountable institutions that are able to protect human rights and basic freedoms.

The UNDP has also argued that countries can promote human development for all only when they have governance systems that are fully accountable to all people, and when all people can participate in the debates and decisions that shape their lives.[66] Views such as these have encouraged the belief that democratic governance is not only valuable in its own right, but that it can also advance human development, at least for two reasons. First, enjoying political freedom and participating in the decisions that shape one's life are fundamental human rights. These are essential components of human development in their own right, as Amartya Sen has argued with much originality.[68] Secondly, democratic governance can trigger a virtuous cycle of development, as political freedom empowers people to press for policies that expand social and economic opportunities, and as open debates help communities shape their priorities.

As argued in the Human Development Report 2002, democracies also contribute to political stability, providing open space for political opposition and handovers of power. According to the report, between 1950 and 1990 riots and demonstrations were more common in democracies, but were much more destabilizing in dictatorships. Moreover, wars were more frequent in non-democratic regimes and had much higher economic costs.[67] Recent debates have focused on what makes institutions and rules more effective, including transparency, participation, responsiveness, accountability and the rule of law.[68] All of these are important for human development, especially since ineffective institutions usually cause the most harm to poor and vulnerable people.

To be sure, governance for human development is much more than having efficient institutions and rules that promote development. Governance is also about protecting human rights, promoting wider participation in the institutions and rules that affect people's lives and achieving more equitable economic and social outcomes. In other words, governance for human development is not only concerned with efficient, equitable outcomes, but with fair processes.[69] From the human development perspective, good governance is democratic governance.[70] The UNDP elaborates the concept of democratic governance to mean, amongst others,

    (i)   That people's human rights and fundamental free-

doms are respected,

    (ii) That people have a say in decisions that affect their lives

    (iii) That people can hold decision-makers accountable,

(iv) That people are free from discrimination based on race, ethnicity, class, gender or any other attribute,

(v) That the needs of future generations are reflected in current policies,

(vi) That economic and social policies are responsive to people's needs and aspirations; and

(vii) That economic and social policies aim at eradicating poverty and expanding choices that all people have in their lives.

Politics matter for human development because people everywhere want to be free to determine their destinies, express their views and participate in the decisions that shape their lives. To be sure, no positive relationship has yet been established between democracy and economic growth. However, the fact that some of the world's richest countries are also the most democratic does suggest that democracy is compatible with economic growth and prosperity. While democratic governance cannot be a substitute for good governance, both can be mutually reinforcing. What is beyond dispute is that good governance does foster capable states, which are able to provide security and support efficient public institutions to deliver social services to citizens.

One of the more powerful insights into how governance matters for development and security flow from a recent study entitled "The Index of State Weakness in the Developing World"[71] by Susan E. Rice and Stewart Patrick. The study sought to gain a better understanding of the key features of state weakness across the world and the relationship between the state and security and development outcomes. Rice and Stewart reviewed 141 developing countries, ranking them on the basis of performance. The study defines weak states as "countries lacking the capacity and or will to foster an environment conducive to sustainable and equitable growth, to establish and maintain legitimate, transparent and accountable political institutions; to secure their populations from violent conflict and to control their territories; and to meet the basic human needs of their population."[72] The definition seeks to capture government responsibilities commonly considered core functions of statehood.

Although the study sought to examine the phenomenon of state weakness, some of the conclusions underscore the crucial role of governance in generating security and development outcomes. One of such is that developing countries that are more successful at political governance also tend to be better providers of social welfare. The study also found a moderately strong relationship between political governance and the ability to ensure the security of citizens. Flowing from these conclusions, the study argues that "across the developing world as a whole, poor performance in maintaining security or providing social welfare tends to be associated with a lack of democratic governance, whereas stronger economic performance goes hand in hand with more adequate social welfare provision."[73]

Probably inspired by the findings of the Brookings Institution Study, Necla Tschirgi has postulated a "Security – Politics-Development Nexus" to account for good governance and state weakness in sub-Saharan Africa.[74] Tschirgi's proposition that politics matter for development and security is consistent with similar studies, including the United Nations perspectives on development and security in developing countries. Professor Alexandre Lambert of the Geneva School of Diplomacy and

International Relations has also developed what he has called a "triangular security-governance-development nexus" to highlight the interdependent relationships between governance, security, and development.[75] Lambert goes further to segregate the triangular security-governance-development nexus into such sub sets as security-development nexus; security-governance nexus; and governance-development nexus, all of which he considers as two-way streets of mutually reinforcing relationships.

Some researchers have argued that democracies are better guarantors of property rights than non-democracies, and that enforcing property rights and contracts is essential for investment and economic growth. The counter argument that democracy may be bad for growth typically cites the economic success stories of some authoritarian systems by claiming that because dictators are less open to pressure from self-interested pressure groups, they are better able, should they so choose, to focus on nation-building.[76]

While security remains a contested concept, it is beyond dispute that building a functioning state requires a basic level of security. Hegre and others have demonstrated that established democracies are unlikely to experience civil war.[77] As early as 1795, Immanuel Kant, in his essay "Perpetual Peace" had described a "pacific union" established by liberal republics, and argued that democracies were less warlike than other forms of government.[78] Kant identified the constitutional, moral/cultural, and economic factors as the three main pillars underpinning the reluctance of democracies to go to war. Regarding the first, Kant had argued that democracies were representative governments which are elected into power by voters who could also dismiss governments once they failed to deliver what the voters wanted.

According to Kant, wars were expensive undertakings, which necessarily call for increased taxation and austerity. Recognizing that the electorate is never enthusiastic about higher taxes, governments would wish to avoid the austerities that war brings in order not to face the wrath of citizens. As for the economic reasons, the Kantian argument was that since war interferes with commerce and puts profits at risk and undermines the stability of the international trading system, the democracies of his era, which were also the leading trading nations, would be averse to war. The moral argument relates to the destructive power of war, which affects both soldiers and civilians who may be parents and relatives of voters.

Kant's optimism about the pacifism of democracy is not shared by all political theorists and researchers. While proponents such as Michael Doyle and Bruce Russett support it, others such as Steven Chan and Erich Weede oppose it.[79] This debate has, however, produced a consensus on two points. Firstly, that there is little or no difference between democracies and non-democracies in terms of their proneness to war. Second, and crucially, that war between democracies are rare or possibly non-existent. It is this consensus that apparently led Jack Levy to observe that the "absence of war between democratic states comes as close as anything we have to an empirical law in international relations."[80]

The democratic peace thesis has not only engaged the attention of researchers but also the political class as well. For instance, in his 1994 State of the Union Address, U.S President, Bill Clinton, had declared: "ultimately, the best strategy to ensure our security and to build a durable peace is to support the advance of democracy elsewhere. Democracies don't attack each other."[81] Similar sentiments were echoed by former British Prime Minister, Margaret Thatcher who, during a visit to Czechoslovakia in 1990, proposed thus: "if we can create a great area of democracy stretching from the West Coast of the United States to the Far East, that would give us the best guarantee of all for security – because democracies don't go to war with one another."[82]

The belief that democracies do not fight each other challenges the realist world view that nation states are doomed to exist in a state of war. While this conclusion does not suggest that democratic governance is the silver bullet West African countries need to create a safe, predictable and peaceful environment for sustainable development, it does provide evidence that democratic governance constitutes a key element in the security-development nexus.

Notes

1.   Bary Buzan, People, States and Fear: An Agenda for International Security Studies in the Post -Cold War Era, Lynne Rienner, Boulder, 1997, pp.19-20.

2.   Ibid.

3.   Ken Booth, in Ken Booth, ed.; New Thinking about Strategy and International Security, Harper, London, 1991, p.87.

4.   Bary Buzan, Ole Weaver, and Jaap De Wilde, eds.; Security: A New Framework for Analysis, Lynne Rienner, Boulder, 1998, p.24.

5.   Ole Weaver, "Securitization and De-securitization, in R. Lipscheitz, ed. On Security, Rowman and Littlefield Publishers, New York, 1986, p.54.

6.   The Report of the Commission on Global Governance, Our Global Neighbourhood, Oxford University Press, 1995, pp. 80-81.

7.   Ibid.

8.   University of British Columbia, Human Security Centre, The Human Security Report 2005: War and Peace in the 21st Century, Oxford University Press, Oxford, 2005, available at www.humansecurityreport.info

9.   United Nations, General Assembly Resolution 60/1 of 2005, paragraph 143.

10.   United Nations, Security Council Resolution 1625 of 2005.

11.   African Union, "Non-Aggression and Common African Defence and Security Policy", Addis Ababa, Ethiopia, July 2004.

12.   Kofi Annan, "Secretary-General Salutes International Workshop on Human Security in Mongolia" Press Release SG/SM/7382, available at www.un.org/News/press/docs/2000/20000508.sgsm738 2.doc.html

13.   University of British Columbia, The Human Security Report 2005.

14.   Commission on Human Security, Human Security Now: Protecting and Empowering People, available online at www.hsrgroup.org/human-security-report.aspx,

15.   ECOWAS/WAEMU: Regional Integration for Growth and Poverty Reduction in West Africa: Strategies and Plan of Action," A Regional Strategy Paper prepared by the WAEMU Commission and the ECOWAS Executive Secretariat, Abuja and Ouagadougou, December 2006, p.6.

16.   Sean Kay, Global Security in the Twenty-First Century: The Quest for Power and the Search for Peace, Rowman and Littlefield Publishers, New York, 2006, p.226.

17.   Ibid.

18.   OAU, "Declaration of the Assembly of Heads of State and Government of the Organisation of African Unity on the Political and Socio-economic Situation in Africa and the Fundamental Changes taking place in the World", Addis Ababa, Ethiopia, July 2002.

19.   ECOWAS/WAEMU, Regional Integration for Growth and Poverty Reduction in West Africa, December 2006, p.6.

20.   Jackie Cilliers, "Human Security in Africa, A Conceptual Framework for Review," Monograph for the African Human Security Initiative, available at www.africanreview.org,

21.   Keith Krause, "Towards a Practical Agenda of Human Security," Geneva Centre for the Democratic Control of Armed Forces, (DCAF) Geneva, Policy Paper No.26, 2007, p.13.

22.   See Jackie Cilliers, "Human Security in Africa," p.13.

23.   E. Wayne Nafzinger, Economic Development, Cambridge University Press, Cambridge, p.48.

24.   Ibid.

25.   Walter W. Rostow, The Stages of Growth, A Non-Communist Manifesto, Cambridge University Press, Cambridge, 1997, p.4.
26.   Andre Gunder Franck, Capitalism and Underdevelopment in Latin America: Historical Studies of Chile and Brazil, Monthly Press Review, New York, 1969.
27.   See E. Wayne Nafzinger, 2006, p.149.
28.   Pedro-Pablo Kuazynski, and John Williamson, eds.; After the Washington Consensus: Restarting Growth and Reform in Latin America, IIE, Washington DC, 2003, pp. 323-331.
29.   Amartya Sen, Development as Freedom, Anchor Books, London, 1993, p.3.
30.   Ibid.
31.   Lansana Kouyate, "Introduction," ECOWAS Annual Report 2000, ECOWAS Executive Secretariat, Abuja, 2000.
32.   Ibid.
33.   Frances Stewart, "Development and Security," Conflict, Security and Development, Vol.4, No.3, December 2004.
34.   Ibid.
35.   Ken Menkhaus, "Vicious Cycles and the Security – Development Nexus in Somalia", Conflict, Security and Development, Vol.2, No.4, August 2004, pp. 150-151.
36.   Ibid.
37.   NeclaTschirgi, "The Security-Politics – Development Nexus: The Lessons of State Building in Sub-Saharan Africa," European Report for Development Workshop, Florence, Italy, 16-17 April 2009.
38.   United Nations, "World Summit Outcome Document", A/60/L.I, 20 September 2005, New York, available online at http://www.un.org.
39.   Ibid.

40.	See Human Development Report, 2002

41.	Ibid.

42.	Paul Collier, "Doing Well Out of War: An Economic Perspective", in Mats Berdal and David M. Mallone, eds.; Greed and Grievance, An Economic Agenda in Civil Wars, Lynne Rienner, Boulder, 2000.

43.	Samuel P. Huntington, The Clash of Civilizations and the Remaking of World Order, Simon and Schuster, London, 2002, p.28.

44.	Robert D. Kaplan, "The Coming Anarchy: How Scarcity, Crime, Over-population, Tribalism, and Disease are Rapidly Destroying the Social Fabric of our Planet," Atlantic Monthly, Vol. 273, February 1994, pp. 44-76.

45.	Nicholas Sambanis, "Poverty and the Organization of Political Violence: A Review and Some Conjectures," Unpublished Paper, Yale University, July 2004, p. 50.

46.	United Nations, "2005 World Summit Outcome Document", A/60/L.I, 20 September 2005, New York. Online: http://www.un.org.

47.	Kofi Annan, "In Larger Freedom: Towards development, security and human rights for all," Report of the Secretary-General, New York. 2005.

48.	Kehinde Olayode, "Reinventing the African State: Issues and Challenges for Building a Developmental State," paper presented at the 11th General Assembly of the Council for the Development of Social Science in Africa, Maputo, Mozambique, 6-10 December, 2005, p.3.

49.	Peter Ekeh, "Colonial Rule and the Two Publics in Africa," Comparative Studies in Society and History, Vol.17, No.1, 1975.

50.	See Kehinde Oloyede, 2005, p.4.

51.	Ibid.

52.	Ibid.

53.   Robin Theobold, "Patrimonialism," World Politics, Vol.34, 1992, p.559.

54.   Christopher Clapham, Third World Politics: An Introduction, University of Wisconsin, Madison, 1985, pp.34-35.

55.   Richard Joseph, Democracy and Prebendal Politics in Nigeria: The Rise and Fall of the Second Republic, Cambridge University Press, Cambridge, 1987, p.8.

56.   Wayne E. Nafzinger, 2006, p.19.

57.   Claude Ake, Democracy and Development, The Brookings Institution, Washington, D.C., 1996, p.42.

58.   See Kehinde Olayode, 2005, p.6.

59.   See Robin Theobold, 1992, pp. 548 – 549.

60.   United Nations, Human Development Report 2002, Deepening Democracy in a Fragmented World, Oxford University Press, Oxford and New York, 2002, p.51

61.   Ibid.

62.   Kofi Annan, "In Larger Freedom: Towards Development, Security, and Human Rights for All", Report of the Secretary-General, New York, September 2005.

63.   Ibid.

64.   See UN General Assembly Resolution 55/2, paragraphs 12-13 of 2000.

65.   See Concept and Measurement of Human Development, 1990, Oxford University Press, Oxford, 1990.

66.   Ibid.

67.   See Amartyn Sen, Development as Freedom, 1999.

68.   UNDP, 2002, p.3.

69.   Ibid.

70.   Ibid.

71.   Ibid.

72.	Susan Rice and Stewart Patrick, "The Index of State Weakness in the Developing World," The Brookings Institution, Washington D.C; 2008.

73.	Ibid.

74.	Ibid.

75.	Necla Tschirgi, "The Security-Politics-Development Nexus, The Lessons of State Building in Sub-Saharan Africa," paper prepared for the European Report for Development Workshop, Florence, Italy, 16-17 April 2009.

76.	Critique of Author's draft doctoral dissertation by Professor Alexandre Lambert, Geneva School of Diplomacy and International Relations, Geneva, Switzerland.

77.	UNDP, Human Development Report 2002, p.56.

78.	Havard Hegre, Tanja Ellingsen, Scott Gates and Nils Peter Gleditsch, "Towards a Democratic Civil Peace? Democracy, Political Change, and Civil War, 1816-1992," American Political Science Review, Vol.95 No.1, 2001, pp.33-48.

79.	See Michael Sheehan, International Security: An Analytical Survey, for a full account of Kant's Democratic Peace Thesis.

80.	See Michael D. Sheehan, 2005, pp. 33-34.

81.	Jack S. Levy, "Domestic Politics and War," Journal of Interdisciplinary History, No. 18, 1998, pp. 653-673.

82.	Quoted in Michael Sheehan, 2005, p.32.

Chapter Four

THE GEOPOLITICS OF WEST AFRICA

Introducing the Regional Dynamics

The pattern of cooperation and dissonance in West Africa has been marked in a most remarkable manner by the legacies of its colonial past. Among the various sub-regions of Africa, none is as polarized as West Africa. Indeed, the sub-region has been described as the most varied in Africa in terms of the size of the countries, colonially inherited cultures, the levels of economic development and linkages, both internal and external. Of the 16 countries of the sub-region, nine are Francophone, five Anglophone and two Lusophone. In no other sub-region are there so many countries with a mixture of colonial experiences and legacies, all of which continue to dictate the nature, direction and intensity of regional cooperation and dissonance.

Historically, Great Britain and France were the dominant regional powers by virtue of their colonial penetration and subjugation of the countries of the sub-region. However, their approaches to colonial rule in their territories were markedly dissimilar, and these are strikingly reflected in the region's post-colonial legacies. For instance, although Britain had a long and intense contact with West Africa, this was dictated more by commercial rather than political impulses. However, the competition which British merchants had to face from other European adventurers necessarily led to the establishment of bases on the West Coast, followed by gradual expansion into the hinterland. For the British, therefore, it could be said that mercantilism preceded and propelled territorial acquisition.

On the other hand, the French saw their mission as an absolute necessity for maintaining France's status as a major global power, hence the integration of the colonial territories through the policy of assimilation as outposts of metropolitan France. The development of a commercial policy towards the colonies, including the consolidation of military power came after the great period of colonial expansion, whose primary motivation was the political ambition to create a Greater France in order to enhance its role and status as a world power.

These contrasting motives explain why Britain was rather quick to reconcile itself to the prospect of independence of its West African colonies, and while the French were fundamentally opposed to the idea of independence for its colonial possessions. France's African empire, which of course includes its prized possessions in West Africa, was seen by France's political elites as an important manifestation of state power and prestige.

Even if Britain was not without the desire to maintain some form of control after independence, it did not, except in the ill-fated defence pact with Nigeria, seek to formalize such links. Thus, it was easy for the Anglophone West Africa States to cut off what little links that existed between them and Britain on attainment of independence. By contrast, and in accordance with what was virtually a conditionality for independence, every Francophone West African State maintained what was termed a 'Co-operative Agreement' with France. As argued by Olu Adeniji, a former Foreign Minister of Nigeria, the new type of relationship with France in the name of cooperation was aimed to temper the process of independence, which had become irreversible, and to prolong the multifarious presence of the former colonizer.[1]

Whereas the British presence, though not insignificant in the economic domain, was less obtrusive and politically uncoordinated, the French shadow loomed large and has persisted rather decisively in the post-colonial pattern of cooperation and dissonance in West Africa. For instance, the so-called 'Cooperative Agreements' found expression not only in the conventional sense of development cooperation, but also included defence agreements by which the West African states signatories are obliged to call in French security assistance whenever there is a need to do so.

The historical context of external involvement in West Africa's political economy reveals two contrasting models. While one colonial power's influence looms large, that of the other – Britain – had been on the wane since its colonies achieved independence in the 1960s. However, it must be understood France and Britain are not the only dominant powers in the sub-region. Whereas France remains a key player on the West African political landscape, Nigeria's influence is large and growing. Until the United States post

9/11 global war on terror, the U.S. has maintained a benign interest in the region largely centred on Nigeria's oil resources. However, recent U.S. focus on state building and democracy promotion as a means to create capable states able to provide security and stability and assist in the so-called war on terror has rekindled U.S interest in the region.

China has also lately been a major player in the sub-region, also on account of its growing appetite for the region's vast mineral resources. The European Union completes a complex and conflicting mix of major internal and external actors shaping events in West Africa. To this list, however, we must add the phenomenon of resource wars because of the profound impact of resource conflicts not only on the trajectory of security and development, but also on economic cooperation in the sub-region.

France: An Extra-Regional Power

In granting independence to its African colonies from the 1960s, France attempted to replace direct domination with indirect hegemony. Indeed, maintaining France's influence in Africa was considered to be one of the preconditions for Paris to hold on to its pre-eminent status in world politics, and to maintain its international status as a global power, expressed in the notion of "grandeur de la France."[2] Way back in 1957, Francois Mitterrand, who was to become French President in 1981, had underscored Africa's central importance to post war France by declaring: "without Africa, France will no longer have a history in the twenty-first century."[3] Years later, President Omar Bongo of Gabon, replied in kind when he declared: "Africa without France is like a car without a driver, France without Africa is like a car without fuel."[4]

The philosophy of 'grandeur de la France' was ideologically rooted in the messianic notion of France's civilizing mission in its relations with its colonies. Politically, it meant that France could entertain a clientele of African States. Strategically, this special relationship gave Paris access to minerals, such as uranium and oil, crucial to the pursuit of an independent foreign policy. Culturally, the Francophonie was an additional bond between France and Francophone African Countries. In other words, even though economic considerations were important, the main drivers of this relationship were political and strategic.[5]

The international clientelism model provides the best analytical tool for understanding the nature of these relations. One of the specificities of this model is that the patron and the client control unequal resources. It follows, therefore, that the patron gives more to the client than the client gives to the patron. Each individual client depends more on its patron than the patron on the client. At the root of this unequal relationship is the structural dependency of the client. Thus, in return for political and economic favours critical to the client's survival, the client gives political support and loyalty to the patron – in this case, France.[6] Critics of this analytical model may object that since the patron-client relationship is a personal one, such a relationship cannot exist between states. Such an objection, however, ignores the fact that Franco- African relations have often been rooted and strengthened by strong interpersonal ties between French and African elites.

This system of Franco-African relations, as set up by President Charles de Gaulle, largely survived under succeeding French Presidents and political majorities from the political right and the left without fundamental changes until 1994, when the relationship went through a deep crisis which brought about some transformations.[7] Some of the notable new trends included a progressive decline in the quantity of French aid to Francophone Africa, a more economically oriented French policy and an opening towards other African countries. The Franco-African Summit is an illustration of this trend.

At the policy level, several trends in French policy, particularly towards Francophone Africa – its traditional sphere of influence – became evident in the 1990s. First, there was a drastic decline in French bilateral economic aid, from Euro 3.8 billion in 1996 to Euro 2.9 billion in 2001. At the same time that French bilateral aid was declining, its share of multilateral aid increased, with the largest chunk of this channelled through European institutions. This marked a clear change in French policy towards Africa. For France, involving Europe in Africa has been an advantage, allowing France to maintain its traditional influence, while Europe shares the aid burden.[8]

Another major shift in France's Africa policy in recent times has been the privileging of economic neo-colonialism over military influence, ostensibly under the guise of promoting democracy and good governance.[9] This is consistent with post-Cold War prioritization of economic imperialism over military imperialism and proxy wars by Western powers. For decades France had viewed post-colonial Africa as an exclusive sphere of influence. Indeed, France still maintains military influence and stations thousands of its troops across the continent, from Senegal to the Horn of Africa. France has, however, folded many of its African missions into multinational operations since its unhappy experience in Rwanda in 1994, when French troops failed to intervene in the opening days of that nation's genocide. Be that as it may, recent small-scale interventions in Chad and Cote d'Ivoire indicate Paris has not forfeited the right of unilateral military action in areas it considers as falling under its traditional spheres of influence in Africa.

From the commercial perspective, France has an intense business relationship with Africa. For instance, Africa accounts for 5 percent of France's exports, and French statistics indicate some 240,000 of its nationals live in Africa.[10] Though France has diversified its sources of raw materials, Africa remains an important supplier of oil and metals. The Omar Bongo metaphor in the preceding paragraph illustrates this relationship. In contrast to France's historical sense of imperial grandeur and civilizing mission, the new French policy has stressed the importance of encouraging regional stability, development and support of democratic institutions. As Andre Dulait, a French Parliamentarian noted during a recent debate on Africa, "the African continent is our neighbour, and when it is shaken by conflict, we are shaken as well.[11] Of course, not everyone in France is convinced African affairs should be of primary importance to French foreign policy, as exemplified in arguments in some intellectual circles that the resources being spent on Africa could be better placed in Asia and South America, where France's future economic and geopolitical interests are likely to be.[12] Such objections to strong French presence in Africa, however, seem to be the exception rather than the rule. For instance, of some 12,000 French troops engaged in peacekeeping operations across the world, nearly half are deployed in Africa. There are three main French bases in Africa, these are in Djibouti, Dakar (Senegal) and Libreville (Gabon). Their purpose is to promote regional stability.[13]

According to Andrew Hansen of the Council on Foreign Relations, the U.S. foreign policy think tank, France intervened militarily in Africa 19 times between 1962 and 1995.[14] Most of these operations were mounted ostensibly to protect French nationals or subdue uprisings against legitimate governments. Some critics, however, contend that the standard for military support was contingent on an African leader's willingness to support French interests in the particular country. As had been indicated elsewhere in this study, as France's former colonies in African gained their independence in the early 1960s, most signed bilateral treaties pledging various degrees of military cooperation and support with the former colonial master. Quite apart from these formal agreements, France's influence status in Africa derives from cultural, economic and close personal relationships between governing elites in Paris and several French colonies in Africa.

Following the French debacle in Rwanda in 1994, a new African Policy has sought to de-emphasis bilateral security arrangements in favour of military cooperation with international forces and Africa regional bodies. In furtherance of this objective, there is an on-going attempt to 'Europeanize' France's military bases across Africa. However, despite the move toward multilateralism, France has yet to fully abandon its traditional bilateral military structure. The evidence in this is that France has yet revise or renegotiate the secret and public defence treaties it signed long ago with a select number of African countries.[15] Such ambivalence has led to charges that France uses its secret defence treaties, including often ambiguous definitions of what constitute internal and external threats to its African client states, to intervene in furtherance of its geo strategic interests.

However, France's conversion to multilaterism was to receive further impetus under President Nicholas Sarkozy, following his assumption of the French Presidency in 2007. France's new policy in Africa, as enunciated in what has come to be known as the Sarkozy Doctrine, was unveiled by the French President in an address to the South African Parliament in Cape Town on 28 February 2008. In a far ranging speech on Africa-France relations, he declared as follows: "... To help bring about this (African) renaissance, France wants to place its relation with Africa on a new footing. It does not want its involvement in Africa to perpetuate, in different forms, the unequal relations that belong to a past that is over and done with. The relationship between France and Africa can no longer be based on requirements and policies that hack back to a time when the world was very different from what it is now. [16]

The political and security dimensions of the Sarkozy policy have since been elaborated into a coherent package to include, amongst others:

(i)   France's desire to forge new ties of equality, equity and respect, as well as relations based on transparency and accountability with Africa;

(ii)   A recognition that there is an indissoluble linkage between the security and prosperity of France and Europe and those of Africa, given both continent's geographical proximity and historical ties;

(iii)   A definition of the purpose of France's policy in Africa as being the promotion of the unity and rebirth of the entire continent, as against the previous paternalistic relationship with Francophone Africa;

(iv) A policy of not getting involved in local political fights, even in countries with which France has defence agreements.

Some experts have attributed France's conversion to multilateralism in its African policy not only to a series of political missteps in the 1990s, notably the Rwanda debacle, but also to budgetary concerns, including a changing international strategic climate. As Hansen has argued, "structural changes in the armed forces which resulted in sharp reduction in the size of the French Military and bases closures mean that France could no longer maintain the dominance it exercised in the past."[17] In addition to these factors, President Sarkozy himself has not hidden his opposition to France's long-standing practice of propping up dubious regimes in Africa.

Despite the Sarkozy doctrine, France still maintains a heavy presence in West Africa. In Chad, France fields some 1,200 troops, ostensibly to protect French nationals, but in reality to support the Government of President Idris Deby Into, and to provide logistical and intelligence support to Chadian forces. Although, this mission predated the Sarkozy presidency, Sarkozy not recommit his government to this mission when he took office in 2007, France went further to organize a separate 3,700– strong European Union Peace Keeping Force (EUFOR), which deployed in late 2007 after suffering repeated delays. In February 2008, an attempt by Sudanese–backed Chadian rebels to overthrow Deby was beaten back with robust French assistance.

In Cote d'Ivoire, France deploys approximately 3,000 troops, but under a United Nations mandate to patrol the buffer zone between the rebel-controlled northern region and the government –controlled south. The operation is France's largest and most controversial in Africa. Once again, the declared primary motive behind the French mission was to protect French citizens, but the strong French military presence did indirectly help to prop up the fragile government in Abidjan. The French intervention in Cote d'Ivoire does suggest that good old fashioned military intervention by France may never go out of fashion.

Regardless of the motive of the new policy, France's new defence and security policy seems to represent another important phase in the country's roll back from its pretensions as being a global power, which must necessarily maintain its swagger across Africa, as evidence of this status. It must also be understood that these changes are by no means altruistic or borne out of a new policy of good neighbourliness, but rather were adopted as a result of a cool-headed assessment of current geopolitical realities. From all indications, France appears to be retreating from its former Gaullist pretensions of being a great power at par with the United States.

What is relevant to the present study is that the successful implementation of France's new defence and security policy could weaken several West Africa countries, all of which have elaborate security and defence agreements with it. Because these countries have long relied on these secret defence agreements for their security, a retrenchment in France's long-standing African policy may prove disruptive to the security and stability of its African client states. If the new policy does result in a reduction in France's meddlesomeness in the internal affairs of several West African countries, perhaps the resulting security gap could force these countries to pay more attention to regional efforts to construct a viable security architecture for West Africa. Not only would this fit well into the notion of 'African solutions to African problems', it could help in efforts to develop common security and governance norms for the region. Perhaps it is too soon to expect this kind of sea change in West Africa's security environment, not least because there is no shortage of external powers that would readily fill any vacuum created by a French withdrawal from the region.

There is a sense in which it could be said that the evolution of France–African relations represents not only a transition, but a transformation of French policy towards Africa. France is not moving out of Africa, but its presence on the continent is being progressively normalized. Strong ties are developing with non-Francophone countries, such as Nigeria, Ghana and South Africa. In the past, bilateralism and secret defence agreements were at the root of Franco – African clitentelism. The move toward multilateralism is, therefore, significant. While France may no longer have the means to support a clientele of African countries, it still has the means and the will to pull strings and shape economic, political and security outcomes in West Africa.

Nigeria – A Regional Hegemon?

Nigeria has often been described as the "Giant of Africa." Increasingly, it is being seen by many as the local hegemon in West Africa. There is some logic in this assessment. With a population of about 150 million, Nigeria accounts for over 60 percent of the estimated 230 million people in West Africa. Not only does it have the largest and the most sophisticated economy, it accounts for a massive

75 percent of the region's economic strength. The country is the world's sixth largest oil producer and an exporter of over 15 per cent of America's oil needs. It also has an incomparable 95,500 strong army, which it has not shied away from using, either in United Nations and African Union mandated peacekeeping operations, or unilaterally as in several West Africa's peace enforcement operations, notably in Liberia and Sierra Leone.[18]

Recent emphasis on Nigeria's status as a regional power also flows from the international clout and revenues from an oil production that ranges between 1.7 and 2.2 million barrels per day. In addition to these resources, Nigeria also has proven natural gas reserves estimated at 120 trillion cubic feet, making it the ninth largest source of gas reserves in the world. Since the 1990s, the Gulf of Guinea, of which Nigeria belongs, has become one of the world's most promising energy frontiers, turning out a stream of new discoveries for Nigeria. A combination of tremendous human and natural resource endowments, dominance over neighbouring states and the robust diplomatic and military engagements of successive Nigerian regimes in the affairs of Africa may well have led to the widespread perception of Nigeria as a regional power or hegemon, and a natural leader of West Africa.

The concept of hegemony has always conjured up images of domination, bullying behaviour and arrogance on the part of the hegemon— the great power. However, the term is often used to describe the dominant state in a particular region in terms of political and economic clout. It is true that past and present global hegemons, such as Britain during the 19th century, and the U. S. in the 20th century, have often used their awesome power rather aggressively, the former through colonialism, and the latter through military and other forms of domination. On the other hand, one can conceive of constructive hegemony in which the hegemon not only articulates the rules and norms for respective regions, but is able to convince other states to respect such rules. In this sense, hegemony involves leadership and influence, and not dominance for its own sake. Hegemony or leadership is thus based on the general belief in the hegemon's capabilities in the eyes of the subordinate countries, whose interests the hegemon embody and defend. This necessarily requires a certain level of military and financial clout. It also requires the legitimacy of the dominant state in the eyes of its weaker allies. At different times, Britain and the U. S. satisfied these requirements at the global level.

Alongside the global hegemon, there are also regional hegemons. These are states which though are not powerful enough to compete on the global stage, have the necessary military and financial clout sufficient enough to make them dominant and influential in a given region. Nigeria's leadership in Africa in general and West Africa in particular, has often been ascribed to its leading role in Pan-African affairs. Politically, Nigeria has sought to exert its leadership at the U.N, AU and in ECOWAS by speaking loudest and, sometimes, acting strongest on matters of concern to Africa. In addition to its pioneering role in the formation of ECOWAS, Nigeria was the spearhead in the organization's successful peace enforcement operations in Liberia and Sierra Leone. Economically, Nigeria has sought to leverage its leadership in ECOWAS through oil diplomacy, by which it sells oil at heavily discounted rates to West African countries, and also by providing financial assistance to its poorer neighbours. The country is also the single largest contributor to the ECOWAS budget.

A 'Pax Nigeriana' within West Africa is often reflected in utterances by Nigerian politicians and policy makers, all of who appear to share a common belief in Nigeria's manifest destiny with special responsibilities to be a regional 'big brother'. The metaphor of a benevolent older brother who is obliged to protect his younger siblings has often been employed in Nigeria's diplomatic and popular parlance to justify the country's African policy. This 'big brother syndrome' has afflicted Nigeria's leaders since independence, and smacks of a paternalism that had often irritated its neighbours.[19] Some Nigerian politicians and diplomats have even gone further to make an explicit comparison between the country's hegemonic aspirations and the historic role of the U. S. in regional and global affairs. For instance, Shehu Shagari, Nigeria's President between 1979 and 1983 emphatically asserted that: "just as President Monroe proclaimed the American hemisphere free from the military incursions of European empire builders and adventurers, so also do we in Nigeria and in Africa, insist that African affairs be left to Africans to settle."[20] Nigeria's former Ambassador to Washington, Olu Sanu also expressed similar sentiments when he said: "we (Nigeria) have to be recognized as a regional power in West Africa. This is our region and we have the right to go to war. It is a Monroe Doctrine of sort."[21]

There are, indeed, similarities between Nigeria and the United States. Both are large countries that are feared and envied by their neighbours due to their power and relative wealth. Nigerians and Americans are also considered brash and arrogant. However, 'Pax Nigeriana', unlike 'Pax Americana', has not involved military expansion. That is not to suggest that 'Pax Nigeriana' is purely altruistic. As Adekeye Adebajo has argued, "since its Civil War of 1967 – 1970, Nigeria has sought to loosen France's neo-colonial ties in West Africa and to gain more security and larger markets for itself."[22] This perspective seeks to explain away Nigeria's military interventions in Liberia and Sierra Leone in the 1990s as not being driven by military aggrandizement for political control of these two countries, but rather for long-term economic influence in West Africa. Nigeria's interventions in these countries under the platform of ECOMOG were entirely consistent with the country's motive in spearheading the creation of ECOWAS in 1975, namely, to free the region from foreign domination.

In Liberia, as well as in Sierra Leone, Nigeria's intervention represented the country's historic quest for leadership in the West African sub-region. In general, the two ECOWAS interventions in Liberia and Sierra Leone under Nigeria's auspices demonstrated the importance of the country, even its indispensability, to any future regional peacekeeping mission in West Africa. James Jonah, a former United Nations Under-Secretary for Political Affairs has underscored the indispensability of Nigeria to West Africa's security arrangements by arguing that despite the accolades ECOWAS continues to receive for its successes in Liberia and Sierra Leone, those successes were principally Nigeria's achievement.[23] While observing that Nigeria has a comprehensive and achievable policy objective in Africa, Jonah warned that no one should take lightly the capacity of Nigeria to protect its core foreign policy objectives in Africa. On this basis, the former United Nations top man suggested that perhaps there was a real need to "recognize Nigeria as a benign hegemon on the continent".[24]

Adekeye Adebajo, a Nigerian Scholar, has used the metaphor of "Gulliver" to refer to Nigeria's overwhelming stature in West Africa, while describing the smaller and relatively weak states in the region as Lilliputians.[25] The Gulliver and the Lilliputians metaphor, as adapted from Jonathan Swift's classic, Gulliver's Travels, sought to contrast Nigeria's overwhelming strength against the vast member of tiny, and military insignificant or 'Lilliputian' states of West Africa. Adebajo goes on to suggest that the absence of the Nigerian Gulliver from ECOWAS intervention force in Guinea-Bissau, which comprised 'Lilliputian' peacekeepers from Benin Republic, the Gambia, Niger and Togo, accounted for the failure and premature end of the peacekeeping mission in that country after only four months. On the contrary, in Liberia and Sierra Leone, the Nigerian led ECOMOG forces were able to overcome initial logistical shortcomings to protect Monrovia and Freetown from being overrun by rebels in 1992 and 1999 respectively. Nigeria, acting alone, was also able to repel Liberian rebel forces from Monrovia in 1990 and to restore President Kabbah to power in Freetown in 1998, after he was chased from power by rebels. According to Adebajo, not only do these two instances validate the Gulliver and the Lilliputians metaphor, but significantly prove the "indispensability of Nigeria's military and financial muscle to regional peacekeeping efforts in West Africa".[26]

The French Scholar, Daniel Bach, who largely agrees with this assessment, has argued that from the decision by ECOWAS to intervene in the Liberian war in 1990 up to the temporary solution of the conflict seven years later, Nigeria's diplomatic, financial and military involvement shaped processes and outcomes in a decisive fashion.[27] According to Bach, the ECOMOG intervention in Sierra Leone offered yet another testing ground for Nigeria's projection of military power, adding that, as had been the case in Liberia, "Nigerian involvement was decisive, since the bulk of the forces were formed by Nigerian troops, and all force commanders were Nigerians."[28] It is hard to contemplate a viable economic community or security architecture in West Africa without Nigeria's leadership.

Nigeria-France Rivalries

For geo-political reasons, France is the natural rival of Nigeria in West Africa. Indeed, for both camps, this rivalry is self-evident. Nigeria is located at the heart of France's "sphere of influence" in Africa, and is surrounded by four Francophone countries namely, Niger, Chad, Benin and Cameroun. For France, the demographic and resource endowments of Nigeria in contrast to the sparsely populated and not so wealthy surrounding Francophone countries constitute a threat in itself to the former's dominance of the West African political and economic landscape.

Historically, Nigerian politicians and policy elites have shared a mortal fear of France. For instance, Bassey Ate has noted that French involvement in West Africa impedes the natural emergence of Nigeria as the regional power.[29] Another Nigerian Scholar, Jibrin Ibrahim, has spoken of France as "a source of worry for Nigeria".[30] While the source of this fear has been elaborated elsewhere in this study, the strategic contest for regional leadership in West Africa is much more deeply rooted. As Nigeria was spearheading the formation of ECOWAS, France was encouraging its West African allies to form a parallel organization. From the French perspective, the establishment of ECOWAS represented an attempt by Nigeria to destabilize Francophone countries of West Africa.[31] Consequently, rather than support ECOWAS, France instead promoted the establishment of the wholly French speaking CEAO in 1973. Naturally, Nigeria not only attempted to weaken all French sponsored organizations in West Africa, but proceeded to create a broad-based organization in the mould of ECOWAS. Anecdotal evidence suggests that France was afraid that, under the pretext of bringing peace to West Africa, Nigeria aimed to establish its regional military hegemony through the imbalance of military power with its neighbours – all of which are French-speaking. For Nigeria, the problem was almost the same, namely, the need to counter the economic and military influence of France in West Africa.

It is important to observe that, over time, some accommodation has been worked out between these two rivals for power in West Africa. Not only has France come to recognize and accept Nigeria's regional leadership, Nigeria, on its part, now looks up to France to contribute effectively to the prevention of conflicts and peacekeeping operations in the region.[32] In contrast to political relations, economic relations between Nigeria and France have been robust and quite substantial. While Nigeria has long been France's most important trading partner in sub-Saharan Africa, French investments in Nigeria are larger than its investments in all the countries of Francophone West Africa combined.[33] On its part, France is Nigeria's fourth largest economic partner after the U. S, Britain and Germany.

What is particularly revealing in Nigeria-France strategic relations is how economic and political relations are disconnected. Perceptive observers of the turbulent Nigeria – France strategic relationship have suggested that,
with the continuing conflicts in West Africa, France's priority should no longer be about who is the leading power in this region, but rather about how to prevent West Africa's zone of turmoil and insecurity from expanding. It is also in Nigeria's interest that peace and stability reign in West Africa. The rapprochement between France and Nigeria is, therefore, a healthy development that can only benefit the cause of regionalism in West Africa.

The United States: A Global Power in West Africa

Historically, Africa has never been central to U. S foreign policy, talk less to be of any strategic value to the super power. At a general level, official U.S. attitudes and policies toward Africa have been marked by neglect at best and indifference, at worst, which was the case more of the time. In other words, historically, the United States has treated Africa as a policy backwater, as measured by the policy attention and resources allocated to the continent in comparison with other regions of the world.

During the Cold War, U.S. policy makers had consistently defined the country's vital national interest as fighting and containing communism whenever it appeared. In furtherance of this objective, a consistent axiom of U.S. foreign policy and strategic engagement at the time was: "we have no permanent friends or enemies, but only permanent interests." This attitude clearly defined U.S. policies toward Africa. For instance, when the U.S. believed it could benefit in a geostrategic or economically material manner by engaging or disengaging with one or the other

African country, it took the necessary steps to do so. In sum, therefore, beginning with the Cold War, the U. S. followed a policy of selective engagement towards Africa. It selectively engaged countries in which it felt U.S. national interests were at stake, and ignored those countries with the least to offer along a broad spectrum of interests deemed strategic to the U.S.

Despite conducting at least 20 military operations in Africa during the 1990s, it was fashionable among defence planners in the United States during the period to maintain that the U.S. had "very little traditional strategic interest in Africa.[34] In 1998, President Bill Clinton's National Security Strategy of the United States listed Africa last in its inventory of integrated regional approaches to U.S security.[35] During the 2000 presidential election campaign, candidate George W. Bush noted that "while Africa may be important, it doesn't fit into American national strategic interests, as far as I can see them."[36] Since 2001, however, Africa has steadily gained strategic importance in the eyes of American policy makers. One reason for this is the heightened awareness of the international security dimension of the continent's multiple challenges on its so-called 'war on terrorism.' Second, U.S foreign investment in the region is growing, almost all of it related to the development of petroleum resources in West Africa's offshore waters.

The role of the United States in West Africa is increasing in proportion to the region's offshore oil boom. Several factors account for West Africa's rising importance to the U.S. energy needs. First, West Africa holds in excess of 60 billion barrels of proven oil reserves; the region currently supplies 15 percent of U.S oil imports and could supply as much as one quarter of U. S. imports by 2015.[37] Second, West Africa's oil production is projected to increase by 50 percent or more by 2020. The increase will primarily be driven by the development of deep-water discoveries in the Gulf of Guinea, mainly from Nigeria, Equatorial Guinea and Chad. According to ECON analysis, a Norwegian energy policy group, the growth potential of West Africa's oil field exceeds those of Russia, the Caspian Basin and South America.[38] ECON also estimates that investment in the region's deep-water fields will exceed 50 billion dollars by 2020, making the Gulf of Guinea the world's largest recipient of offshore hydrocarbon capital investment.[39] Third, while West Africa's overall output will represent 7 – 9 percent of global daily oil production by the end of 2010, the region's position as an incremental supplier will be even stronger. ECON Analysis estimates that West Africa will add 2 to 3 million barrels per day of oil to the global market by the end of 2020. These volumes will represent 20 percent of new worldwide production capacity, meaning that one in five new barrels of oil brought into the market will come from West Africa.[40]

The growth in West Africa's oil output has coincided with a renewed urgency among leading oil importing countries, notably U.S, to diversify their supplies from sources outside the Persian Gulf. In terms of energy security, the comparative advantages of West Africa have become increasingly apparent. This ranges from openness to foreign investment, reduced political risk on account of high offshore production, high quality of oil and proximity to U.S markets.[41] Such extraordinary growth in West African energy sector is prompting Washington to reassess its strategic and security priorities in the region in particular, and in Sub-Saharan Africa, in general. An African Oil Policy

Initiative Group (AOPIG), a U.S. private energy lobby group, describes West Africa's strategic importance in the following words: "West Africa is a swing production region that allows oil companies to leverage production capabilities to meet the fluctuating world demands. West African oil is of high quality, is easily accessed offshore, and is well positioned to supply the North American market. Already, Nigeria provides as much oil to the U.S as Venezuela or Mexico, making it of strategic importance."[42]

According to the influential AOPIG, American energy security would be well-served by a coherent strategy that recognizes the unique advantages West Africa offers, and hence utilizes it as a means of diversification and price stabilization in the world energy market. The Bush administration probably bought into AOPIG's advice, because by 2007 President Bush had rolled out an energy policy which stressed the importance of diversification of energy sources. According to Bush, "we (America) need to strengthen our trade alliances, to deepen our dialogue with major oil producers, and to work for greater oil production in the Western Hemisphere, in Africa, the Caspian Basin, and in other regions with abundant oil resources."[43] By implication, President Bush was espousing a policy for greater U.S diplomatic, financial and military involvement in the affairs of oil exporting countries and regions. The overall purpose of the Bush policy was to assure that the economy of the U.S is served with uninterrupted supply of oil in terms and conditions that support domestic growth and prosperity. The policy also sought to assure that the U.S can pursue its foreign policy and national security interests without being constrained by energy shortages.

A major strategic fallout from the Bush policy was the establishment, in 2007, of the United States Africa Command (AFRICOM). Officially, AFRICOM is intended to enhance U. S security relationships with African governments, their militaries, and related regional organizations, and to expand their capacities to address regional instability and crises. As President George W. Bush stated at the inauguration of AFRICOM, "this new command will strengthen our security cooperation with Africa, and help to create new opportunities to bolster the capabilities of our partners in Africa. AFRICOM will enhance our efforts to help bring peace and security to the people of Africa and to promote our common goals of development, health, education, democracy and economic growth in Africa."[44] Unofficially, AFRICOM will help provide a stable environment for U.S oil exploration and uninterrupted supplies to the U.S market.

Several senior officials of the U.S government have justified President Bush's decision to establish AFRICOM as a reflection of the rising strategic importance of Africa to U.S interests. They have argued that the U.S. has a strong interest in bolstering peace and stability in Africa, increasing regional capacity to address crises and deter aggression, expanding and ensuring America's access to energy resources, preventing the spread of terrorism in weak and broken states, and addressing traditional concerns. Claudia Anyaso, Director of the Office of Public Diplomacy and Public Affairs for Africa at the State Department underlined the security focus of AFRICOM in the following words: "The Africa Command will foster security, stability and safety, all of which promote economic prosperity and stability on the African Continent."[45] According to Anyaso, if done right, AFRICOM can prevent problems from turning into crises and crises from turning into conflicts."[46]

AFRICOM's focus on non-security challenges reflects a broader U.S objective to promote development by addressing root causes of conflict and instability in Africa. This perhaps explains why administration officials have characterized AFRICOM as a "Combatant Command Plus", in reference to the command's mandate which comprises traditional military roles as well as a broader soft power mandate aimed at "winning hearts and minds," and building a stable security environment for economic growth and prosperity. Despite understandable U.S enthusiasm for the fledging AFRICOM, not all in Africa are united in support of enhanced U.S military presence in Africa. Some of the objections to AFRICOM range from the lack of a common definition and appreciation of what security means for both the U.S and Africa. There are also serious concerns that AFRICOM represents the militarization of U.S foreign policy and diplomacy in Africa, including the fear that the AFRICOM platform could be used to prop up "friendly" repressive regimes, and to effect regime change in countries not so friendly and accommodating to U. S overtures.

Within ECOWAS there is no unified response to AFRICOM. Different ECOWAS States have manifested contradictory levels of support and opposition to the new U.S security initiative. Whereas Liberia offered to host AFRICOM's Headquarters, others including Nigeria have opposed a full blown American military presence in the region. Partly in response to the announcement by Umaru Musa Yar'Adua, Nigeria's President, that Nigeria would oppose a U. S military garrison and headquarters in West

Africa in 2007, the U. S dramatically dropped its plans to locate AFRICOM's headquarters in Africa, preferring to run it from Germany.

While supporters see AFRICOM as a guarantor of stability, regime survival, including access to new U.S. patrimonial resources, opponents are united in the belief that AFRICOM is primarily a vehicle for the advancement of strategic U.S interests, with African security coming a distant second. Within ECOWAS, key actors involved in regional security are largely receptive, perceiving AFRICOM as an opportunity to build and enhance the peacekeeping capabilities of West Africa's armies and ECOWAS peacekeeping unit. The reasoning is that AFRICOM would support the principle of "African solutions to African problems" by providing training, equipment and logistical support to the region's militaries, as well as providing opportunity for joint deployment of peacekeeping troops in West Africa's bad neighbourhood.

Some in West Africa have attributed opposition to Liberia's offer to host AFRICOM's African headquarters to concerns that AFRICOM's presence will set up West Africa as a target for terrorists, since terrorists tend to follow America wherever it goes. While it is true that the U.S military had long operated in the Gulf of Guinea, such offshore presence shielded the troops from contact with local populations. On the contrary, the AFRICOM headquarters in West Africa will represent the symbol and icon of U.S military power and influence, hence an attractive target for terrorists.

On a different level, academics and civil society actors see AFRICOM as a strategic military and diplomatic offensive to counter and contain China's growing influence in the region. Some have argued that the predatory competition between China and the U.S over West Africa's oil and mineral resources would affect the region in profound ways; either provoking a new Cold War or resource war, or encouraging the propping up of friendly regimes. Either way, the battle of the 'giants' in West Africa will neither be in the interest of West Africa security nor developmental needs.

China: A growing force in West Africa

Given the dynamism and intensity of China's growing engagement with Africa, it is easy to think that this relationship is new. Quite to the contrary, China has had a long history of engagement with Africa that predated the continent's independence era. In the early period of Africa's independence, China's intentions were primarily diplomatic. China increased diplomatic overtures to African countries to counter the possibility of the recognition of Taiwan, and to shore up votes for the eventual rejection of Taiwan's China credentials in the United Nations.

In this early period, China encouraged wars of national liberation across the continent, granted long term low-interest loans, provided aid to neglected areas, and promoted 'benevolent trade' by, for instance, buying up large coffee and tobacco surpluses from Tanzania. The aim of Chinese aid to Africa during the period was essentially to embarrass the West.[47] By the mid-1960s, perceiving a regional threat from Moscow, China competed directly with the Soviet Union in Africa by supporting rebel groups across the continent. China's involvement in Africa' liberation struggle closely paralleled its competition with Taiwan for international recognition. Beijing's efforts were to pay handsome dividends when dozens of African governments provided important diplomatic support for the United Nation's General Assembly resolution admitting the People's Republic of China to the world body in October 1971.[48] Chinese aid to African countries was, therefore, an important geopolitical tool in its contest with Taiwan.

Following the success of the decolonization process and China's admission to the UN, Sino-African relations suffered a decline, but not for too long. The decade following the end of the Cold War saw a rejuvenated Sino-African relationship. While the fall of communism in Europe reconfigured China's place in the international pecking-order, it also ignited growing Western criticism of China for its poor human right records. To fend off these attacks, which rose to a crescendo following the Tiananmen crackdown, China once again turned to Africa for support, with its policy shifting from benign neglect to one of renewed emphasis.[49] Unsurprisingly, the post-Tiananmen period witnessed renewed diplomatic and economic engagements between China and Africa.

The characteristic features of Sino-African relations during this period relate to their strategic and indirect focus. Whereas Chinese foreign policy towards Africa has historically exhibited consistent aims, policy engagement has been largely inconsistent. This is because China's interests in the Third World as a whole were indirect ones, even if they were projected with a consistent rhetoric of south-south solidarity.[50] As Philip Snow has argued, "China's tendency to employ the services of African countries to checkmate other powers display a policy focus that see Africa in strategic terms.[51] For instance, in the 1950s and 1960s, China's main concerns were the threat of American imperialism and the business of challenging Taiwan for a United Nations seat; during the 1970s and up to the early 1980s, the focus was on the Soviet threat. As these threats abated during the late 1980s, and as China turned inwards to an ambitious modernization programme at home that prioritized relations with the industrialized world, its presence in Africa correspondently diminished. However, as the prospect of a post-Cold War liberal global order interfering in its domestic affairs seem large following the end of the Cold War and the emergence of the United States as the global superpower, China again returned to Africa, only this time in a big way.[52]

It would seem, therefore, that when China's policy towards the major powers changes, so also does its strategic engagement with Africa. However, China's predominant foreign policy aim – to protect its sovereign interests from imperialism and hegemony – remains germane in its dealing with Africa. Significantly, this policy reflects the principles of non-interference in the internal affairs of countries, anti-hegemony and pluralistic human rights that were reaffirmed in the so-called Beijing Declaration of 12 October, 2000, the outcome of the inaugural forum on China-Africa cooperation. This history of China's foreign policy and its underlying foundation are essential to understanding China's increasingly complex and intense engagement with West Africa. Jin Yongjian, China's Ambassador to South Africa, made an important connection between history and the present when he noted in May 2005 as follows: "The Chinese people will never forget that in 1971 it was African countries that helped restore the legitimate seat of the People's Republic of China in the UN.... As China is the largest developing country in the world and Africa has more developing nations than any other continent, China-Africa cooperation constitutes an important part and parcel of South-South cooperation.[53]

As China becomes a 'rising global power', the indirect nature of its engagement with Africa appears to be showing signs of change. Although its African policy constitutes but a small part of its overall global engagement, China is assuming a pre-eminent presence on the continent. Moreover, its interests are markedly different from those which underpinned its inconsistent engagement with Africa in the past. Contemporary dynamics in China's relationship with Africa are prompted by more direct interests in the interconnected realms of strategic, economic and political relations.

A discernible trend in China's latest engagement with Africa relates to access to natural resources. Across Africa, China is acquiring control of natural resource assets, outbidding Western firms on major infrastructural projects, and providing soft loans and other incentives to bolster its competitive advantage. As the world's second largest importer of oil, China imports as much as 28 per cent of its oil from Africa. China has more recently become a significant player in the oil sector on the West Coast of Africa, particularly in Nigeria, where it is investing heavily in the sector. China is also active in many parts of Africa, seeking exploration rights, ownership of facilities and import agreement.[54]

China's presence in Africa has expanded dramatically in the last decade. For instance, between 1977 and 2006, the value of China-Africa trade rose ten-fold, from US$5.7 billion in 1997 to US$56 billion in 2006. In 2008, the figure exceeded US$100 billion. Similarly, China's investments in Africa have increased almost six-fold, from US$56 million in 1996 to US$379 million in 2006.[55] China's political and military engagements on the continent have also deepened considerably in recent years.

President Hu Jintao and Premier Wen Jiabao, between them, made five high profile visits to Africa from 2003 – 2007. Building on this political momentum, Beijing hosted 41 African Heads of State and Government in November 2006 under the auspices of the Forum on China-Africa Cooperation. In the realm of education, considered an important tool of China's soft power projection, Africa has also featured prominently on China's radar. Beijing currently awards 4000 scholarships to students from Africa to study in Chinese universities.[56]

China's diplomatic engagement in Africa is driven by the country's growing need for resources to ensure economic growth. Oil is the leading commodity that China imports from Africa, but China's policies encompass strategic goals other than merely securing oil, other natural resources and new export market. China's heightened level of activity in Africa is part of the country's overall strategy to promote an image of a peacefully rising, constructive and responsible major power.[57] When describing Sino-African relations, China's political leaders often refer to 50 years of friendly ties between China and Africa. Official statements also stress mutual benefit and mutual respect for state sovereignty and non-interference in the domestic affairs of states as guiding principles of the international system.[58]

In sum, from Beijing's point of view, Africa is vital for China's continued economic growth, as well being an important component in shaping China's influence and prestige as a rising major power. From Africa's point of view, the relationship with China is multifaceted; African governments welcome China's growing involvement in Africa because increased trade, investment, aid and debt relief have resulted in expanded economic opportunities.

In particular, Chinese aid has become a timely alternative to the aid from Western countries and international organizations which often come with stringent conditionality. From the point of view of Western countries, China's growing engagement in Africa constitutes competition for resources, markets and competition for political and military influence on the continent.

Overall, China's is still a marginal force in Africa, if one compares trade and investment volumes of China with those of Western countries. However, the very rapid pace with which China has increased its activities in all spheres in Africa has given rise to growing anxiety in Europe and in the United States over China's real intentions in Africa, especially in regard to the possibility that China's interests will undermine those of Europe and America. Judging by the present scenario, the world's two largest energy consumers – the US and China – appear to be heading toward a fierce competition for oil in Africa, especially in West Africa, which is Africa's fastest growing oil region.

In addition to its growing appetite for Africa's mineral and oil resources, China's food security concerns are also driving investments in Africa. Despite Africa's food deficit, China is investing heavily in agricultural production across Africa to argument food production in mainland China. In Nigeria, for instance, China has entered into joint fishery ventures and secured supply contracts for palm oil and non-oil commodities. Both countries have also agreed to prioritize investment and technology transfer as part of efforts to strengthen their strategic partnership.[59]

Politically, China's engagement with Africa is now part of a wider approach to strategic cooperation under the auspices of the inter-governmental forum on China – Africa Cooperation (FOCAC). The impetus for China's African policy is its 'five principles of peaceful co-existence, which emphasizes China's solidarity and cooperation with African countries as an important component of its independent foreign policy of peace, as well as China and Africa's common history of colonialism and liberation.[60] This shared sense of history is important for the powerful imagery it provokes, namely that China and Africa belong in the developing world and face common enemies and threats. The sentiments of Sino-African solidarity, forged in the crucible of independence members and the struggle against neo-colonialism, have thus provided an important political foundation for the evolving China – African strategic relationship.

In its engagement with Africa, China has also invoked the symbolism of south-south cooperation in its efforts to oppose Western hegemony and unilateral global dominance.[61] The key political platform for China's efforts to diminish and contain the influence of hegemonic powers, especially American hegemony, has been the Non-Aligned Movement, of which African countries constitute the dominant bloc. As China's powers rise in proportion to its economic prosperity, the country has lately promoted the idea of multi-polarity in world affairs.

China's advancement of the concept of multi-polarity, defined as the construction of more or less flexible alliances to contain every form of hegemony, and to build a new and just international order has often driven its engagement in Africa.[62] The ideological basis of a world view grounded on the principle of peaceful co-existence and solidarity was espoused by President Hu Jintao in his address to the 17th Congress of the Chinese Communist Party as follows: "…. for developed countries, we will continue to strengthen strategic dialogue, enhance mutual trust, deepen cooperation and properly manage differences to promote long-term, stable and sound development of bilateral relations… for developing countries, we will continue to increase solidarity and cooperation with them, cement traditional friendship, expand practical cooperation, provide assistance to them within our ability, and uphold the legitimate demands and common interests of developing countries. We will continue to take an active part in multilateral affairs, assume our due international obligations, play a constructive role, and work to make the international order fairer and more equitable. We will also continue to conduct exchanges and cooperation with the political parties and organizations of other countries."[63]

These general principles are reiterated in China's more focused five principles of African policy, which, as we have argued elsewhere in this study, is premised on respect for sovereignty and non-interference in national political processes. China's emphasis on sovereignty, non-aggression and mutual interdependence differentiates its policy substantially from those of Western powers, which often come with political conditionality. This is the basis of China's attraction to Africa governments. This kind of rhetoric is particularly reassuring to African governments because it encourages the impression that China is not imposing its political views, ideas or principles on its African partners.

Ironically, it is precisely the lack of political conditionality to Chinese aid to African countries that has attracted strident criticisms from the West, which accuses China of opportunism in its dealing with authoritarian regimes in Africa. Critics of China's growing influence in Africa have pointed to China's easy and comfortable relationship with several autocratic regimes in Africa as evidence that the country's resource-driven policy has little room for morality. Western apprehension that China's rapid and significant emergence in Africa exacerbate the governance crisis in Africa reverberated at a U.S Congressional hearing on China's presence in Africa on 28 July, 2005, when Chris Smith, the Chair of the African sub-committee, spoke of China as follows: "China is playing an increasingly influential role on the continent of Africa, and there is concern that the Chinese intend to aid and abet African dictators, gain a stranglehold on precious African natural resources, and undo much of the progress that has been made on democracy and governance in the last 15 years."[64]

While Congressman Smith's depiction of China's destabilizing intent in Africa may be rather harsh, it goes to demonstrate the considerable unease in Western countries about China's growing influence in Africa. Growing competition over fossil fuel in the Gulf of Guinea is more probable the cause of Western fears than a concern for democracy in Africa. After all, the same Western governments had consorted with African dictators in the past when the Chinese presence was marginal.

As a prelude to the confrontation that may come, Western governments, especially the US, have attacked China's no strings-attached aid policy as capable of undermining attempts to link aid to good governance and to support sustainable development in Africa. China, in turn, has dismissed this criticism by pointing out that Africa has not benefited from several decades of Western aid policies loaded with political conditionality. There are both African and Western observers who agree with the Chinese argument. Furthermore, the Chinese government's emphasis on equality and mutual respect in China's relations with African governments resonates well on the continent, even among those who are sceptical about the motives driving China's new African polices.

It would be a mistake for Western powers to consider China as an adversary in Africa. Like other growing economies, China is a legitimate competitor for natural resources whenever they may be available in the world. The most important thing to note is that the rise of China and its increasing penetration of West Africa have changed the strategic, political and economic environment of the region in fundamental ways. For centuries, Western powers have exercised unrivalled influence in West Africa.

In the current environment, the US and Europe cannot consider Africa their spoil, as France once saw Francophone Africa. The rules of the road are changing, as China seeks not only to gain access to resources, but also to control resources production, perhaps positioning itself for priority access as these resources become less available, as eventually they would. In all of this, China is only a competitor, as are the other major powers scrambling for a piece of the African pie. From an African perspective, this is good for Africa because, for once, it is no longer a take it or leave it situation. Now, African governments can negotiate and expect to get better outcomes from their strategic partners than before China's entry into the fray.

As China's policies toward Africa evolve, it is possible to make at least one tentative judgment. This relates to China's capacity to adhere to its long-standing principles of non-interference in national political processes. It is difficult to see how China can sustain this principle as the commercial interests and the corresponding need for the Chinese government to protect these investments and the security and safety of its citizen grow. In other to protect these interests, it is possible to see China actively trying to influence policies in African countries, just as Western powers have been doing for decades. In other words, as its economic, political and military clout grow, it is possible that Beijing's inclination to be selfish could strengthen. On the other hand, it is also possible that China's desire to be regarded as a responsible major international player will force it to abandon some of the traditional principles governing its engagement with Africa, particularly the principle of non-interference in national political processes. If this proves to be the case, then the enthusiastic embrace of China by governments across West Africa may have been premature.

The European Union

Africa and Europe have a long history of dialogue and strategic engagement that has occurred at many levels and in different forms. In general, the framework for the Europe – Africa relationship was fragmented for historical and geo-strategic reasons, characteristics which reflect colonial dominance and so-called spheres of influence. For West Africa, this engagement had for long been conducted under the framework of the Cotonou Partnership Agreement, which defines the various aspects of the relationship between African, Caribbean and Pacific countries and the European Union. This agreement stresses development cooperation, political and trade issues. All West African countries are party to the Cotonou Partnership Agreement.

Since the 1990s, however, shifting economic and political interests and new common problem have created a compelling need for new strategies and new solutions to tackle complex post-Cold War security challenges with far-reaching ramifications on both Europe and Africa. Such challenge as the proliferation of small arms and light weapons in West Africa, terrorism, intra-state violent conflicts, drugs, human trafficking and transnational criminal networks have forged closer cooperation between Europe and Africa.

It is to Europe's credit that its leaders were quick to recognize that it has a stake in a peaceful and stable Africa, not least because, if regional problems of Africa are left unresolved, they could spill over and pose security risks to Europe. Since 9/11, fears that underdevelopment in Africa could multiply the incidence of failed states which could provide breeding grounds and safe havens for international terrorist networks have further accelerated Europe – Africa links. Within Europe, at least, a growing awareness of the security- development nexus forced a re-examination of Europe's relationship with Africa. Hence forth, Europe whose involvement with Africa had hitherto been defined essentially in terms of trade and development assistance began to re-classify its relationship with Africa in strategic terms.

While development approaches to security have long been seen as integral to the EU's distinctive international identify, since 9/11 this has been backed up by firmer policy commitments and new instruments. Increasingly, the EU has elevated a two-way link between development and security as a core tenet of its foreign policy.[65]

Increasingly, also, the European Union is focusing on governance reforms as a potential link between security and development. For example, while the European Security Strategy (ESS) substantially focuses on traditional security issues such as the proliferation of weapons of mass destruction, the need for tighter control over the movement and financing of transnational criminal networks, counter terrorism cooperation with security forces in developing countries, the central thesis of this strategy is built around a three – way linkage between security, development and governance reforms.[66] The European Consensus on development agreed in 2006, also reiterates a conviction in the two-way linkage between security and development: development is said to be necessary for security, while security is necessary for development. While affirming that "insecurity and violent conflict are amongst the biggest obstacles to achieving the Millennium Development Goals (MDGs), and that security and development are important and complementary aspects of European Union relations with third countries," the Consensus pledges to promote the security development nexus in both crisis management and in post-crisis contexts. [67]

From the EU perspective, the key link between development and security is judged to lie in support for democratic governance, which is stipulated in the Consensus as "fundamental for poverty reduction, and whose absence is part of the root causes of violent conflict".[68] Consequently, the solution to the fragility of conflict-prone states, such as there are in West Africa, requires an approach based on governance reforms, the rule of law, anti-corruption measures and the building of viable state institutions."[69] This is the policy and institutional context that frames the EU's engagement with West Africa.

Much of the security challenges and strategic ambitions expressed in the ESS have necessarily impacted on emerging EU – ECOWAS relations in many important ways. One reason for this is that, since the early 1990s, ECOWAS has emerged as a security actor to a certain extent, not least in the field of crisis management, a conspicuous objective of the EU. ECOWAS credentials as a credible security actor were burnished with successful interventions by the ECOWAS Monitoring Group (ECOMOG) in several conflicts in the region since the early 1990s. As enunciated in the ESS, some of the EU's strategic ambitions relate to its desire to deal with new threats, such as state failure and organized crime, willingness and commitment to contribute to the prevention and settlement of regional conflicts, including capacity to contribute to the stabilization and security sector reform processes in other regions and, or, countries.[70]

In furtherance of its strategic ambitions, the EU has sought an expanded role in the search for regional stability, conflict prevention and peace building in West Africa. Using mainly development tools, the EU Strategy has targeted support for economic and regional integration and the integration of West Africa into world trade networks. The rational for this kind of structural stabilization focusing on economic integration aims essentially to address "structural causes of conflicts.[71] In other words, the EU is increasingly applying development tools to address structural causes of conflict in West Africa.

The EU has also been active in crisis management in West Africa. Either at national level, or under the auspices of UN Missions, EU member States have taken part in several peacekeeping operations in West Africa since 1990. While direct involvement in peacekeeping missions remain largely at national level in the region, with the United Kingdom having intervened in Sierra Leone and France in Cote d'Ivoire in 1988 and 2006 respectively, other EU States have occasionally supported troops deployed by ECOWAS or those under United Nations mandate.

The EU has recently also emerged as an important supporter of initiatives and processes to strengthen ECOWAS efforts to control the spread of illicit small arms across West Africa. In trying to solve the problem of illicit arms in the region, ECOWAS had declared a moratorium on the importation, Exportation and Manufacture of Small Arms and Light Weapons (SALW) in October 1998, as an attempt to tackle collectively and regionally the spread of illicit proliferation of such armaments. This has since been upgraded into the ECOWAS Convention on Small Arms and Light Weapons and their Ammunitions.

Given the extensive nature of EU – ECOWAS collaboration, it would be tempting to describe this relationship as a partnership. However, such a description appears not to take account that this is essentially an unequal relationship in which the EU sets the agenda. For instance, the prominence giving to terrorism on the EU-ECOWAS agenda in the aftermath of 9/11 indicates where the priorities emanate from. Furthermore, the emphasis on issues of moral or political importance to the EU on this agenda, such as gender equality, minority rights, respect for human rights, good governance and transparency goes to prove that local priorities do not drive this relationship.

Likewise, the debates on conflict, security and development in Africa have been dominated by concepts and discourses that originate in Europe and North America. Despite lip service to the need for African 'partnership' and even 'ownership' of these discourses and processes, the reality remains that the African input has been disappointingly low.

To be of any use, this partnership would have to be based on mutual respect and sensitivity to local needs. On its part, West African governments must be serious about the promotion of good governance and domestic accountability as a way to build social cohesion. On its part, Europe would have to address some of its contradictory security and development policies in West Africa, so as to improve its credentials as an honest and credible partner. For instance, the partnership would be better served if the EU could impose certain measure of coherence among the various security frameworks between it and West Africa, including security cooperation among some EU member States and individual West African countries.

Furthermore, EU-West Africa security relations could also benefit from conceptual clarity on what may be regarded as security challenges requiring joint efforts to combat. For instance, in Europe, security concerns many cover such issues as terrorism and migration, while for West Africans, the some concept may apply to the activities of a dictator, civil insurrection and ethnic nationalism. While the EU remains a key player in West Africa, the conflicting priorities in what is essentially an unequal partnership has created considerable mistrust in EU-ECOWAS relations so much so as to render this relationship largely ineffectual.

West Africa's 'Resource Wars'

Nearly 125 years ago, at the beginning of the European scramble for Africa, European empires competed with each other to take over Africa and plunder it for its resources. Today, the Europeans are gone, but the battle over control of resources in Africa rages on as fiercely as it was among the European adventurers. The big difference now is that these resource wars are largely being fought by Africans themselves, though with occasional encouragement from multinational companies and brokers who act as patrons to local interest groups, including warlords and militias ostensibly fighting against political marginalization but who may, in fact, be fighting for control over resource-rich territories.

The West African sub-region is particularly endowed with vast mineral resources, ranging from oil in Nigeria to diamond in Sierra Leone, cocoa in Cote d'Ivoire and gold in Ghana. Liberia is also rich in rubber. The characteristic feature of the West Africa's political economy is that several of the resource-rich countries have been embroiled in one form of violent conflict or the other over the past two decades. While Liberia and Sierra Leone have only just emerged from a protracted and brutal civil war, the fate of Cote d'Ivoire still hangs in the balance, with the country effectively divided between rebels in the north with the government controlling the south. In Nigeria, a long-standing insurgency in the oil-rich Niger Delta may only now be resolved if a government initiative to end the conflict through an amnesty programme succeeds.

What is common to all these conflicts is that, while they lasted, they were driven or exacerbated by fight over control of a dominant resource in each country. In the case of both

Sierra Leone and Liberia, the conflicts were fuelled principally from revenues from diamond extraction and logging and sale of timber, respectively. In both cases, the largest rebel factions – Sierra Leone's Revolutionary United Front (RUF) and the National Patriotic Front of Liberia (NPFL) fought brutal battles against their respective governments and other factions for control of areas rich in economic resources, including diamond, gold, timber, rubber and iron ore. In Liberia, for instance, the rebel leader, Charles Taylor, who has been indicted for war crimes and is now standing trials at The Hague, is reported to have amassed $450 million from illicit export of resources, mainly diamond and timber, in territories he controlled during the war. In Sierra Leone, RUF rebels and rogue military officers controlled an estimated $250 million annual diamond trade.[72] In both cases, the existence of economic resources prolonged the war and complicated peace-making efforts, as rebels were able to sell extracted resources to enrich themselves and also to buy weapons to prosecute their wars.[73]

In the case of Nigeria, control over oil resources is the primary driver of the conflict in the country's oil rich Niger Delta region. Indeed, in Nigeria, locals actually refer to the low-intensity conflict in the Niger Delta region as 'resource control'. The basis of the conflict derives from the fact that, while oil from the Niger Delta provides over80 per cent of Nigeria's federal revenues and 95 per cent of national exports, the states and communities that produce this vital resource are among the most destitute and marginalized in the federation. In response, the youth in the region have, since the early 1990s, waged a low-intensity insurgency against federal authorities for control of what they see as their own resources.

A number of studies have analysed the paradox of bountiful natural resource endowment, poverty and wars. The metaphor of the 'resource curse' or 'resource war' emerged in the early 1990s to describe how natural resource-endowed states were unable to use their wealth to boost their developmental fortunes. On the contrary, these countries were characterized by indicators of underdevelopment. For some of these countries, resource plenty has proved to be a curse, rather than a blessing.[74] The same metaphor of resource curse or 'paradox of plenty' has been used to explain why some rentier states have not experienced significant socio-economic development and good governance and, conversely, why this state of affairs serves as a potential motivation for conflict. For instance, Terry Karl has proposed that:

"Abundant supplies of valuable natural resources create incentives for conflict groups to form and fight to capture them. This may spawn attempts by regional warlord and rebel organizations to cleave off resource-rich territories, or violently hijack the state. Once seized, control over valuable natural resources fuels conflict escalation by allowing the parties to purchase weaponry and mobilize potential recruits."[75]

Terry Karl is not alone in linking resource abundance to conflict. Different theories, with varied explanatory powers and contextual relevance, have also tried to explain the paradox and analyse the key drivers of conflict. One of the early and most compelling arguments on the economic rationale for conflict and civil wars was developed by Paul Collier, who posits that the incidence of civil war increases with the dependence of a state on natural resource exports, which include all forms of rentable and exportable endowments, namely, agriculture and mineral exports.[76] In regard to the enabling environment for the economy of war, Collier suggests that "a country with large natural resources, many young men and little education is very much more at risk of conflict than one with opposite characteristics.[77] Thus, he concludes that economic agendas or greed, rather than political factors, or grievance, constitute the key causal factor in most recent civil wars. According to Collier, warlords and rebel forces are driven by the opportunities of notable resource rent as a means of survival and perpetuating the war economy.[78]

Collier's greed and grievance thesis has attracted a number of criticisms, one of which was elaborated by Michael Ross.[79] While admitting that economies that are highly dependent upon natural resources do experience problems, Rose nevertheless argues that it is impossible to say with certainty whether their resources lead to the observed political and economic consequences, or whether the direction of causality runs in the opposite direction.
Other scholars have adopted a middle ground with suggestions that any given conflict is brought about by a complex set of events. Often poverty, ethnic or religious grievances and unstable governments play major roles in a variety of conflicts in transitional societies. Jacques Lesourne, for instance, has argued that even after these factors have been taken into account, "natural resources heighten the risk that a civil war will be more difficult to resolve."[80]

While a growing number of scholars have come to question Collier's analytical framework as not providing a sufficient explanation for the conflict-risk propensity of resource-rich countries, the evolution of the Liberian and Sierra Leonean civil wars seem to validate the Collier thesis.

In both cases, while control over resources may not have precipitated the crises, the evidence on the ground suggests that once the wars started, fighting over control of resources certainly contributed to their intensification and sustenance.

Despite the proliferation of several explanatory models, all tend to establish some degree of positive correlation between the structure of extractive economies dependent on primary commodity export, on the one hand, and patrimonial corruption, inter group struggle for 260 Jacques Lesourne, Governance of Oil in Africa: Unfinished Business, IFRI, Paris and Brussels, 2009, pp. 11-12. resources and dysfunctional conflicts, on the other.81 These positive linkages are consistent with the notion of the rentier state, which Terry Karl has described as "one which is largely dependent on extractive resource rents, taxes and loyalties paid by transnational companies (TNCs), and on profits from its equity stakes in TNCs investments."[82]

A rentier state generally lacks a productive economy, in the sense that revenues from natural resources contribute a substantial proportion of the gross domestic product and dominates national income distribution, usually at the expense of the real productive sectors of the economy. What results from this is usually referred to as 'rentierism, which is the condition or syndrome of rent accumulation and rent dependency, a phenomenon mostly associated with the extractive economies of the global South.[83]

In general, conflicts associated with rentierism are not only complex and dysfunctional, but also protracted and seemingly intractable. This state of conflict is well captured in the resource wars metaphor in contemporary political economy. Nigeria, Liberia and Sierra Leone, all in West

Africa, are some of the contemporary illustrations of the countries where abundant natural resource endowments have not enhanced sustainable development and security, but instead aggravated the frontiers and scale of dysfunctional conflicts.

It must be said that there are rentier economies where the patterns of conflict have been comparatively less virulent and more or less manageable, for example, in places like Libya, United Arab Emirates, Oman, Qatar and Kuwait. In all these cases, the governments have largely succeeded in managing conflict by undertaking extensive distributive and developmental initiatives for the benefit of their citizens. In other words, governing rentier elites in these states have tried consciously to align rentierism with development, with the aim of improving the well-being of the underprivileged classes. While this tendency may not permanently obliterate the structure of dysfunctional conflicts, it apparently helps to ensure a broad measure of consensus necessary to reproduce the legitimizing ideology and hegemony of the governing elites.

Beyond the conflicts associated with internal structures and contradictions in domestic political economies, rentierism is also linked to some wider geopolitical conflicts that can have profound regional and international resonance. This category of conflicts is mostly connected with the interventionist roles of powerful external actors from developed economies, who regard certain extractive resources in the developing world as part of their strategic national interests and, as such, feel no qualms about enforcing their unimpeded access to, or control of these resources, using all means possible, including war. Dating from the early years of post-colonial rule to the present, external interest in extractive rentier economies of developing countries have led to the involvement of different external actors or patrons in the politics of many rentier states through strategies such as:

(i)   Propping up unpopular, repressive and corrupt clientelist regimes,

(ii)   Complicity in reactionary coup d'état and assassination of key anti-imperialist or nationalist leaders,

(iii)   Strategic defence partnerships and provision of military aid to strengthen the coercive capacity of clientelist regimes,

(iv)   Mobilization of diplomatic support for clientelist regimes facing justifiable international opprobrium for wrongdoing and, conversely, international sanctions against defiant rentier regimes; and

(v)   Outright military invasion, occupation and regime change to pave way for uninterrupted access to strategic resources.[84]

The links between the rentier state and wider geopolitical interests resonated in a recent study by Michael T. Klare. In 'Resource Wars: The New Landscape of Global Conflict',Klare argues that the theatres of war in the future will shift away from the Cold War era's focus on confrontation zones in a divided Europe toward areas of the world that are rich in resources. According to Klare, the wars of the future will largely be fought over the possession and control of vital economic goods – especially resources needed for the functioning of modern industrial societies."[85] While many countries in the past had sought access to valuable natural resources by conquering other nation's territories, Klare argues that more intense competition for resources, such as oil, timber, water and minerals will make resource security the main focus of military policy for some nations in the coming decades.

While Collier's analytical framework does provide an insight into much of the internal conflicts that have ravaged West Africa in the past two decades, Klare's furnishes a geostrategic explanation of essentially the same phenomenon.

Within a local context, and regardless of the remote or immediate cause of conflict, once a rebellion has erupted, the fighting often evolves into a resource conflict. The reason being that, to pay their troops and obtain money for arms and ammunition, rebel commanders naturally seek to gain control over territories containing valuable resources. Once in possession of such prized territories, they can continue fighting indefinitely, even if defeated in battles conducted elsewhere in the country.

They do not have to gain control over the entire country so long as they can keep the resource-rich area, no matter how small in size. Overtime, many of these leaders acquire the status of warlords – local despots who dominate a particular region by terrorizing populations and extracting rent from the resources they control. On its part, the government is just as likely to fight for control of these same resources both to pay its war bills and also to ensure the continued happiness and loyalty of prominent cliques and interest groups.

With arms and cash coming into their hands on a regular basis, the leaders of ethnic and insurgent factions have no incentive to sue for peace, or to reach a compromise at the bargaining table. On the contrary, their interests are best served by prolonging the conflict. This is the essential logic of the Collier thesis. It suggests that ruthless and greedy personalities or factions in poor and weak states are prepared to provoke civil war or otherwise employ violence in the pursuit of valuable resources. Both the RUL and NPFL typified these tendencies in the protracted Sierra Leonean and Liberian civil wars from the late 1980s to late 1990s.

Although conflicts over resources were not unknown during the Cold War era, these were normally suppressed by Washington and Moscow. To reduce the threat of insurgency, both superpowers readily provided their respective allies with substantial military and economic assistance. With the end of the Cold War, however, this type of assistance have largely disappeared, making the former recipients of such aid vulnerable to internal challenges.

The growing presence of transnational firms in areas of conflict is responsible for another distinctive feature of resource conflicts in much of West Africa. This relates to the role of private military companies (PMCs). These firms, often composed of demobilized soldiers, are engaged to provide protection for large oil and mining companies and, in some cases, assist governments in their efforts to suppress rebel movements. As would be expected, such companies do not seek resolution of conflicts; rather, their interests are best served by allowing the fighting to continue as long as possible. Among the Western countries, there is evidence of convergence of interests, notably in their coordinated approach to providing maritime security in the oil-rich Gulf of Guinea. More specifically, British energy policy in West Africa is also shaped by the special relationship between the country and the United States and the converging commercial interests of major British and American oil companies in West Africa.

In regard to this special relationship, a United States policy document revealed in 2001 that "we (United States and Britain) have identified a number of key oil and gas producers in the West African area on which our two governments and major oil and gas companies could cooperate to improve investment conditions, good governance, social and political stability, and thus underpin long term security of supply."[86] The report identified the petroleum producing areas where the US and Britain could work together to leverage resources effectively and avoid duplication of effort as "Nigeria, Sao Tome and Principe, Angola and Equatorial Guinea, all of which belong to the Gulf of Guinea Commission."[87]

At the geostrategic level, the resource wars among the great powers in West Africa are still tactical than conflictual. The context revolves around which companies and, by implication, which countries will win the most lucrative oil blocks and mining concessions. While there seems to be a convergence of interest among the Western powers, who also dominate the energy sector in West Africa, China's entry into the region is increasingly being viewed with apprehension by the Western countries. As far as the Western countries are concerned, China is an intruder, which should be avoided by the local regimes.

Criticisms against China's support for egregious regimes in Africa, including sharp business practices by Chinese companies, are rampant, the motive being apparently to demonize the Chinese among local governing elites. On its part, China is responding in kind, throwing generous economic aid packages at several African governments. It is yet too early to know how the competition between China and Western countries will evolve in West Africa. One thing though is evident: the competition has all the trappings of a new scramble for Africa. If so, this can only be to the detriment of West Africa's security and development.

Notes

1.   Olu Adedeji, "Mechanisms for Conflict Management in West Africa: Politics of Harmonization," paper delivered at the AFSTRAG Workshop on Conflict Management Mechanism in West Africa, Abuja, 21-23 May 1997.

2.   Jean- Francois Medard, "Crisis, Change and Continuity" in Adekeye Adebajo and Abdul Raufu Mustapha, eds.; Gulliver's Troubles, Nigeria's Foreign Policy after the Cold War, KZN Press, Scottsoille, South Africa, 2008, P. 306.

3.   Quoted in Kaye Whiteman and Douglas Yates, "France, Britain and the Limited States", in Adekeye Adebajo and Ismail Rashid, eds.; West Africa's Security Challenges, Lynne Rienner, Boulder and London, 2004, p. 351.

4.   Jeune Afrique, 25 -31 January 1996, p.11.

5.   See Jean – Francois Medard, "Crisis, Change and Continuity," 2004, p.316.

6.   Ibid.

7.   Ibid.

8.   Ibid.

9.   See Kaye Whiteman and Douglas Yates in Gulliver's Troubles, Nigeria's Foreign Policy after the Cold War, p. 361.

10.   Andrew Hansen, "The French Military in Africa," Council on Foreign Relations, CFR.org/French Military – in – Africa.html, accessed on 2 August 2010.

11.   Ibid.

12.   Ibid.

13.   Ibid.

14.   Ibid.

15.   Ibid.

16.   Nicholas Sarkozy, Address to South African Parliament, Cape Town, South Africa, 28 February 2008, available online at http://www.ambafrance-uk.org/president-sarkozy-s-speech-to-the-html.

17.   See Andrew Hansen, p.20.

18.   Adekeye Adebajo, "Hegemony on a Shoestring," in Adekeye Adebajo and Abdul Raufu Mustapha, eds.; Gulliver's Troubles, Lynne Rienner, Boulder and London, 2004, p.12.

19.   Ibid.

20.   Shehu Shagari, My Vision of Nigeria, Frank Cass, London and Toronto, 1981, pp.75 – 76.

21.   Karl Magyar and Earl Conteh – Morgan, eds.; Peacekeeping in Africa: ECOMOG in Liberia, Macmillan and St. Martin Press, London and New York, 1998, p.12.

22.   See Adekeye Adebajo, "Hegemony on a Shoestring," p.14.

23.   James O. C. Jonah, "The United Nations" in Adekeye Adebajo and Ismail Rashid eds.; West Africa's Security Challenges, Lynne Rienner, 2004, p.340.

24.   Ibid.

25.   See Adekeye Adebajo, "Hegemony on a shoestring," p.1.

26.   Ibid.

27.   Daniel Bach, "Nigeria's Manifest Destiny in West Africa: Dominance without Power," AfriKa Spectrum, Hamburg, No.2, 2007, pp.301 -32.

28.   Ibid.

29.   Bassey E. Ate, "The Presence of France as a Fundamental problem for Nigeria," in Bassey E. Ate and Bola Akinteriwa, eds.; Nigeria and its Immediate Neighbours: Constraints as Prospects of Sub-regional Security in the 1990s, NIIA, Lagos, 1992, pp.11 – 30.

30.	Jibrin Ibrahim, "Toward a Nigerian perspective on the French problematic", in Bassey E. Ate and Bola Akinteriwa, eds, 1992, p.14.

31.	Jean – Francois Medard, "Crisis, Change and Continuity," in Adekeye Adebajo and Abdul Raufu Mustapha eds.; Gulliver's Troubles, 2008, p.327.

32.	Ibid.

33.	Ibid.

34.	Robert G. Berschinski "Africa's Dilemma: The Global War on Terrorism, Capacity Building, Humanitarianism and the future of U. S. Security Policy in Africa," Strategic Studies Institute, November 2007, p4, available at http://www.StrategicStudiesInstitute.army.mil/

35.	Ibid.

36.	Ibid.

37.	Steve Kretzman, "Oil, Security and War: The Geopolitics of U.S Energy Planning," Multinational Monitor, January/February, 2003.

38.	ECON Analysis AS, "Geopolitics, Energy, Security, and West Africa", ECON Report No. 2004-063, September 2004. p.7.

39.	Ibid.

40.	Ibid.

41.	Ibid.

42.	Quoted in "African Oil: A Priority for U.S National Security and African Development," An AOPIG Publication, Washington, D.C, 2001.

43.	Ibid.

44.	News release, "President Bush Creates a Department of Defence Unified Combatant Command for Africa," The White House, February 6, 2007, available online at www.whitehouse.gov.news/releases/2007/02/20070206-3/html

45.   Claudia Anyaso, "AFRICOM's Historic Step in U. S – Africa Relationship," address at conference at Arlington, Virginia, 21 April, 2008, available at America.gov/.../2008 0423140127 wcyero

46.   Ibid.

47.   Sharath Srinivasan, "A Rising Great Power Embraces Africa," in Adekeye Adebajo and Abdul Raufu Mustapha, eds.; Gulliver's Troubles, 2008, p.336.

48.   Ibid.

49.   Ibid.

50.   Ibid.

51.   Philip Snow, "China and Africa: Consensus and Camouflage," in Thomas W. Robinson and David Shambaugh, eds.; China Foreign Policy: Theory and Practice, Clarendon Press, Oxford, 1994, p.156.

52.   See Sharatt Srinivasan, "A Rising Great Power Embraces Africa", in Gulliver's Troubles, p.339.

53.   Jin Yongjian, "China's Economic Development: New Opportunities for the Sino-African Relations," Specch delivered at Africa Institute of South Africa Seminar, 17 May, 2005.

54.   Council on Foreign Relations, "More than Humanitarianism: A Strategic U.S Approach towards Africa," An Independent Task Force Report, No.56, 2006, p.43.

55.   Linda Jackobson, "China's Diplomacy toward Africa: Drivers and Constraints," International Relations of the Asia-Pacific, Vol.9, 2009, pp.403-433.

56.   Ibid.

57.   Ibid.

58.   Ibid.

59.   Ibid.

60.   Ibid.

---

61.   Marcus Power and Gils Mohan, "The Geopolitics of China's Engagement with African Development," Paper presented at the POLIS and BISA supported Workshop on New Directions in IR and Africa, The Open University, July 9, 2008.

62.   Ibid.

63.   Quoted in Marcus Power and Giles Mohan, "The Geopolitics of China's Engagement with African Development."

64.   Jim Fisher – Thompson, "China, No threat to the United States, US Official says," US State Department Information Service, 28 July, 2005, available online at http://usinfo.state.gov/eap/Archive/2005/Jul/29-550683. html.

65.   Richard Young, "Fusing Security and Development: Just another Euro-Platitude," CEPs Working Document, No.277/ October 2007.

66.   Ibid.

67.   Ibid.

68.   Ibid.

69.   Ibid.

70.   Javier Solana, A Secure Europe in a Better World: European Security Strategy, Brussels, December, 2003.

71.   Bastien Nivet, "Security by proxy? The EU and (Sub-) Regional Organizations: The Case of ECOWAS", an ISS Occasional Paper, No. 63, March 2006, p. 24.

72.   Ibid.

73.   See Adekeye Adebajo, "Introduction" in Adekeye Adebajo, and Ismail Rashid, eds.; West Africa Security Challenges, Building Peace in a Troubled Region,2004, p.14.

74.   Richard Auty, Sustaining Development in Mineral Economies: The Resource Curse Thesis, Routledge, London, 1993, p.8.

75.   Terry L. Karl, The Paradox of Plenty: Oil Boom and Petro-States, University of California Press, Berkeley, 1979.

76.   Paul Collier, "Doing Well out of War: An Economic Perspective," in Mats Berdal and David M. Malone, eds.; Greed and Grievance: Economic Agendas in Civil Wars, Lynne Rienner, Boulder, 2000, pp.91 – 111.

77.   Ibid.

78.   Ibid.

79.   Michael L. Ross, "The Political Economy of the Resource Curse," World Politics, No.51, pp.297 -322.

80.   Jacques Lesourne, Governance of Oil in Africa: Unfinished Business, IFRI, Paris and Brussels, 2009, pp. 11-12.

81.   Kenneth Omeje, ed., Extractive Economies and Conflicts in the Global South: Multi-Regional Perspectives on Rentier Politics, Ash gate, Aldershot, U.K., 2008, p.2.

82.   See Terry L. Karl, The Paradox of Plenty: Oil Boom and Petro-States, 1977, p. 34.

83.   See Kenneth Omeje, 2008, p.5.

84.   Ibid.

85.   Michael T. Klare, Resource Wars: The New Landscape of Global Conflict, Metropolitan/Owl Books, London, 2001.

86.   United Sates National Energy Policy, "Strengthening Global Alliances: Enhancing National Energy Security and International Relationships," May 2001.

87.   Ibid.

Chapter Five

SECURITY GOVERNANCE IN WEST AFRICA

Conflict Dynamics in West Africa

Violent conflict arises from a host of causes, including disputes over ideology, land, access to resources and power of the state, gross inequality, ethno-religious and identity issues among others. Any list of causes is bound to be incomplete, but there is at least some consensus with regard to general types of sources of conflict that are common. These are sometimes categorized as fitting within four broad groupings, namely, insecurity, inequality, private incentives and perceptions. These factors may well work in tandem, and may interact in a variety of ways across time and space.[1] The categories are useful in describing the issues but do not contribute to an understanding of whether the risk of conflict is high, low, or somewhere in between. Although many would argue that conflict does not necessarily progress in a linear or even cyclical fashion, it can be useful to talk about the causes of conflict in terms of root or structural causes, proximate causes, and triggers. This categorization recognizes that different causes will be of varying importance at different stages in the escalation or de-escalation of a particular conflict situation. From the point of view of policy, it also facilitates the design of conflict prevention strategies that are responsive to the particular dynamics at play.[2]

Root or structural causes, as the name suggests, are underlying sources of discontents. Many structural causes are linked to the relationship between the State and its citizens, the legitimacy of the government, and its ability to provide basic services, or what are called public goods. Perhaps paradoxically, both overly weak and overly strong governments are problematic in their propensity to generate conflict. In general, structural causes of conflict can include inequality, discrimination, breakdown of the rule of law, and unequal access to means of production and services, such as education and health care. In practice, all these may be associated with the quality of governance. Structural causes may also include relative or absolute poverty, although there is considerable debate as to the role of either in provoking conflict. While some level of inequality and discrimination is present in most societies, not all are experiencing violent conflict or are even likely to experience one in the near future. Similarly, poverty and weak or corrupt state institutions are seldom sufficient to provoke conflict. Proximate causes are generally necessary to move a society closer to conflict, be it widespread or isolated.[3]

Proximate causes, which might vary from root causes only in degrees, include the entrenching of discrimination, for example, in the introduction of quotas for entrance to universities, the loss of citizenship for specific groups, the manipulation of group identities for political purposes, systematic corruption in governance or in the electoral system, mismanagement of state resources, corrupt and abusive security forces, and widespread human rights violations. Even where significant root and proximate causes are present in a country, conflict may not necessarily be a by-product. Often, there must also be an event that is more difficult to predict and thus more difficult to prevent – a mobilizing or triggering event.[4] Triggers may include a host of events, from the violent removal of a leader from office to wide-scale election fraud and specific abuses by key institutions or leaders, including the destruction or desecration of important cultural or religious sites, among many others.

Looking at the causes of conflict in terms of root or structural causes, proximate causes and triggers is helpful to this study precisely because not only does it illuminate the complex conflicts that have ravaged much of West Africa in the past decades, but it helps in understanding the logic behind the ECOWAS conflict prevention mechanisms, as we would see later in this section. In regions such as West Africa, where there is a history of conflicts, there is always a regional dimension to the causes of these conflicts. In general, however, conflicts in a given region often have similar causes that can be linked to a host of historical, political, economic and geostrategic factors.[5]

Conflicts can also become regionalized, spilling over across national borders, as is also the case in West Africa's recent tragic history. In West Africa, several sources of conflict are shared across the sub-region. One common source of conflict in the sub-region relates to the nature of the post-colonial state in West Africa, all of which emerged from colonial rule with highly centralized and elite-driven governance structures and regimes. Not only does this governance regime create a wide gulf between the urban elites and the peripheral rural poor, it also significantly transforms the states into unaccountable, repressive and predatory institutions. With the end of the Cold War, weak regimes which proliferate in the region, several of which were propped up by external patrons, began to collapse, unable to withstand pressures for democratization, institutional and economic reforms.

For countries in the region, weak economies and a lack of opportunities have contributed to the rise of criminality and violence, all of which are fuelled by the easy availability of small arms and light weapons. Furthermore, internal and external actors, driven by economic incentives, took advantage of the weakness of the state to plunder natural resources, using revenue from these resources to capture the state, leading to a vicious cycle of violence, underdevelopment and state collapse. In other instances, where grievances from prior conflicts are left unaddressed, these have festered on and consequently precipitated new conflicts.

West Africa is one of the world's most unstable regions. Since 1957, when Ghana became the first State in the region to gain independence, West Africa has been beset with violent conflicts that have caused a vast number of deaths and created massive refuges flows and internally displaced persons.6 Between 1960 and 1990, thirty-seven of seventy-two successful military coups in Africa occurred in West Africa, a region comprising less than a third of all African States.7 In 1963, only six years after Ghana's independence, neighbouring Togo experienced Africa's first coup, and four years later, civil war broke out in Nigeria. Civil war started in Liberia in 1989, restarted in2000, and intensified in 2003; Sierra Leone endured a brutal civil conflict from 1991 to 2002, while violence engulfed Guinea-Bissau in 1998. Cote d'Ivoire, once a bastion of stability in an otherwise turbulent region, has slipped into conflict since 2002.

As for Nigeria, West Africa's most influential state, it has been slipping in and out of one crisis and conflict to another, the most notable being the conflict in the oil-rich Niger Delta region. This crisis has only just abated, thanks to a shaky presidential amnesty and promises to address the grievances of the militants who have waged a low intensity war against the federal authorities since the mid-1990s.

To be sure, not all of West Africa is in crises. Countries like Ghana, Benin Republic, and Senegal have been relatively stable. It is also important to understand that conflicts in West Africa vary in their sources, dynamics and complexity. For example, there are local and particular manifestations of conflict that are associated with the distinct historical experiences of colonial rule in each context, the challenge of nation-building, and levels of social -economic development of each state. Conflicts also have their own histories and specific characteristics, making it difficult to offer broad generalizations or conclusions about why conflict proliferates in the region.

However, while there is no consensus on the causes and dynamics of conflict in the region, it is possible to reach some general conclusions, especially in relation to those conflicts that are essentially internal. Traditional explanations that link conflict to issues of ethnicity and tribalism remain relevant, as demonstrated in the emergence of conflict in Cote d'Ivoire in September 2002. However, on their own, such factors do not provide a sufficient explanation, and only furnish a modest picture of an often complex situation. This is why it is helpful to consider the whole complex dynamics at work in particular situations of conflict to gain an understanding of the forces at play, and how those forces interacted to create and re-create dynamic situations of conflict.

For the most part, conflicts in West Africa have not occurred between States, but rather within States, although there is a definite trend towards their regionalization and spill over across the region. This is contrary to what might have been expected at independence, given the artificiality of Africa's colonially imposed state boundaries. Despite the arbitrary nature of Africa's borders, the continent has not experienced significant border changes, yet border issues have seldom been a driving force behind West Africa's conflicts. According to Jeffrey Herbst, "African leaders recognized in the early 1960s that a potentially large number of groups would want to secede from the states they are presently in to join others or create entirely new ones. In order to prevent the continent from being thrown into the chaos of large scale boundary changes in which the stability and integrity of any state could be threatened, they created a system of explicit norms, propounded by the Organization of African Unity in 1963, which declared any change in the inherited colonial boundaries to be illegitimate.[8]

These norms have held over time, and, consequently, spared Africa from large scale interstate conflicts. In West Africa, the several relatively small border skirmishes, such as between Mali and Burkina Faso, have been easily brought under control. At the root of conflicts in West Africa are the insidious legacies of colonial rule, exacerbated by the failure of post-colonial leaders and their civilian and military heirs to construct and manage public institutions and govern effectively, while eschewing corruption and nepotism.9 It is these failures that have created the widespread discontent among citizens, which self-serving and cynical political entrepreneurs, both civilian and military, have exploited to cause the perennial conflict that have characterized West Africa's political landscape since the 1960s.

In many West African countries, attempts at state building have effectively failed, and what is left behind is a highly centralized, often personalized state incapable of providing basic goods and services. These states, severally emasculated, tend to operate on a patronage basis and serving only a relative few who are either connected to the ruling families, or are members of favoured ethnic, religious or regional groupings. Thus, the starting point for understanding the causes of conflict in West Africa at the national level is the legacy of colonialism, a phenomenon that failed to build strong and democratic institutions and norms in colonial territories.

A key component of colonial administration in West Africa was an emphasis on developing and exploiting coastal regions, which left much of the interior underdeveloped. Consequently, political and economic power became centralized around capital cities, which were almost always located in the coastal regions of littoral states. This spatial concentration of development and political power in coastal regions reproduced itself at the level of national political governance in that post-colonial leaders found it expedient to concentrate power in their own hands rather than devolve power to local administrations in rural communities. These communities were therefore marginalized politically and economically.

This neglect necessarily created tensions between urban political elites and local or rural dwellers, who rightly felt alienated. In many cases, young adults reacted by challenging central authorities, or were available to be recruited by factions of the governing elite to cause public disorder in furtherance of their self-serving agendas. The colonial legacy not only explains the patently flawed post-independence development model privileging export of primary products over integrated development, it also accounts for the deep-seated animosities and mistrust that have come to characterize inter-governmental relations in the region.

The gradual politicization of security forces is a common phenomenon in West Africa, a clearly undesirable development which has contributed to a number of conflicts. Since the beginning of the colonial period, African security forces have frequently been a source of insecurity for both the state and its citizens, rather than an instrument for public safety and protection. One notable manifestation of the threat posed by West Africa's security forces is that, very often, divisions within the military establishment have led to coups, counter coups and mutinies.[10] For another, the politicization of the military, and its leadership in particular, has led to armies operating as the personal tool of the Head of State, not a few of who have used this tool inappropriately to decimate opponents or to oppress a restive population. In several instances, strong armies have been used either to impose sectional hegemonic rule, or to prop ineffective and corrupt leaders, such as Nigeria's General Sani Abacha from 1994 to 1998.

Other conflict dynamics arise in relation to citizenship, by which some communities are identified either as 'natives' or settlers' in various West African countries. Indeed, these pernicious distinctions are in some cases given constitutional legitimacy, while in others, they may exist only by custom or tradition. Regardless of the forms in which they exist in particular countries, they can be smoking guns of conflict. These divisions can play a role in causing or exacerbating conflict by emphasizing differences between groups, rather than emphasizing the commonalities that bind and mould communities into a nation. In situations such as these, political contests have come to be determined by the relative population size of the various groups in the community, as people would naturally vote for candidates from their group rather than for reasons of competence. As would be expected, when such a candidate emerges victorious, his or her loyalty often lies with the supportive group and not with the larger community or the country as a whole.

If the candidate is elected into a powerful executive office, his natural reflex is to make important appointments, including the awarding of government contracts and patronages, to his kin group. This necessarily breeds discontent and a feeling of marginalization among the less favoured groups, once again creating tension and avoidable conflicts. At the regional level, one of the more notable manifestations of the colonial legacy is the Francophone – Anglophone divide, a veritable obstacle to mutual understanding and cooperation in West Africa. This problem has not only proved subversive of regional integration efforts, but its persistence says a lot about the health of ECOWAS integration efforts.

Much of West Africa's political and social pathologies are directly linked to the vast natural resources that abound in the region. The region's geographical location, environmental and demographic variable complete the first basket of countervailing factors. As it had been argued in the penultimate chapter, the resource curse or 'paradox of plenty' provides a necessary explanation of West Africa's tragic development process and, by implication, much of its modern-day security challenges.

It should, however, be understood that the 'resource curse' thesis, no matter how compelling, does not provide a sufficient explanation of West Africa's diverse and complex conflicts. As the civil wars in Liberia and Sierra Leone and the conflict in Nigeria's Niger Delta region typify, struggle over control of resources can be a major cause of conflicts, but resources by themselves do not necessarily cause conflicts In resource-rich countries facing crises, the role of resources is essentially instrumental, namely, the intensification and sustenance of the conflict.

In much of West Africa's recent conflicts, issues of political and economic marginalization, as well as social exclusion, identity and citizenship have combined and have provided the spark to conflicts, which are then fed and reinforced by fight over the control of resources, both for the sustenance of the war and for the personal aggrandizement of warlords and political elites on both sides of the conflict.

While West Africa's location along the Gulf of Guinea has been a blessing in terms of its oil and mineral riches, its proximity and easy access to the Americas – the same factor that makes it a high value source of oil for the United States – has transformed the Gulf of Guinea into a favourite trans -shipment zone for Latin American narco-cartels seeking less protected routes into Europe and the United States.11 Thus far, West Africa has been used mainly as a transit point for the narco-trade. While this represents a security threat in itself, the real problem relates to the capacity of powerful drug barons to deploy their vast resources to undermine state authority through orchestrated violence, as it is increasingly the case in Guinea Bissau, an emergent narco-state.

Given that most states in the region are weak with highly penetrable borders, it may not be long before narco barons and turf battles compound the already fragile stability in West Africa. In other words, the sudden rise in drug trafficking through West Africa indisputably has negative implications for governance, security, and development in the region. As with the case of resource availability, drug trafficking is not a cause of conflict and state fragility, but rather is a symptom of the pre-existence of these conditions in countries in the region. What the drug traffickers and their patrons are doing is simply to exploit West Africa's fragile security environment to capture and criminalize the state, creating a vicious cycle of criminality, violence, state fragility and underdevelopment.

If securing West Africa's territorial waters is beyond the capacity of the littoral states, the security challenges along the region's northern frontiers are even more daunting. The Sahel-Sahara divide that stretches from north-western Chad through northern Niger and Mali to Mauritania epitomizes the rising challenges of complex emergencies in West Africa.[12] The latest low intensity conflicts in West Africa are located in this increasingly vulnerable belt. In Niger, the insurgent Tuareg group-Movement Nigerien Pour la Justice (MNI) is locked in a deadly conflict with the government over autonomy and uranium revenues. As in similar conflicts in West Africa over the last two decades, genuine grievances have been adulterated with banditry, terrorism, arms trafficking, human and drug trafficking, including the usual export of refugees and internally displaced persons.

As in land and maritime insecurity, West Africa's environmental challenge is just as vast and potentially destabilizing, reason being that the region is prone to extremes of climate change, which alternate between severe cyclical droughts and heavy flooding. In the Sahel region, for instance, the southward encroachment of the desert is adding an environmental dimension to the precarious livelihoods of the pastoralists and nomads, injecting an incendiary element into age-old conflicts with the largely sedentary farmers further south.

In addition, as water shortages increase in the arid northern fringes of West Africa, common water sources are turning into combustible sources of conflicts. Given that warlords and unscrupulous politicians have often manipulated ethnic divisions and rivalries over control of scarce natural resources, it is not improbable to conceive land and water wars to dominate the local (internal) and cross-border (regional) conflict landscape in West Africa in the very near future. Managing these regional commons so that they do not provoke another cycle of conflict will task ECOWAS in the years ahead.

Another source of insecurity relates to internal and regional governance processes. Several scholars have pointed to Africa's stifling and closed political space, sectional and patrimonial politics as being responsible for much of the political violence and instability that have ravaged West Africa in the last two decades. The privatization and criminalization of politics, in short, poor governance, is perhaps the single most critical factor in West Africa's crisis of insecurity and development. Since policies and practices at the national level exert considerable influence on human security both at national and regional levels, good governance has come to be seen as the panacea to much of West Africa's developmental and security challenges. This recognition probably accounts for the greater salience governance has assumed in development and collective security initiatives at the regional level in West Africa in the past decades.

As this analysis seeks to demonstrate, the principal sources of conflict in West Africa are to be found within nation states. Perhaps this is so, not least because Africa and its sub-regions are often considered peripheral in the international system. Nonetheless, changes in the international system, most notably the end of the Cold War, have had a profound effect on West Africa and must necessarily be taken into account when assessing sources of conflict in the region. In addition to the end of the Cold War, other international changes aggravating pre-existing tensions and contributing to conflict in the region include the proliferation of small arms, the regionalization of conflicts and the role of external profiteers and influence seekers.[13]

The Cold War and the East West rivalry it fostered provided an organizing principle and stability for the international system. Its end in the late 1980s encouraged chaotic tendencies, including across West Africa. In 1997, UN Secretary General, Kofi Annan, had stated that "across Africa, undemocratic and oppressive regimes were supported and sustained by the competing superpowers in the name of their broader goals but, when the Cold War ended, Africa was suddenly left to fend for itself".[14] The end of the Cold War meant a restructuring of military and political assistance to former client states which contributed to a number of tumultuous and violent clashes in various corners of the world. In West Africa, a region in which the seeming order imposed by the Cold War was always mixed with anarchy, the end of the East-West rivalry and the retrenchment of the superpowers' interests in the region provoked a groundswell of anarchy and state decomposition.

The immediate effect was that Africa leaders could no longer rely on outside powers to frighten or crush armed opposition groups; nor could West African leaders continue to exploit superpower rivalry to garner unprecedented quantities of military and financial aid for their security services.[15] As William Reno has graphically described, "weak state sovereignty after the Cold War no longer guarantees external military or financial support to state bureaucracies to battle armed rebels and control militaries composed of disgruntled youth and others long marginalized in postcolonial politics.[16]

The withdrawal of military and financial support from the United States and the Soviet Union had critical, mostly destabilizing, consequences on West Africa as the region's insecure leaders became increasingly vulnerable to internal revolt. It is no coincidence that some of West Africa's most brutal and long-running conflicts, such as the Liberian and Sierra Leonean civil wars, erupted as the Cold War was unravelling. The new world order which the end of the Cold War has unleashed, also explains Cote d'Ivoire's implosion in 2002, following France's reluctance to protect President Henri Konan Bedie's divisive rule. On a cautionary note, it is important not to overemphasize the effect of the Cold War on West Africa's decent into chaos in the past two decades. While the consequences of the end of the Cold War set the stage for increased conflict in West Africa, it only exposed structural weakness of the states in the region, weaknesses that were already present but were suppressed by the stabilizing presence of the superpowers.

Related to the end of the Cold War was the emergence of a new phenomenon of external power seekers who sought to fill the void left by the superpowers. The 1990s also saw an increasingly influential role for external profiteers, whose actions sustain and exacerbated conflict in the region.[17] The new actors include mercenaries, arms dealers, and others with an interest in meddling in West Africa, such as Libya's eccentric strongman, Muammar Qaddafi. At the heart of the civil wars in Sierra Leone and Liberia was the geostrategic machinations of Muammar Qaddafi, who has sought diligently to remove Western, especially United States', influence throughout Africa through the instrumentality of financial support to cash-strapped regimes. His meddling in West African affairs has included backing groups claiming to have radical revolutionary agendas, including Charles Taylor's NPFL and Foday Sankoh's RUF in Sierra Leone.[18]

Another trend, perhaps most visible in Sierra Leone's civil war, was the use of and dependence on mercenaries or, to use the popular euphemism, "private military companies." Since the end of the Cold War, both rebels groups and governments in transition societies have regularly tapped into clandestine mercenary networks to argument their fighting forces. For instance, the government of Valentine Strasser in Sierra Leone famously hired the South African mercenary firm, Executive Outcomes, to train Sierra Leonean troops, and also to fight for the government.[19] As the Sierra Leonean government could not afford to pay Executive Outcomes' costly salaries, it granted the company unrestricted access to Sierra Leone diamond mines, an arrangement that proved quite profitable for the firm.

On the other side of the conflict, RUF rebels tapped into mercenaries from Burkina Faso and Liberia. Thus, the civil war in Sierra Leone also became a proxy war, in the mould of Cold War proxy wars, between South African mercenaries on one side and Burkinabe and Liberian war entrepreneurs, on the other. This complex dynamics not only prolonged the war but further destabilized the entire sub -region, as victorious factions in each country attempt to settle the score by supporting rebel movements in states that had supplied mercenaries to fight them. Similarly, in the Ivorian crisis that began in September 2002, President Gbagbo had relied heavily on mercenaries from France, South Africa and Eastern Europe in his attempts to defeat various rebels groups ranged against his government.[20]

Accompanying the proliferation of mercenaries is the proliferation of the small arms that are commonly used in these conflicts. By themselves, small arms do not cause conflicts. However, they facilitate conflicts and thus are rightly considered among the sources of conflict. According to a 2000 UN report, approximately 7 million small arms and light weapons, which include assault rifles, light and heavy machine guns, rocket-propelled grenades, individually portable mortars and missiles, and anti-personnel landmines are in circulation in West Africa, of which more than 40 per cent is believed to have been acquired through illicit means.[21]

The end of the Cold War led to an increase in the flow of small arms in the region, as the superpowers and their allies began to reduce their arms stockpiles. For a small price, small arms could be procured either from rogue regimes or from arms dealers, making them an important factor in sustaining and fuelling conflicts. Small arms are extreme tools of violence in West Africa for several reasons: they are durable, highly portable, easily concealed, simple to use, extremely lethal and possess legitimate military, police and civilian use. They are also cheap, widely available and light weight, and so can be used by child soldiers, who have played such a significant role in recent conflicts in West Africa.[22] Arms provided by a network of dealers across the region and the considerable surplus of arms left over from previous conflicts were particularly influential in both the Sierra Leonean and Liberian conflicts.

The ECOWAS Convention on Small Arms and Light Weapons, Their Ammunition and Other Related Materials is the primary means by which ECOWAS countries have sought to control the flow of small arms into and within the region. As an instrument for the promotion of collective and human security in the region, the Convention constitutes a critical component of the broader ECOWAS conflict prevention framework.

Without a capable state to provide for their security and welfare, civilians in conflict as well as in non-conflict states have sought to fill the void by arming themselves in order to ensure their own security and safety in what could be likened to a Hobbesian state of nature. While the affluent could hire private security for their protection and safety, the more impoverished majority has often organized themselves into militias and self-help civilian defence organizations. Ostensibly established to provide security where the state has failed, these groups have often developed into politically sensitive, murderous and extortionist urban guerrilla gangs. In Nigeria, for instance, groups like the Odua People's Congress and the Bakassi Boys have grown into well-armed private armies of powerful individuals who often use them to settle personal scores. Such is the deleterious consequences of small arms on human security in West Africa.

Conflicts in West Africa: Five Case Studies

Despite their seeming divergences and localized agendas, West Africa's conflict of the past three decades share more in common than they differ from each other. For instance, the Liberian insurrection was waged from inside bases in Cote d'Ivoire by a mix of Liberian, Burkinabe and Ivorian insurgents. When the Revolutionary United Front of Sierra Leone launched its own 'revolution' in Sierra Leone in 1991, not only did it receive help from about 200 Burkinabe regular soldiers and veterans of the Liberian conflict, Charles Taylor also provided an operational base inside Liberia for the fledging rebel movement. Furthermore, both armed insurrections in Liberia and Sierra Leone were notorious for their brutality and mindless targeting of defenceless civilians, including the use of child soldiers.

This inter-dependence runs deep, and may suggest that there are factors which are responsible for the post-Cold War upsurge of violence and armed conflicts in West Africa. There are no easy answers to explain the culture of violence across West Africa, as journalistic and academic writings on the phenomenon are contested. Robert Kaplan, for example, attributed West Africa's conflicts to social tension, youth delinquency and environmental depletion.[23] While Paul Collier and others have proposed the greed thesis, much of Africa's political theorists have attributed conflicts in West Africa, as indeed much of Africa, to bad governance. On the other hand, for David Keen, West African' conflicts can be understood through rational choice theory and market-centred analyses in which struggles for personal control, appropriation and exchange of resources and commercial networks, rather than state power and institutions, provide the primary motivation for rebel movements seeking to seize control of the State. For social anthropologists, Africa's wars invoke another dimension of the 'crisis of modernity,' a dimension that can only be understood by being sensitive to the esoteric, psychological and religious foundations of different cultures.[24]

Given the contested nature of these explanations, this study would seek understanding of five of West Africa's legacy conflicts that erupted in the late 1980s and persisted into the new Millennium by investigating their history and sociology. The investigation necessarily focuses on the centrality of politics, precisely because the history, character and dynamics of rebels, militants and insurgent groups in West Africa suggest they are initially propelled by political conditions in their countries. The evidence of political motivation resides in their demands for inclusivity, openness, and democracy in the determination of how decisions are made and resources allocated in individual countries. As it is often the case in West Africa, the formulation of political objectives and strategies by rebels and insurgent groups are not static, but rather are part of a process that includes the dynamic interplay between local and international politics, changes in the configurations of power and alliances both at the national and regional levels, and shifts in the relationships among different protagonists. All of these make the environment of conflict in the region intensely political.

Liberia

Liberia, a republic of 2.5 million inhabitants on West Africa's coast, was founded by freed black American slaves in 1847. Despite constituting only 5 per cent of the population, the Americo-Liberian elites, as the freed slaves are called, established an oligarchy that excluded and oppressed the indigenous inhabitants. The 133 year rule of the Americo-Liberian oligarchy created deep-seated resentment and divisions within Liberia society.[25] In the midst of growing economic difficulties in the 1970s, the government of William Tolbert was confronted with unprecedented political challenges from a bourgeoning opposition movement. Towards the end of the decade, public disaffection had reached the boiling point, paving the way for Samuel Doe, a low-ranking indigenous army sergeant, to stage a coup in April 1980. The spontaneous jubilation by indigenous Liberians following the success of the coup symbolized the level of hostility that had accumulated against the Americo-Liberian privilege class.

However, the brutality of Doe's rule was matched only by his parochialism and ineptitude. Not only did he order the execution of William Tolbert and several leading Americo-Liberian politicians, over the next four years he all but eliminated all potential rivals through assassinations or enforced exile. Human rights abuses were widespread, and any who challenged Doe's rule was a legitimate target for an increasingly paranoid government. Whereas the Americo-

Liberians were hated for their marginalization of other Liberians, Doe perpetuated his sectional rule by filling the most important military and government positions, including the cabinet, with fellow members of his Krahn ethnic group, purging the military of America-Liberians and other indigenous clans. Thus, he effectively turned the military, a supposedly national institution, into a Krahn-dominated instrument of oppression.

Following an increasingly brutal phase in Doe's rule, he was challenged in a failed military coup in 1985. Doe not only executed General Thomas Quiwonkpa, the leader of the failed coup plot and other putschists, his Krahn-dominated army took revenge against other clans whose members featured in the failed coup, killing as many as 3,000 members of the Gios and Manos clan.[26] This single event, perhaps more than any other, set the stage for the exploitation of ethnic rivalries that would eventually culminate in Liberia's brutal civil war.

The ground for Liberia's descent into chaos was, however, laid by Doe's refusal to concede to popular demands for the democratization of Liberia's politics. To hold on to power in the midst of growing demands for democratization, Doe transformed from a military dictator to a civilian presidential candidate and, by 1985, had banned, bullied and brutalized all his opponents to submission. Not surprisingly, he easily won the presidential election in the process.[27]

In 1989, Charles Taylor, backed principally by Cote d'Ivoire and Burkina Faso, launched an invasion against Doe's government. Right from the start, Taylor's armed band consisted of individuals drawn from many West African countries. Several of his senior commanders were Sierra Leoneans and Gambians, who had joined the Taylor organization in Libya. Libya was to remain a major backer of Charles Taylor throughout the long-drawn conflict.

Partly as a result of the unfolding humanitarian crisis, but also to prevent Liberia from becoming a Libyan revolutionary outpost in West Africa, ECOWAS countries, led by Nigeria, set up the ECOWAS Military Observer Group (ECOMOG) to counter the destabilizing consequences of the invasion of Liberia by Charles Taylor's National Patriotic Front of Liberia (NPFL). The ECOMOG intervention denied Charles Taylor victory, but remnants of his troops did succeed in capturing and killing President Doe in September 1990.[28] Following a ceasefire in 1996 and flawed elections characterized by threats from Charles Taylor that only his electoral victory would guarantee peace in Liberia, the rebel leader ascended the presidency in 1997. Overall, the 1989 invasion of Liberia by Charles Taylor's NPFL, which sparked the Liberian Civil wars, resulted in an estimated 200,000 deaths, and well over one million refugees and internally displaced persons.[29]

The Liberian conflicts spanned a period of 14 years, from December 1989 to August 2003, and can be divided into two distinct periods. The first war, from 1989 and 1996, began with rebellion that rapidly escalated and resulted in the complete collapse of the state of Liberia. This phase of the conflict involved at least eight armed factions, all fighting for the control of Liberia in the absence of a central authority. This first Civil War also attracted regional and United Nations' peacekeeping missions, from 1990 to 1997. The second Civil War from 1999 to 2003 was waged by elements of the Liberian opposition against the elected government of Charles Taylor, the former rebel leader. This phase of the conflict did not attract any international intervention until ECOWAS leaders forced Taylor to step down in August 2003 as part of a process of national reconciliation.

Because coups have occurred rather too frequently in West Africa, many did not appreciate the full implications of the Samuel Doe-led military takeover of 1980. The military coup not only uprooted a flawed century-old governance system dominated by the Americo-Liberian oligarchy, it created the combustible environment of ethnic polarization, including a rapacious and unprofessional military, whose off shoots became the instrument of violence, plunder and pillage, making Liberia the epicentre of a system of violent conflict in West Africa.[30] Amos Sawyer, the Liberian intellectual who was to head an interim administration in Liberia preparatory to UN supervised elections in 2006 had described elements in the Doe's regime as "bounty hunters, fortune seekers and ethnicists",[31] a view shared by Ibrahim Abdullah and Ismail Rashid, both of who described the Doe regime as lacking "a programme, common agenda and political discipline."[32] As for Charles Taylor, the general view is that he was just a political entrepreneur for who politics was merely an instrument for personal aggrandizement.

Just like Doe before him, Charles Taylor and his entourage mobilized key institutions of the state, filling them up with his cronies and fellow-travellers. After having purged the Liberian army of several officers from the Krahn Clan – Doe's ethnic group –he proceeded to fill his security forces with loyal lieutenants, a replay of Doe's fatal mistakes. In doing this, it could be argued Taylor was only following a popular tradition in contemporary African politics by which insecure leaders place their kinsmen at the helm of strategic public institutions, including the military.

However, by filling key institutions of state and the military with ethnic loyalists and using the security forces as a tool to silence political opponents, Taylor did create conditions for the mobilisation of other ethnic groups to protect their own people against a partisan government.

Thus, the institutionalisation of violence, which was the hallmark of the Doe's regime, continued unabated under Charles Taylor's presidency and fed into a combustible mix of perceptions of marginalisation, poverty, corruption, and under-development, all of which are manifestations of poor governance. Taylor himself admitted this much in an interview he granted West Africa Magazine in 2000. According to Taylor, "once you are in, (in power) because of the chaos created from outside, you become undemocratic in the preservation of power. It is almost like the survival of the fittest".[33]

For Taylor and much of the political leadership in West Africa, indeed across Africa, the state is not merely an extension of the leader's own personal power, security of the state is conflated with regime or personal security of the Head of Government. Such a conception of the state not only provides an existential justification for the criminalisation of the state, it can often leave marginalized groups with no legitimate avenue for the expression of grievances other than violence.

Sierra Leone

Sierra Leone achieved independence from Britain in April 1961. Like Liberia, Sierra Leone is rich in mineral resources, principally diamond, gold, iron ore and bauxite. Compared to other West African countries, Sierra Leone enjoyed relative peace and stability until the early 1990s, even though ethnic disputes were not uncommon in the country. Historically, conflict between the Creole elite and other less favoured tribes defined post-colonial politics. The seemingly tranquil Sierra Leonean polity, however, masked a history of militarization and consistent mismanagement of the country's wealth and social relations.[34]

Since independence, Sierra Leone's politics had been dominated by the Sierra Leone People's Party (SLPP) until 1967 when the All People's Congress (APC), headed by the charismatic Siaka Stevens, won the polls. Stevens ran a populist campaign in which he mobilized rural communities against an inept and corrupt alliance of urban elites and rural chiefs.[35] A pre-emptive military coup had prevented Stevens from taking power until a counter coup in 1968 restored his presidential mandate. Consistent with Africa's patrimonial politics, Stevens established a staggeringly corrupt patrimonial system in which he doled out patronage to loyal clients to buy political support.[36] By 1978, Sierra Leone had been transformed into a de-jure one-party state with a rubber stamp parliament to legitimize Steven's decrees.

Under the president's supervision, the army was weakened, with all senior officers APC loyalists. Steven's seventeen-year rule also diminished the role of civil society in the political life of Serra Leone, as he ensured that all trade unions, business and professional organizations were effectively under government control. Steven's governance failures were exacerbated by rampant corruption and a harsh international economic environment. A rapacious political class and a parasitic Lebanese business clique combined to loot the country's diamond revenues, even as agricultural production collapsed. When Stevens came to power in 1968, Sierra Leone was earning about U.S $200 million from annual diamond sales. By the time he left office in 1985, only about U.S $100,000 of diamond revenues were entering government coffers annually.[37] The steep declines in diamond revenues thus completed Sierra Leone's misery and ignited mass discontent and revolt.

Apparently unable to bribe his way through, Stevens handed over the reins of power to his loyal army chief, General Joseph Momoh, who inherited a divided and demoralized APC, a weak army and an economic mess.[38] Throughout the late 1980s, international efforts to revive the ailing economy were spearheaded by the African Development Bank (ADB) and the Bretton Woods Institutions, whose Structural Adjustment Programme (SAP) only created more misery and deprivations for the ordinary poor people of Sierra Leone. These rescue missions failed partly because of structural deficiencies in the Sierra Leonean economy, but also because of a deteriorating security environment, both within Sierra Leone and also across the border in Liberia.

Sierra Leone's civil war erupted in March 1991, when RUF rebels and remnants of Charles Taylor's NPFL of Liberia were joined by mercenaries from Burkina Faso to invade the diamond-rich south-eastern Sierra Leone from their base in Liberia. As was the case with the NPFL's invasion of Monrovia, in 1989, ECOWAS had promptly deployed troops under the auspices of ECOMOG to defend the capital Freetown from falling into rebels hands. ECOMOG's did succeed in protecting the capital from falling into rebels hands but failed to stabilize the volatile political situation in the country. In the end, General Momoh was forced to step down for another military junta headed by Captain Valentine Strasser, which itself was soon overthrown by yet another military faction headed by General Julius Bio. Under international pressure, Bio's regime yielded power to a democratically elected civilian administration headed by Ahmed Tejan Kabbah in 1996.[39]

The involvement of ECOMOG in Sierra Leone was to increase dramatically in 1997 when Nigeria diverted its peacekeepers from the concluding Liberian Mission to Sierra Leone in an attempt to crush a military coup against the democratically elected Ahmed Tejan Kabbah, barely one year after his inauguration. By early February 2008, a Nigerian -led ECOMOG had reversed the coup and restored Kabbah to power.[40]

The roots of the Sierra Leone civil war go far back to the political misrule of Siaka Stevens (1966 – 1985) and General Joseph Momoh (1985 – 1992). This was exacerbated by corruption, collapse of the country's diamond revenues and deteriorating economic conditions. This situation combined with incredible socio-economic inequalities between an opulent urban elite and impoverished youths in the country side who had limited access to education and employment and were thus denied the opportunity of social mobility. A potent cocktail of political autocracy, corruption and economic decay produced a mass of disaffected and angry youth in the countryside, many of who were to form the nucleus of the RUF rebels, either with their consent or by forceful recruitment. The youth saw the war as a chance to improve their social position through plunder of diamond fields. In other words, they hoped the war would provide them with an escape route from their wretched existence.

What the foregoing analysis suggests is that Sierra

Leone, just like Liberia, descended into violence and state collapse through extraordinary leadership failure and disintegration of patrimonial politics. In other words, in Sierra Leone, socio-political disintegration and decay caused by governance failure constituted the combustible spark for the violence and human misery that characterized the Sierra Leonean state all through the period of the civil war, from 1991 through 1999. Self-serving political elites, armed bands and assorted revolutionaries cynically exploited public discontent to pursue private agendas of plunder and pillage through the instrumentality of terror. Sierra Leone's notorious rebel leader, Foday Sankoh, was one such person who succeeded brilliantly in framing personal agendas in ideological and messianic slogans.

As in Liberia, poor governance precipitated the conflict, in which assorted rebels and government security forces fought over control of territory to protect access to natural resources, especially diamond, whose revenues were used to fuel more conflicts in a vicious cycle of war, murder and social deprivation and state collapse. With so much to plunder, there was little incentive to stop the war and end the humanitarian disaster associated with it.

Guinea-Bissau

Guinea-Bissau is a tiny country of about 1.6 million people located on West Africa's Atlantic coast. As well as being one of the poorest countries in the world, a decade of political and military instability has worsened domestic social and economic problems. In the 1970s, Guinea-Bissau was widely seen as a political and economic model of a successful African peasant revolution. Under the charismatic leadership of Amilcar Cabral, a largely peasant army of about 6,000 had forced the withdrawal of some 30,000 Portuguese troops, paving way for independence in September 1974. Following the assassination of Amilcar Cabral in 1973, Luis Cabral, his brother, look over leadership of the Partido Africano da Independence da Guinea Cabo Verde (PAIGC), the revolutionary movement which transformed into the ruling party following independence.[41]

Once in government, the PAIGC appropriated and centralized power such that the party soon became indistinguishable from the state. Before long, Luis Cabral had built up a repressive state and centralized power in a close-knit cabal. By the time he was overthrown in a military coup in 1980, his autocratic style and misrule have created deep fissures in Guinea-Bissau's social fabric. Whereas during the independence struggle there was no distinction between a Guinea Bissau and a Cape Verdean, another Portuguese Island State, Cabral's misrule ensured that identity issues became prominent in Guinea Bissau society.

Cape Verdeans were the leading lights in Guinea-Bissau's independence struggle, including the Cabral brothers themselves. Because of shared political and cultural history, several Cape Verdeans made successful careers in Guinea-Bissau's public service, creating a groundswell of resentment among the indigenous population. The fact that many of the senior officers in the country's army were of Cape Verdean descent was also a source of tension.[42] These tensions were to culminate in the coup of 1980 which led to a two-decade rule by Joa Bernando Viera. Viera's rule was to prove no different from that of his predecessor, as be continued in the repressive and autocratic style of the deposed Luis Cabral. Not only did Viera disband the National Assembly, he quickly established firm control over the army and security services, often asserting power through periodic purges of so-called fifth columnists' and suspected coup plotters.[43]

After years of autocratic rule, Guinea-Bissau's first multiparty election was held in July 1984 in which President Viera participated and won. This election which was designed to legitimize Veira's rule, largely failed to calm social tension, as discontentment grew amid charges of cronyism and corruption. Within four years of its first multiparty election, Guinea-Bissau's political and economic anomie became sharper, forcing the country to collapse into civil war between 1988 and 1999. The economic decline continued after the civil war amidst charges of mismanagement of the economy and poor governance. Despite the great expectations of independence, governance in Guinea-Bissau since then has degenerated into an orgy of corruption, repressive rule and wanton killings of political opponents.

The causes of current instability in Guinea-Bissau are therefore the result of the inability of the country's leaders to confront dysfunctional tendencies that have characterized the history of the country since independence. These include:

(i)   The militarization and personalization of the state during the last four decades, which led to the steady criminalization of the state, as reflected in such political tendencies as the elimination of rivals and the orchestration of vengeance schemes;

(ii)   The normalization of violence at the state level, which creates a culture of impunity. Violent conflict and murder proliferate due to the non-functioning of the formal institutions of the state, such as law and order and the justice system; and

(iii)   The criminalisation of the state, which has created a complex web of patronage and corruption, and reinforced a political system based on alliances among ethnic and religious factions.[44].

As in much of West Africa, governance deficit is at the root of Guinea-Bissau's recurrent political crisis. For instance, the first coup d'état after six years of independence was a direct result of nepotism and a client-based power structure created by the sole political party. This has remained the model of reference for future leaders, all of who have centralized power and deployed the army and security forces in furtherance of self-serving and often parochial agendas.

Cote d'Ivoire

Cote d'Ivoire offers an example of the political manipulation of identity as a driver of conflict in West Africa. Historically, a stable country by the standards of West Africa, Cote d'Ivoire experienced its first military coup only in December 1999. A failed coup attempt in September 2002 was to trigger nine months of sustained violence. The immediate spark for the 2002 rebellion was disagreement over a demobilization drive by the government of President Laurent Gbagbo designed to rid the army of soldiers recruited by General Robert Guei, the former military leader who took power after the 1999 coup. However, the mutiny by a group of soldiers fearful of the imminent demobilization exercise was merely reflective of a deeper national crisis resulting from the absence of effective leadership and pandering to patrimonial instincts. For example, all the leaders who have held power since

1993, following the death of Cote d'Ivoire's long-running post-independence leader, Houphouet-Boigny, blatantly used and abused ethnic, religious and parochial identities to secure and maintain power.[45]

Houphouet-Boigny, Cote d'Ivoire's patriarchal leader led the country for thirty-three years until his death in December 1993. He was no democrat, but he combined charisma, autocratic one-party rule with policies that sought to prevent destabilizing divisions in Cote d'Ivoire's body politics. He was sensitive to issues of diversity, and his administration included ministers from different ethnic, regional and religious backgrounds. He opened the country to migrant workers from other West African states, who contributed to the building of what became the third largest economy in sub-Saharan Africa, after South Africa and Nigeria. But when Houphouet-Boigny died, apparently so did his policy of diversity in political and economic life.

Instability emerged when Henri Konan Bedie, Houphouet-Boigny's chosen successor, introduced the policy of Ivoirite, which roughly translates to 'Ivorianness' in order to exclude his main political rival, Alassane Quattara, a northerner, from participating in the 1995 presidential election. Under the policy of Ivoirite, Quattara was supposedly not a native Ivorian. Although Quattara had served as Prime Minister under Houphouet-Boigny, the legislation introduced by President Bedie effectively disqualified him from running for the presidency, ostensibly because he is not an Ivorian.

Bedie, out of fear of a possible northern backlash, took further measures to marginalize the north from Ivorian society, including the gradual removal of northerners from powerful positions in the security forces. He also attacked migrant workers, blaming them for the economic failures and the massive unemployment crises that clouded his presidency in the mid-1990s. By his policies, Bedie implied that northerners, whose ethnic affinities stretched across Cote d'Ivoire's borders into Burkina Faso, Guinea, Mali and Niger, were at the root of the country's economic problems. In the process, northerners were subjected to systematic and coordinated harassment and marginalization, as President Bedie strove to concentrate power in the centre and south of the country.[46]

Amid such divisive politics of discrimination and xenophobia, disaffected soldiers led a bloodless coup against Bedie in December 1999 and installed General Robert Guei as president. However, Guei's rule was violent in a way previously unknown in Ivorian politics.[47] Rather than undo the divisive policies of Bedie, he not only went ahead to revise the constitution to prevent Quattara from competing in the 2000 presidential election, he significantly marginalized northern politicians of Burkinabe, Malian, or Guinea descent. Consequently, the run-up to the election was marred by ethnic and political violence. Guei tried to steal the election by prematurely ending the vote count, but a combination of mass protest and the loss of support of the army forced him to flee into exile in Benin Republic.[48]

Guei's forced departure paved the way for Laurent Gbagbo to assume the presidency, but his rule was marred by violence surrounding the December 2000 parliamentary election, which included clashes between the President's supporters, mainly of southern extraction, and those of Quattara's, mainly from the north. Prior to the parliamentary vote, Gbagbo had rejected calls to review Quattara's eligibility to run for President. In the manner of his predecessors, Gbagbo had used national identity to protect and consolidate his power.

Following sustained mass pressure, Quattara's citizenship was restored in July 2002, but remained barred from running for president. While maintaining his hostility and divisive policies towards immigrants, Gbagbo promoted members of his ethnic group, particularly within the army and the security services, an act which further inflamed tensions. As was with his predecessors, Gbagbo did nothing to promote ethnic reconciliation, and the violence of 2002 and 2003 were the direct consequences of these divisive policies.

As it has become the pattern in much of West Africa's recent conflicts, the government of Cote-d'Ivoire accused Burkina Faso and Liberia of fomenting the rebellion. In a confusing web of accusations and counter accusations, Charles Taylor, Liberia's President at the time accused Cote d'Ivoire of supporting the Liberian rebel group – the Movement of Democracy in Liberia. Despite these accusations and counter accusations, the conflict in Cote d'Ivoire spilled over 125,000 Ivorian refugees into Liberia, Ghana, Guinea, Mali and Burkina Faso.[49] As Adekeye Adebajo has argued, the alleged involvement of rebel elements from Liberia and Sierra Leone in the conflict in Cote d'Ivoire may well mean the case of regional chickens coming home to roost.[50]

The Ivorian conflict once again demonstrated the pivotal role of governance in building stable communities and stabilising society. While ethnic and identity politics is not uncommon in much of Africa, the Cote d'Ivoire conflict spoke to what has become a desperate attempt by West African politicians to manipulate ethnic cleavages for short term political gain. In Cote d'Ivoire, immigrants have long been welcomed in the country right from the early days of independence when President Houphouet-Boigny encouraged them to settle in the country and cultivate lands to boost agricultural production. Since then, immigrants, mostly from Burkina Faso, have settled in the country, several of who have fully integrated and had been accepted as bonafide Ivorian citizens. For instance, Alassane Quattara whose exclusion from the 2000 presidential election had precipitated the conflict had previously served as Prime Minister of the country. Questions could be asked why a former Prime Minister could be ruled ineligible to contest presidential election for being a non-national in the same country he had previously served as Prime Minister.

The only plausible explanation for the Ivoirian political debacle may well be that after 33 years of Houphouet-Boigny's autocratic rule ended with his demise in 1993, Cote d'Ivoire was forced to grapple with the democratic process for the first time. Apparently lacking the charisma and statesmanship of Houphouet-Boigny, his political heirs were forced to take refuge in ethnic enclaves to boost their electoral prospects. The xenophobic policy of Ivoirite which precipitated the political crisis in Cote d'Ivoire is consistent with tribal and patrimonial politics in much of West Africa.

Nigeria
Nigeria is the most populous country in Africa and one of the most endowed on account of its vast petroleum and gas resources. Nigeria gained independence from Britain in 1960, and is generally regarded as West Africa's hegemon. For all its enormous resource endowment, Nigeria is still a poor country, economically backward, politically unstable and notable for its egregious corruption.

By 1995, there had been nine military coups d'état, three of which were abortive. Before that, there was the civil war, which was provoked by a secessionist attempt by one of the country's major ethnic groups, and lasted from July 1967 to January 1970 and claimed hundreds of thousands of lives. Nigeria's post-independence history has been characterized by long military rule and short civilian interregnums, which were always displaced by yet another military rule. Since 1999, however, the country has returned to democratic rule, a feat unmatched in the country's turbulent political history. In general, military rule, the civil war and the oil rents which flow into the coffers of the central government have facilitated the centralization of authority and power and, with it, pervasive corruption. As a rentier economy, control of the state not only translates to power over the allocation of strategic resources, but also provides opportunities for state capture and profit-making. This is the context that has made the struggle for control of the Nigerian state often fierce and vicious.

There is an absence of fundamental cleavages among Nigeria's political class, whether military or civilian, which means that the struggle for power is always less about competing policies or ideals, but with who and which group should secure power and control the disposition of its spoils. In this kind of situation, political contest can become more or less a game of musical chairs, a negative condition that does not rule out violence, but merely ensures that such conflict mostly destroys individuals and not the state. Writing on the state of politics in Nigeria in the mid1980, a Presidential Transition Committee had observed as follows:

"The 'new morality,' which has emerged from the military era, is such that there is general acceptance among most members of the power elite that power is for profit, rather than for responsible exercise of its privileges or for service. This philosophy has legitimized the privileges of power being used for pillage. The new morality encourages and protects chaos because members of the new elite have vested interest in chaos despite its long term danger to social stability and their real or permanent interests."[51]

In a tragic sense, the Presidential Transition Committee's perceptive assessment of Nigeria's political economy elegantly sums up the crisis of governance in Nigeria: massive corruption, mismanagement, political chicanery, and epidemic violence. These pathologies have reproduced themselves with the same intensity and venality regardless of the type of regime, whether civilian or military. This perhaps explains why democracy has proven elusive, if not chimerical, in Nigeria, as cycles of civilian and military governments have scandalously failed to unite the country and to ensure that revenues from oil trickle down to the vast majority of Nigerians who remain poor. It also explains the source of the current conflict in Nigeria's oil-rich Delta region.

The conflict in the Niger Delta, also known as the Niger Delta crisis, arose in the early 1990s over perceptions of neglect by minority ethnic groups in the Niger Delta. The basis of the conflict derives from the fact that, while oil from the Niger Delta region provides over 80 per cent of national export revenues, the states and communities that produce this oil are among the most destitute and marginalized in the entire federation.[52]These communities have also suffered adverse effects from widespread oil exploration, which has degraded the environment, including communal livelihoods. In order to maximize oil production and the revenues that accrue to the federal government, production relations are so organized as to disempower host communities. For instance, legislation in 1978 and 1979 placed ownership of all land, including all off-shore minerals, in the hands of the federal government, thus stripping local communities and states not only access to oil revenues, but also of any form of control over oil companies and their operations. In Nigeria, oil and related environmental matters are treated as "national security" issues, foreclosing transparency and accountability.

The historical neglect of the Niger Delta and the federal government's increasingly militaristic response to the public expression of these grievances climaxed in 1995 with the hanging, by the government, of the writer and environmentalist, Ken Saro-Wiwa, and eight of his colleagues from the Ogoni ethnic group. The Ogoni protest had been cleverly linked to environmental concerns and with the broader national struggle against militarism and authoritarianism, as epitomized in the repressive regime of General Sani Abacha.[53] The government's clampdown on the Ogoni and Niger Delta minority groups has transformed large parts of the Niger Delta into a militarized and heavily garrisoned area. The Nigerian government's militarized response to the Niger Delta crisis has created a culture of violence and criminality in the region, with government troops fighting militants, and the militants turning to criminal activities such as kidnapping and oil theft to raise money to finance their struggle against the government.

As with much of West Africa's conflicts, there is as much ethnicity in Nigeria's oil politics as in the Niger Delta conflict. At the level of national politics, there is a perception among the Niger Delta's minority ethnic groups that the three majority ethnic groups – the Hausa Fulani, Yoruba, and the Igbo – are benefiting from the oil riches at the expense of the oil communities due to their control of, and greater representation in, the federal government. For many members of these communities, "there appears no justifiable reason why an area that produces so much wealth for the nation wallows in abject poverty while other parts of the country without oil resources are being developed with oil revenues.[54] At the local level, the oil communities themselves are in rivalry against one another along ethnic divides over the little resources that are earmarked for the oil communities. This development is entirely consistent with the prevailing elite practice of pandering to ethnic and religious cleavages in order to create protected fiefdoms for sub-elites, and to demobilize and confuse subaltern interests, rather than seeking to build a coherent and united nation based on equity, justice and fair distribution of resources.[55]

The profound social dilemma at the heart of Nigeria's political economy can, therefore, be attributed to economic malaise, corruption and communal polarization, all of which are manifestations of poor governance. The assessment by the Presidential Transition Committee, quoted in the opening paragraphs of this section, had aptly described these pathologies as the "new morality" of Nigerian politics. This "new morality" which is, in fact, the organizing principle of national political engagement, necessarily views access to the State as essential for sectional opportunities and claims on resources. As a result, strategies for communal advancement aggressively focus on securing control of government, or gaining important representation through electoral office, cabinet appointments, or powerful positions in the civil service or other public enterprises. Thus, having a "son of the soil" in high position is the only assured channel for advancing group interests.

Furthermore, the concentration of political and economic power enables a particular sectional group to consolidate its dominance over rival groups. Political authority is, therefore, seen in instrumental, zero-sum terms: state position are used to direct resources towards one's group, while denying access to competing ethnic groups. As Peter M. Lewis has argued, "elites in power are motivated not only by the patronage demands of their particular constituencies, but also by a desire to prevent other groups from gaining access to the state.[56] The reflex tendency among all groups to privatize the state not only speaks to a profound crisis of government, but also a recipe for crisis and instability – features that have characterized Nigerian politics for much of her post-independence history.

The five case studies examined in this study highlight the interdependence of security in West Africa and the importance of a regional approach to conflict management. For example, the civil war in Liberia was staged from Cote d'Ivoire and the invading rebels received military aid and logistical support from Burkina Faso, and also from Libya, an extra- regional power. The fighting spilled over 750,000 refugees into Cote d'Ivoire, Guinea, Sierra Leone, Ghana and Nigeria. In the same vein, military incursions were launched into Cote d'Ivoire and Guinea at various times by Liberian factions. Also at various times, governments of Guinea-Conakry and Sierra Leone had supported Liberia rebels in the country's northern Lofa country.[57]

The independence of security in West Africa was further

underscored when Sierra Leone's RUF aligned with Charles Taylor's NPFL of Liberia to invade Sierra Leone in March 1991. This invasion triggered the decade-long civil war in which Nigeria, Ghana and Guinea had to send in troops to support the regime in Freetown. Over 500,000 Sierra Leonean refugees spilled over into neighbouring Guinea and Liberia as a direct result of this particular civil war. Furthermore, in Guinea-Bissau, troops from Senegal and Guinea-Conakry intervened militarily in a civil conflict that spilled refugees into Senegal, Guinea, and the Gambia. Over 3,000 refugees have entered Guinea-Bissau from Senegal as a result of fighting in Senegal's Casamance region. The separatist movement in Senegal's Casamance region had used Guinea-Bissau as a base to launch their attacks, forcing Senegal to intervene militarily in the civil conflict in the former. Finally, the management of the civil wars in Liberia and Sierra Leone led to deep political splits within ECOWAS, with much of the Francophone states opposing the Nigerian-led interventions.

These Case Studies suggest that while conflicts in West Africa tend to have multiple causes, the single most important cause is poor governance, coupled with frustrated aspiration for political change, often occurring in the context of profound state debilitation. In the longer view, violent struggles for control of the state and, by implication, resources in these weak states should be seen to result from conflict at least as much as they cause it. As it is evident from these case studies, to challenge the state is to challenge state control over resources, and vice versa. State mismanagement of resources, such as diamond in Sierra Leone and Liberia and oil in Nigeria, has given rise to persistent conflict over distributional issues.

While conflicts are normal in political society, it is the responsibility of politics to resolve conflicting interests, particularly distributional issues, to prevent them from boiling over. In West Africa, these issues boil over into violent conflicts because of failure of governance to manage or mediate between contending interests in society. At an ECOWAS Conference on Peace and Conflict Prevention in Monrovia in 2010, Liberian President, Ellen John Sirleaf, was emphatic on the causes of conflict in West Africa, declaring that: "The root causes of conflict in the region are bad governance, lack of respect for human rights, social-economic and political marginalization and grinding poverty."[58]

On what provoked the Liberia conflict, Sirleaf explained that significant portions of the society were systematically excluded and marginalized from institutions of political governance and access to key economic assets. From this perspective, governance remains the major challenge confronting member states of ECOWAS. However, on account of their pauperization effects and regional externalities, conflicts pose formidable developmental challenges, because development can only be pursued in a secure and stable environment. In essence, therefore, proliferating conflicts and poor governance in West Africa are the reason why there is so much poverty and human insecurity in much of the sub-region, a situation that clearly negates ECOWAS overarching goal of working to improve the living conditions of community citizens. It is for this reason that conflict prevention and resolution and issues of governance are increasingly becoming top priorities for ECOWAS.

Defining Security Governance

The notion of governance is relatively new, and has come into use in the context of globalization, reflecting a shift in perspective from government to governance. In its basic meaning, governance refers to the structures and processes by which a social organisation, from the family, corporate business to international institution, – steers itself, ranging from centralized control to self-regulation.

As a political phenomenon, governance however covers a wide range of rather different developments, such as the introduction of self-government at the local level, or in certain policy sectors; the outsourcing of central government functions to the private sector, including security functions to private military and security companies; the increasing network-type of cooperation between states, international organizations and private actors, as illustrated by the transitional governance of post-conflict societies under international auspices.[59] What these developments have in common is that they reflect the fragmentation of political authority among public and private actors on multiple levels of governance, as well as the emergence of formal and informal cooperative problem-solving arrangements and activities.

The governance concept thus contains both horizontal and vertical dimensions. Horizontally, it refers to the multiplicity of non-state actors, such as international organizations and private actors, with the latter ranging from non-governmental organizations (NGOs) to multinational corporations and even armed groups. Vertically, it signals the growing interaction of these actors at various territorial levels – national as well as sub-national and international – a trend that is well captured in the notion of multi-level governance.

At the state and sub-state levels, governance is largely exercised by governments, except for weak states or so-called failed states, where the government is so feeble that it is forced to share power with other actors, be they international organizations, foreign powers, armed rebel or insurgent groups and criminal organizations. At the level of the international system, including within a regional context such as in ECOWAS, governance takes the form of shared responsibility among multiple governments through the mechanism of rule-based cooperation among the various national governments, international organizations as well as transnational private actors.[60]

What emerges from the forgoing analysis is that governance is a more encompassing concept than government, precisely because the former offers a conceptual perspective which helps to grapple with the complexity of the contemporary world in which, while governments are still the central actors, they are increasingly sharing power with non-state actors or through multiple levels of interaction. In summary, it is useful to restate that the concept of governance has been applied to different levels or geographic spaces, as in national, regional or international, to different types and constellations of actors, as in corporate governance, private governance or multi-level governance, and to normative issues as in economic, environmental, health, human rights, governance, and security governance, the last being the focus of this section.

Security governance is observable at the different levels of analysis in the preceding paragraphs, namely, at the global, regional, national and local levels. For instance, at the global level, the frame of reference is the United Nations system, which provides the most universal structures for dealing with security issues, ranging from arms control, disarmament and non-proliferation of nuclear weapons, to conflict prevention, peace-making, peace enforcement, peace keeping and post-conflict peace building.

In general, global security governance is dominated by nation states and inter-governmental actors, although the role and influence of non-governmental organisations (NGOs) are growing, particularly in areas such as in disarmament, control of small arms and light weapons, and post-conflict peace building. At the regional level, security governance refers to broad dynamics in the development of security arrangement in the given region. Although ECOWAS is part of the African Union's, peace and security architecture, for the purpose of this study, security governance in ECOWAS, would be construed to mean regional security arrangements in place in the West African sub-region.

Measured by the degree of fragmentation of authority in security policy making, the West African sub-region is way far behind Western Europe, which has witnessed the greatest transformation of the security sector in terms of evolution from government to governance. In Europe, not only have regional governments and regional organizations such as the OSCE, NATO and the EU expanded their security functions considerably, a variety of private actors, ranging from charities to private security companies, have emerged in local, regional and trans-regional security governance.[61]

At the national level, security governance refers to the organization and management of the security sector, whereas the security sector is taken to comprise all the bodies whose main responsibilities are the protection of the state and its constituent communities. These bodies comprise such core structures such as the armed forces, police and intelligence agencies to those institutions that formulate, implement and oversee internal and external security policy, such as the executive branch and parliament. More often than not, non-state actors, armed groups as well as civil society organizations also play important roles in national security governance – the former by providing or jeopardizing security, the later by strengthening security governance mechanisms.[62] In the emerging literature on the subject, security governance at the national level is generally referred to as "security sector governance".

Finally, at the local level, security governance refers to the relevant internal security arrangements which may be dominated by national security forces, local police, or as in failed or war-torn states by armed non-state actors, such as rebel groups or forces controlled by war lords and criminal gangs. In the peculiar security environment of West Africa, in which intrastate conflicts often spill over to neighbouring states, security governance at the national level must be sensitive to regional norms and practices. It is partly because of the externalities of most of West Africa's intra-state conflicts that ECOWAS has developed copious conflict prevention and resolution mechanisms, including normative governance principles of democratic rule and respect for human rights, all of which constitute the broad framework of ECOWAS conflict prevention mechanism.

ECOWAS Security Governance Mechanisms

When it was set up in 1975, ECOWAS was not intended to play any role in the security arena. In its founder's minds, economic integration was to be its primary and overarching goal. Indeed, the Treaty of ECOWAS (1975) declared the central goal of the organization as the "promotion of trade liberalization and the harmonization of economic, agricultural and fiscal policies."[64] In other words, what the founders had in mind was to create a custom or monetary union to promote trade and to facilitate the economic development of Member States of ECOWAS. However, the recurrence of intrastate conflicts sparked by a host of factors, as have been identified in this study, led to the adoption of the Protocols on Non-Aggression and Mutual Assistance in Defence Matters way back in 1978 and 1981, respectively. However, security did not become a formal pre-occupation of ECOWAS until the 1990s when the organization made a fundamental policy shift, insisting on the intrinsic relationship between security, democratic governance and development.[65] This policy shift was formally captured in the Revised Treaty of 1993, which not only sought to strengthen ECOWAS and is institutions, but made explicit reference to regional security arrangements, including obligations on member states to adhere to the organisation's Declaration of political principles and the African Charter on Human and Peoples' Rights.

In regard to regional security, Article 58 obliges Member States to "work to safeguard and consolidate relations conducive to the maintenance of peace, stability and security within the region." The same Article also calls on Member States to "cooperate with the Community in establishing and strengthening appropriate mechanisms for the timely prevention and resolution of intra-state and inter-state conflicts, including the establishment of a regional peace and security observation system and peacekeeping forces, where appropriate."[66]

Following this paradigm shift, all through the 1990s, ECOWAS not only crafted and adopted a flurry of protocols and declarations, but reinforced this with frequent peace prevention and peace-making missions to conflict areas and also to states in which tensions were dangerously high. In these instruments and declarations, ECOWAS identified and prescribed core security and governance principles to reducing regional tensions and also to nurture domestic peace and stability. As ECOWAS Executive Secretary, Mohammed Ibn Chambas, has observed, in these protocols and declarations, ECOWAS set out "guiding principles for intrastate relations that would help foster participatory democracy, good governance, the rule of law, respect for human rights, and a balanced and equitable distribution of resources, among a host of others – all issues the neglect of which result in instability within states.[67]

What emerges from this policy shift was an attempt by ECOWAS to securitize democracy and good governance. By securitizing democracy and good governance, ECOWAS was being honest in admitting that poor governance was at the root of much of the conflicts that have caused so much human insecurity across the region. Consequently, a characteristic feature of ECOWAS security governance regime is the deliberate creation of normative frameworks on conflict prevention, resolution and peace keeping, including on democratic governance, good governance of the security sector, as well as the control of small arms and light weapons into and within the region. The evolving instruments also created a standing mediation structure through which the organization strives to stay on top of developing crises, including troop contributions for peace keeping and, when necessary, peace enforcement in Member States.

Early in the life of ECOWAS, the principles of cooperation, mutual assistance and non-aggression have provided the ethos for organizational behaviour within the community. It is within this context that ECOWAS adopted the Protocol on Non -Aggression way back in 1978 and the related Protocol on Mutual Assistance in Defence Matters in 1981. Building on these foundation documents, the Community has adopted ground-breaking instruments, protocols and declarations in response to the challenges of conflict prevention, resolution and peace building in the region. Some of these instruments created organs and tools such as the early warning system, the Mediation and Security Council, Office of the Special Representative, the Council of the Wise and Special Mediators.

Starting with the revised Treaty of ECOWAS of 1993 which conferred the status of supra-nationality on the Organization, the organization has created an impressive body of normative frameworks for confronting the threats to peace and human security in the region. Thus Article 58 of the revised Treaty which commits Member States to cooperate for the purpose of reinforcing the appropriate mechanisms to ensure the timely prevention and resolution of inter and intra-state conflicts provide the entry point for ECOWAS increasingly dominant role in regional security.

The principal objective of the Declaration of the Moratorium on the Importation, Exportation and Manufacture of Light Weapons of 1998 was to deny war mongers, especially non-state actors, access to weaponry through preventive disarmament initiatives. The moratorium had since been transformed into a legally

binding instrument as the Convention on Small Arms and
 Light Weapons, Their Ammunition and other Related
Materials. As a mechanism to promote human security
within the region, the Convention imposes far-reaching
duties on states including, for example, duty to avoid gross
violation of international human rights law and
international humanitarian law. Article 6 (6) (a) provides
that "a transfer shall not be authorized if the arms are
destined to be used for the violation of international
humanitarian law or infringement of human and people's
rights and freedoms, or for the purpose of oppression"[68].

In the same vein, Article 6 (3) (b) stipulates that "a
transfer shall not be authorized if the arms are destined to
be used for the commission of serious violations of
international humanitarian law, genocide or crimes against
humanity"[69]. There is also the duty on States to avoid
aggravating regional insecurity and instability. Article 6
(4)(a) stipulates that "a transfer shall not be authorized if it
is destined to adversely affect regional security, endanger
peace, contribute to destabilizing or uncontrolled
accumulation of arms or military capabilities into the region
or otherwise contribute to regional instability.[70]

The Protocol Relating to the Mechanism for Conflict
Prevention, Management, Resolution, Peace keeping and
Security, which was adopted in December, 1999, constitutes
the most comprehensive normative framework for
confronting the threats to peace and security in the region
by boosting the conflict prevention capabilities of
ECOWAS to pre-empt potential outbreak of violence,
resolve conflict when they occur, and to engage more
effectively in post-conflict peace building. The mechanism
not only tasks ECOWAS Member States with responsibility

to manage and resolve internal and inter-state conflicts, it effectively establishes inextricable links between the raison d'être of the organization, namely: the economic and social advancement of ECOWAS citizens and their security. The mechanism also creates institutions and organs which would be responsible for implementing its provisions, including procedures for doing so.

These organs include the Mediation and Security Council, Defence and Security Commission, and Council of Elders. The Mediation and Security Council comprises ten members, and takes decisions on the bases of two-thirds majority of six members. Its principal duty is to accelerate decision making in crisis situations by taking prompt decisions on the deployment of military and political missions and informing the UN and AU on behalf of the ECOWAS Authority of the Heads of States.

The Defence and the Security Commission serves as the technical advisory body to the Mediation and Security Council. It comprises Army Chiefs of Staff, Police Chiefs and experts from foreign ministries of member states, including responsible officers from customs and immigration services, when necessary. The duty of the Commission is to advise the Mediation and Security Council on mandates, terms of reference and the appointment of force commanders for military operations. Finally, the Council of Elders, which is composed of eminent personalities from within and outside of Africa, including women, traditional, religious and political leaders, plays an advisory but important role in regional peace-making efforts.

In general, the Protocol calls for improved cooperation in early warning, conflict prevention, and peace-keeping operations. It also seeks coordinated regional responses to cross-border crimes, particularly trafficking in small arms. The protocol also broadened the powers of the ECOWAS Executive Secretary such as to allow the office holder take far-reaching initiatives for the prevention and management of conflicts, including fact-finding, mediation, facilitation, negotiation and reconciliation.

The Protocol Relating to the Mechanism for Conflict Prevention, Management, Resolution, Peace keeping and Security seeks to correct certain flaws that had emerged from ECOWAS previous military deployments in Liberia, Sierra Leone and Guinea Bissau. One of these flaws relate to the need to keep the ECOWAS force commander under the operational control of the ECOWAS Executive Secretary, rather than under field commanders who are inclined to report to their national military high command, as were the cases in the Liberian, Sierra Leonean and Guinea Bissau deployments.[71] The Protocol also sought to provide regional legitimacy to future peace keeping operations by involving a broad section of Member States in decisions relating to the composition, deployment and control of troops in the field. This was to guide against unilateral deployment and control of future ECOMOG operations, as was the case with Nigeria's dominance of ECCOMOG operations in Liberia and Sierra Leone.

At the apex of ECOWAS regional security architecture is the ECOWAS Conflict Prevention Framework (ECPF). The overall aim of the ECPF is to strengthen the human security architecture in West Africa. For instance, according to section VI of the ECPF: "The immediate purpose is to create space within the ECOWAS system and in Member States for cooperative interaction within the region and with external partners to push conflict prevention and peace keeping up the political agenda of Member States in a manner that will trigger timely and targeted multi-actor and multi-dimensional action to diffuse or eliminate potential and real threats to human security in a predictable and institutional manner.[72]"

Whereas military intervention has been the traditional tool of choice in conflict prevention in West Africa, the ECPF aims to make military intervention a measure of last resort, as it should be, promoting instead conflict prevention and peace building, including the strengthening of sustainable development and the culture of democracy.[73]The ECPF therefore encompasses all initiatives for enhancing human security, as well as the security of Member States and institutions in the region. Some of its key objectives include:

(i)   The mainstreaming of conflict prevention into ECOWAS policies and programmes,

(ii)   Increasing understanding of the conceptual basis of conflict prevention and, in so doing, interrelate conflict prevention activities with development and humanitarian crisis prevention and preparedness,

(iii)   Increase understanding of opportunities, tools and resources related to conflict prevention and peace keeping at technical and political levels with ECOWAS Member States and in the ECOWAS system as well; and

(iv)   Enhance ECOWAS anticipation and planning capabilities in relation to regional tensions.

In general, ECOWAS security governance principles and frameworks developed before 1990 appear to have been inspired by the normative principle of non-interference in the domestic affairs of Member States, as was espoused in the Charter of the defunct Organization of African Unity (OAU), and in the United Nations Charter. For instance, in 1978, ECOWAS established a collective security framework by adopting a protocol on Non-Aggression. The focal point of this Protocol was to bring into operation a framework that was specific on non-interference, akin to article 2(7) of the UN Charter and article 3(2) of the OAU. The 1978 on effectively barred ECOWAS Member States from employing means that are inconsistent with both the Charters of the UN and the OAU.

Furthermore, the 1981 Protocol Relating to Mutual Assistance in Defence sought to deter attack from extra-regional powers. The language in the protocol not only suggests ECOWAS was already thinking of itself as a security community, but betrays a lack of understanding of the major sources of threats facing the community, which are within the region, rather than from extra-regional sources. For instance, Article 2 of Chapter 11 declares that "a threat or aggression directed against any member shall constitute a threat or aggression against the community"[74] On the other hand, the security principles and frameworks that were developed after 1990 marked a major shift in ECOWAS policy formulation. First, these new documents reflect an attempt to focus on addressing the emerging challenges of intrastate conflicts with a coordinated sub-regional approach. Second, these frameworks and protocols also sought to link the pursuit of security and conflict prevention with development objectives. This shift makes sense in the context of the nature of the region's conflicts and the global recognition of the intrinsic link between security and development.

At the same time ECOWAS was putting in place its elaborate security mechanisms, it was also making progress in developing its normative democratic governance frameworks. Partly as a result of donor pressure but also because of growing intrastate conflicts, ECOWAS had, since the beginning of the 1990s, recognized the asymmetrical relationship between governance, security and development. Since then, the Organisation has elaborated various texts and declarations stressing the importance of democratic governance as a central element in the achievement of human security and development in the region.

In this regard, the ECOWAS Declaration on Political Principles of 1991 marked the beginning of a conceptual rethink in the regional approach to development and security in West Africa. The Declaration reflects a determination by Member States of ECOWAS to recognize, if not in practice, but at least in theory, that the era of military dictatorship and autocratic rule that were in fashion across the region during the Cold War era were no longer sustainable. This marked the beginning of what has been described in West Africa, as indeed in the broader context of Africa peace and security policy, as a period of transition from the systems of authoritarian civilian and military dictatorships to a general embrace of democratic system of governance. In practice, this transition has been uneven across the region, with some countries progressing along the democracy spectrum, while others have stagnated, even regressed, as in Guinea Bissau, Guinea-Conakry, Cote d'Ivoire and, most recently, in Mali.

The ECOWAS Declaration on Political Principles affirms the determination of Member States to promote democracy based on political pluralism and respect for fundamental human rights. For instance, Articles 4 and 5 affirm member states' resolve to promote fundamental human rights and freedoms, including freedom of speech, conscience and association. There is also a commitment to encourage the promotion of political, economic, social and cultural rights as means toward the progressive development of the human person, in effect the promotion of human security. Quite significantly, Article 6 declares the right of the individual to participate by means of "free and democratic processes in the framing of the society he/she lives in".[75] By seeking to promote multiparty politics and representative institutions, the Declaration of Political principles set the tone for a good governance regime in West Africa. Although human security was not explicitly mentioned in the document, it nevertheless laid the building blocks for ECOWAS subsequent efforts to promote human security in West Africa.

The most elaborate and far-reaching, in terms of its explicit linkage of security, good governance and development, is the 2001 Protocol on Democracy and Good Governance. To underscore ECOWAS recognition of the mutually reinforcing relationship between security-democratic governance and development, the Protocol on Democracy and Good Governance appropriately supplemented the Protocol Relating to the Mechanism for Conflict Prevention, Management, Resolution, Peacekeeping and Security. This is significant precisely because it demonstrates the evolution of policy in ECOWAS in regard to the security governance-development nexus.

The protocol explicitly formulates democratic requirements for ECOWAS Member States, including division of power and responsibilities among the three branches of government – the executive, legislature, and the judiciary. It also prescribes free elections, participatory democracy, civilian control of the armed forces, freedom of the press and of assembly, protection against discrimination and perhaps, most significantly, zero tolerance for power obtained or maintained by unconstitutional means.

Specifically, Article 32 declares that "good governance and press freedom are essential for preserving social justice, preventing conflict, guaranteeing political stability and peace and for strengthening democracy."[76] A major innovation relates to the provisions on sanctions in two specific instances, namely, violent overthrow of constitutional authority and massive violations of human rights.

According to Article 45, "in the event that democracy is abruptly brought to an end by any means or where there are massive violations of human rights in a Member State, ECOWAS may impose sanctions on the State concerned."[77] The same Article 45 goes on to prescribe a graduated range of sanctions against offender states, including refusal to support candidates presented by the Member State concerned for elective posts in international organizations; refusal to organize ECOWAS meetings in the Member State concerned, and suspension of the Member State from all ECOWAS decision-making bodies.

In recent times, ECOWAS has invoked this article to sanction errant Member States of Guinea-Conakry and Niger, two states where democracy was abruptly terminated by military coupists. The application of this provision to Mauritania, following a forceful change of government, led to that country's withdrawal from ECOWAS in 2006.

Among the most recent instruments ECOWAS has adopted to promote security, development and democratic governance in West Arica is the 2003 Declaration on a Sub-regional Approach to Peace and Security. In this Declaration, Member States restated the imperative of a regional approach to peace, security and stability, including commitment to democratic consolidation and the rejection of force as a means to pursue or maintain political power. The evolution of a regime of good governance and defence of democratic principles and institutions reflect a response to a legacy of poor governance, autocratic and one-party rule, including the syndrome of life presidencies across much of Africa. The vicious civil wars and state collapse that have become common in African since the end of the Cold War accelerated the process of change leading to the emergence of new norms of democratic governance.

The end of the Cold War which led to the withdrawal of external support for autocratic regimes in Africa weakened these regimes, making them vulnerable to pressures for democratic change. As Cold War ideological rivalries receded, democracy and good governance have become the new organizing principles in international relations. Henceforth, autocratic regimes in Africa can no longer explain away internal struggles for reforms either as Soviet or Western sponsored subversion. Rather than attribute governance failures to foreign machinations, the focus became more and more fixed on internal deficiencies within the African states, such as failure of leadership and the question of good governance. This shift contrasted with earlier explanations which had attributed Africa's problem to both colonial and neo-colonial legacies. Increasingly, progress towards democratization was accelerated by the conditionalities set by the dominant Western powers and the Bretton Woods Institutions (BWI) as requirements for economic assistance. These pre-conditions gave birth to the curious marriage of economic conditionality of structural adjustment with the political conditionality of good governance.

The OAU, traditionally a conservative organization, was quick to grasp the new rules of international engagement. From its early beginnings in 1963, the OAU did not bother itself with governance issues, either at the regional or national levels; it instead opted to hide under the safety of its Charter provisions on state sovereignty and non-interference in the internal affairs of Member States. The turning point in the OAU's evolution in regard to governance started with the organization's landmark decision to condemn the attempt by the RUF of Sierra Leone to depose President Ahmed Tejan Kabbah's regime in 1997. The OAU not only condemned the coup, but supported ECOWAS efforts to address the resulting political crisis in the country. Nigeria, West Africa's most influential country, did initially try to reverse the coup but failed. However, on a second attempt, a Nigeria-led ECOMOG force defeated the rebels and reinstated Kabbah to power in March 1998.

The position of OAU on the issue of unconstitutional change of government was to set the tone for dealing with similar situations on the continent. At the 35th Assembly of Heads of State and Government in Algiers in July, 1999, the OAU took an even stronger position on the issue. It decided that Member States whose governments had not returned to constitutional rule would not be allowed to attend the summit of the Organization the next year.

Significantly, at its 36th Summit in Lome, Togo, in July 2000, it implemented the previous year's decision by barring Cote d'Ivoire and the Comoros Islands, two recent offenders, from attending the summit. At the Lome Summit, the organization formulated the Declaration on the Framework for an OAU Response to Unconstitutional Changes of Government. This document provided the much needed clarity on several issues, including the articulation of a common set of values and principles of democratic governance in member states, definitions of situations that qualify as constitutional change of government, as well as a set of actions to be taken by the organization in response to such situations.

Additionally, the African leaders at the Lome Summit outlined situations that would constitute unconstitutional change of government. These included military coups against democratically elected governments, interventions by mercenaries to supplant an elected government, take-over of power from a democratically elected government by armed dissident groups and rebel movements, including refusal by an incumbent government to hand over power to a winning party after "free and fair and regular elections"7 The adoption of the landmark Lome Framework ushered in a robust regime of democracy promotion and good governance at the continental level, and sealing a process that began nearly a decade earlier in response to poor governance in Africa. This was a fundamental shift in position by a nominally conservative organization. Since 2000, the OAU had itself been transformed into the African Union (AU) to reflect the emerging normative order.

With the adoption of the Constitutive Act of the AU in 2002, African governments reinforced the new trend in favour of democracy promotion, emphatically declaring that any government which assume power through unconstitutional means would be prevented from participating in the work of the organization. In addition to committing itself to the promotion of peace, security and stability in Africa, the AU pledged to promote democracy and good governance, due process, the rule of law and human rights. In a significant departure from existing norms of sovereignty and non-interference, the AU opened up the possibility of intervention in Member States under grave circumstances of war crimes, genocide and crimes against humanity.[79]

It should be noted that both the Algiers Declaration and the Lomé Framework were part of a growing momentum in favour of instituting good governance in Africa. For example, even before the AU was formally launched in Durban South Africa, in July 2002, the New Partnership for Africa's Development (NEPAD) had largely served notice of the shape of new things to come in regard to governance issues in Africa. NEPAD represents a pledge by African leaders to work towards the achievement of security and development in Africa. It outlines three major preconditions for the sustainable development of Africa, namely, peace and security, democracy and political governance, and economic and corporate governance. Underpinning the NEPAD pledge was the implicit assumption that sustainable development cannot be achieved in the absence of peace, security, democracy and good governance.[80] A significant aspect of the NEPAD plan is the pledge by African leaders to submit their governments to peer review under the framework of the African Peer Review Mechanism (APRM).

The idea of the APRM itself originated from the

Conference on Stability, Security, and Development Cooperation in Africa (CSSDCA), which predates both NEPAD and the African Union, and which was influenced largely by the better known and more effective OSCE.[81] The NEPAD and the African Union's principles of governance and democratic accountability are therefore the culmination of a paradigm shift in the thinking and attitude of African leaders to participatory democracy which was started by the defunct OAU in Algiers in 1999 and consolidated in Lomé, Togo, in 2000.

These initiatives have given impetus to current efforts at regional and continental levels to link governance to security and development. In general, efforts to improve governance in Africa have been conceptualized as the quest for good governance. Central to the notion of good governance is the idea that accountable, transparent, and inclusive governance is both the best promoter and the best producer of development, as well as the best guarantor of security.[82]

Good governance acknowledges three domains of governance, namely, the government, the private sector and civil society. It strives to ensure collaboration among these three different but mutually reinforcing spheres. Prominent among the concerns of good governance, in addition to issues related to the promotion of fundamental human rights and the rule of law, are issues of decentralization of authority, the empowerment of women, civil service reforms, accountable executives, competent, credible and independent judiciary and legislative bodies, and knowledgeable, effective and independent mass media. Good governance strives to promote the empowerment of civil society and to enhance its consultative voice with governments. It also views the private sector as a partner in dialogue with civil society and the government in the pursuit of the common good.[83]

In practice, the quest for good governance in West Africa is essentially an attempt to create capable states with the requisite institutional, technical, administrative, and political capabilities sufficiently to be able to protect citizens and deliver public goods. Such states must also be responsive to societal needs by processing the demands of citizens and civil society. Whereas good governance initiatives designed to improve governance competence are essential, it is important to keep in mind that competent governance is not the same as democratic governance.

Unless capable states develop their democratic potentials, they can easily slide into despotism. This is why Africa's governance agenda must strive from start not only to install competent governments, but also to develop democratic institutions. Therefore, in addition to strengthening capabilities essential for the competent governance of West African states, ECOWAS governance initiatives must seek to deepen processes of democratization at the national level. It must move beyond mere elaboration of protocols, declarations and sloganeering, including feeble attempts to ostracize deviant regimes, to promote political and electoral reforms in individual member states.

At the national level, democratic governance must turn 'governed' citizens into 'governors' making their own political choices and determining their future. This requires that elections are free and fair, allowing citizens to choose freely who should govern them. It requires that political leaderships respect constitutional limits on tenure, and that governing regimes provide space for the political opposition and not to treat them as enemies of the state to be crushed, or eliminated. It also requires creating governance structures that are rooted in constitutional law and that truly devolve governance authority, including the authority to mobilize and dispense resources to local communities. This is especially important to create a sense of belonging for minorities in multi-ethnic and religiously diverse states that proliferate in West Africa. Above all, democratic governance requires the nurturing of an enlightened citizenry and, in this regard, the importance of literacy and education cannot be overstated.

Finally, West Africa's historical experience with centralized autocracies suggest need to avoid a democratic governance strategy that strengthens the state's capabilities without a corresponding counterbalancing strategy of strengthening the capacity of citizens to resist the abuses of the state and also to hold their governments accountable.

In the neo-patrimonial states of West Africa, all too often elections have been instrumentalized, either as means to ensure uninterrupted supply of foreign aid, or as a mechanisms for Presidents to get rid of their unwanted subordinates. In recent times, much of West Africa's leaders have perfected the tactical strategy of letting the electorate do some of their 'dirty work' for them, by entrusting them with the task of ousting from power unwanted, mostly independent-minded members of the political class whose political consolidation might threaten the presidential monopoly of power. In other words, using the instrumentality of flawed elections, political regimes in West Africa have tended to present a façade of democracy to look good in the eyes of external donors, while pursing undemocratic practices at home.

The tendency by some leaders in West Africa to either prolong their tenure or pass on political authority to their children before retiring is much more than a crisis of governance; it is more like having democracies without democrats. Despite copious declarations and protocols affirming faith in democracy and good governance, the states in West Africa still manifest traces of their patrimonial past. Characterized by centralized, personalized and repressive rule, modern West African governance systems have tried but failed to deliver democracy, development and security to citizens. The various coups and counter coups, pervasive poverty and violent conflicts that have characterized the political landscape of West Africa since independence attest to the magnitude of governance failures across the region.

While it is plausible to trace the origins of West Africa's dysfunctional governance regime to the colonial period, it is equally true that the post-colonial ruling class had the opportunity to reform the systems they inherited from the departed colonialists. These systems have been left largely unreformed precisely because they suit the authoritarian instincts of the new ruling class. Failing to deliver development and security within the framework of an international system of unequal exchange and the disruptive forces of globalization, many West African regimes turned autocratic and repressive, causing them to lose popular support, which in turn causes them to be even more repressive in order to maintain control over a restive population.

As West African states failed to deliver development and security, they equally lost their Weberian right of the possession of the monopoly of violence as other actors have taken advantage of the conspicuous weakness of the state to step into the security sphere. Whether it is guerrilla movements, mercenaries, vigilante groups or privately owned security companies, actors other than the state have increasingly become agents of security and insecurity across West Africa.

Notes

1. Chandra Lekha Sriram, and Zoe Nielsen, "Introduction: Why examine Sub-regional Sources and Dynamics of Conflict?" in Chandra Lekha Sriram and Zoe Nielsen, eds.; Exploring Sub-regional Conflict: Opportunities for Conflict Prevention, Lynne Rienner, Boulder, 2002, p.2.

2. Ibid.

3. Ibid.

4. Ibid.

5. Ibid.

6. Ibid.

7. See Adekeye Adebajo, "Toward Pax West Africa," in Adekeye Adebajo and Ismail Rashid, eds.; West Africa's Security Challenges: Building peace in a Troubled Region, 2004, p.6.

8. Jeffrey Herbst, "War and the State in Africa," International Security, Vol.14, No.4, (spring) 1990, p.124.

9. Comfort Ero, and Jonathan Temin, "Sources of Conflict in West Africa," in Chandra Lekha, Sriram and Zoe Nielsen, eds., Exploring Sub-regional Conflicts, p.96.

10. Ibid.

11. Abdul-Fatau Musah, "West Africa: Governance and Security in a Changing Region, Africa Programme", Working Paper Series, International Peace Institute, February 2009, p.3.

12. Ibid.

13. Ibid.

14. United Nations, "The Causes of Conflict and the Promotion of Durable Peace and Sustainable Development in Africa," Report of the Secretary-General, UN DOC.S/1998/318, April 13, 1998.

15. See Comfort Ero, and Jonathan Temin, Sources of Conflict in West Africa, p.106.

16.   William Reno, "War, Markets, and the Reconfiguration of West Africa's Weak States," Comparative Politics, Vol. 29, No.4, July 1997, p.503.
17.   See Comfort Ero, and Jonathan Temin, "Sources of Conflict in West Africa," p.108.
18.   Ibid.
19.   William Reno, Warlord Politics and African States, Lynne Rienner, Boulder, 1999, pp. 130 – 139.
20.   News release by Agence France- Presse, November 23, 2002.
21.   United Nations, "The making of a Moratorium on Light Weapons, United Nations Regional Centre for Peace and Disarmament in Africa", Norwegian Institute of International Affairs and Norwegian Initiative on Small Arms Transfers, Oslo, 2000, p.1.
22.   Frances Languamba Keile, "Small arms and Light weapons transfer in West Africa: A Stock Taking," in Disarmament Forum, United Nations Institute for Disarmament Rescarch, Geneva, No.4, 2008, pp. 5 – 6.
23.   See Robert Kaplan D. "The Coming Anarchy" Atlantic Monthly, Vol. 271, No 2, February 1992, pp. 32-69.
24.   David Keen, "The Economic Functions of Violence in Civil Wars", Adelphi Paper No.320, Oxford University Press, Oxford, 1996.
25.   Paul Richards, "Witches, Cannibals and War in Liberia," Journal of African History, Vol.42, January 2001, p.176.

26.   G. E. SaigbeBoley, Liberia: The Rise and Fall of the First Republic, St. Martin Press, New York, 1983.
27.   Adekeye Adebajo, Building Peace in West Africa: Liberia, Sierra, Leone, and Guinea-Bissau, Lynne Rienner, Boulder, 2002, p.46.

28.   Ibrahim Abdullah, and Ismail Rashid, "Rebel Movements, in Adekeye Adebajo and Ismail Rashid, eds.; West Africa's Security Challenges: Building Peace in a Troubled Region, Lynne, Rienner, Bouler, London, 2004, p.177.

29.   International Crisis Groups: "Liberia: Security Challenges", Africa Report, No.71, November 2003, p.3.

30.   Ibid.

31.   Amos Sawyer, "Violent Conflicts and Governance Challenges in West Africa:' Paper presented at Workshop in Political Theory and Policy Analyses, Indiana University, 2003.

32.   Amos Sawyer, "Effective Immediately: Dictatorship in Liberia, 1980 – 1986: A Personal perspective," Liberia Working Group, Bremen, Germany, 1987, p.16.

33.   Ibrahim Abdullah, and Ismail Rashid, Rebel Movements, 2004, p.177.

34.   Charles Taylor, "The West Wants to Suffocate Liberia" West Africa, No.4251, 6-12 November, 2000, p.11.

35.   Eboe Hutchful and Kwesi Anning, "The Political Economy of Conflict," in Adekeye Adebajo and Ismail Rashid, eds.; West Africa's security Challenges: Building Peace in a Troubled Region, Lynne Rienner, Boulder, 2004, p.210.

36.   See Adekeye Adebajo, Building Peace in West Africa: Liberia, Sierra Leone and Guinea-Bissau, 2002, p.81.

37.   Ibid.

38.   Ibid.

39.   Ibid.

40.   Ibid.

41.   Ibid.

42.   Ibid.

43.   Ibid.

44.   Ibid.

45.   Silvia Rogue, "Peace Building in Guinea-Bissau: A Critical Approach," Centre for Social Studies, University of Columbia, May 2009, p.3.

46.   Adekeye Adebajo, "Pax West Africana, Regional Security Mechanisms," in Adekeye Adebajo, and Ismail Rashid, eds.; West Africa's Security Challenges: Building Peace in a Troubled Region, Lynne Reinner, Boulder and London, 2004, p.299

47.   Ibid.

48.   Ibid.

49.   Ibid.

50.   Ibid.

51.   Ibid.

52.   Federal Government of Nigeria, Report of the Presidential Transition Committee, Lagos, September 1983.

53.   Eboe Hutchful, Kwesi Aning, "The Political Economy of conflict," in Adekeye Adebajo, and Ismail Rashid eds; West Africa's Security challenges: Building peace in a Troubled Region, Lynne Rienner, Boulder and London, 2004, p.211.

54.   Ibid.

55.   Iyabo Olojede, et al, "Nigeria: Oil Pollution, Community Dissatisfaction and Threats to National Peace and Security", Occasional Papers Series, Vol.4, No.3, African Association of Political Science, Harare, 2002.

56.   See Aboe Hutchful, and Kwesi Anning, "The Political Economy of Conflicts", p.21.

57.   Peter M. Lewis, "The Dysfunctional State of Nigeria," available at:
http://216.109.125.130/search/cashe?e.i.;=UTF-8&P= developmental+%2B challenges...,

58.   See Adekeye Adebajo, Building Peace in a West Africa: Liberia, Sierra Leone, and Guinea Bissau, pp.18-19

59.   Ellen Johnson Sirleaf, "Liberian Leader Outlines Root Causes of Conflict in Africa" available online at afriqueavenir.org/.../Liberia-leader.org,

60.   Heiner Hanggi "Approaching Peace building from a Security Governance Perspective" in Allan Bryden and Heiner Hanggi, eds.; Security Governance in Post-Conflict Peace building, Lit VERLAG Munster, 2005, p.7.

61.   Ibid.

62.   E. Krahmann, "Conceptualizing Security Governance", Cooperation and Conflict, Vol. 38, No.1, pp. 5-26.

63.   See Heiner Hanggi, "Approaching Peace-building from a Security Governance Perspective," p.9.

64.   ECOWAS, Treaty of the Economic Community of West African States, Lagos, Nigeria, May 1975.

65.   Mohammed Ibn Chambas, "Forward" in Adekeye Adebajo, and Ismail Rashid, eds. West Africa's Security Challenges: Building peace in a Troubled Region, Lynne Reinner, Boulder, 2004, p. XIII.

66.   ECOWAS Treaty, Article 58 (a), (b), and (f)

67.   Ibid.

68.   Ibid.

69.   Ibid.

70.   Ibid.

71.   See Adekeye Adebajo, Building Peace in West Africa: Liberia, Sierra Leone, and Guinea Bissau, 2002, p.28.

72.   See ECOWAS "Regulation MSC/REG.1/01/08, ECOWAS Conflict Prevention Framework," ECOWAS Commission, Abuja, 2008.p.16.

73.   Ibid.

74.   See ECOWAS, Protocol Relating to Mutual Assistance on Defence, Chapter 11, Article 2, 29 May, 1981.

75.   See ECOWAS, Declaration A/DCL.1/7/91, Political Principles of the Economic Community of West African States, Abuja, 6 July, 1991.

76.   See ECOWAS, Protocol on Democracy and Good Governance, Supplementary to the Protocol Relating to the Mechanism for Conflict Prevention, Management, Resolution, Peacekeeping and Security.

77.   Ibid.

78.   African Union, Constitutional Act of the African Union, Addis Ababa, 2002, Article 4.

79.   Ibid.

80.   NEPAD, Strategic Framework Document, available at http://www.nepad.org/2010/files/documens/inbrief-pdf,

81.   Funmi Olonisakin, "Pan-African Approaches to Civilian Control and Democratic Governance", in Victor-Yves Ghebali and Alexandre Lambert, eds.; Democratic Governance of the Security Sector Beyond the OSCE Area: Regional Approaches in Africa and the Americas, LIT VERLAG GMBH & Co, Zurich and Berlin, 2007, p.30.

82. Amos Sawyer, "Governance and Democratization," in Adekeye Adebajo, and Ismail Rashid eds.; West Africa's Security Challenges: Building Peace in a Trouble Region, Lynne Rienner, Boulder and London, 2004, p.98-99.

83.   Ibid.

Chapter Six

THE FUTURE OF REGIONALISM IN WEST AFRICA

Historically, the political economy of countries in the West African sub region has been characterized by acute crisis. This relates to poor economic performance, debilitating poverty, macroeconomic policy inconsistency, corruption and political instability. For these countries, the debate over an appropriate development model has never been a straight choice between economic growth and social development. While national economic policies continue to stress economic growth, the priority has always been to promote industrialization, eradicate poverty, and to improve the wellbeing of citizens.

Since these countries gained political independence in the 1960s, import substitution, which was the economic model of choice, and which was modified in the 1980s under the framework of SAP, sensationally failed to spur development. On the contrary, the SAP policy only fostered a regime of massive retrenchment of social services, whose consequences have been to push the vast majority of citizens into deeper poverty. The failure of SAP and, before it, the import substitution model, accentuated the crisis of development in West Africa and made the case for regional integration urgent and compelling. These developmental challenges are enormous by any standard of assessment. For instance, a policy document jointly prepared by the ECOWAS Executive Secretariat and the WAEMU (the region's exclusive Francophone bloc of countries) in 2006 identified "poverty as the worst plague in the sub region."[1]

In other words, the main challenge facing countries of the sub-region as a whole is poverty in all its forms. Indeed, the 15 countries of ECOWAS are ranked among the poorest in the world, with more than 50 per cent of the entire population of about 253 million people (2003 estimates) living on less than one dollar per day. Life expectancy at birth is still below 50 years, while close to half of the adult population is still illiterate. Furthermore, more than 50 per cent of the population in rural areas has no access to drinking water.[2] The list of depressing statistics is inexhaustible, but these selected human development indexes illustrate the enormity of the economic crisis in the West African sub region.

By ECOWAS and WAEMU assessment, advances in the fight against poverty in West Africa remain modest, fragile and fall way short of what is required to meet the Millennium Development Goals (MDGs) targets. What emerges from this grim self-assessment by the two regional bodies is that if current trends continue, a large number of West African countries will not be able to achieve the MDG targets by 2015. In the midst of these huge developmental challenges, countries of the West African sub region have had to live through the last two decades with conflicts of various forms and intensities. Yet, to achieve economic growth at a pace that will lift a substantial number of people out of poverty, the region will need a peaceful and stable environment. This necessarily calls for improved governance in countries across the region, reason being that much of the conflicts that have occurred in the region over the past two decades were the direct consequences of poor governance.

Partly in response to globalization, but also because of the grim economic condition of countries in the region, there now appears to be a realization that development underpinned by economic and political reforms, infrastructural expansion, and improved management of public affairs provides the only viable option for these countries. For instance, over the past two decades, many countries in the region have embarked on rapid and significant political reforms, with several abandoning autocratic military and one-party rule in favour of multiparty democracy.

Given the obvious interconnections among countries of the sub region, in which crisis in one country easily spills over across national borders, West African leaders have also come to realize that national efforts alone cannot enable countries attain their objectives of economic growth, poverty reduction and political stability. Among these countries, the trend is to move away from the defective political and economic models that have all but precipitated political instability, destroyed national economies and impoverished citizens.

All across Africa, there is now a much acute awareness of the crucial role regionalism could play in driving economic growth and development. The realization that economic growth, poverty and conflict have significant contagion effects, especially in a crisis-prone region like

West Africa, thus constitute one of the primary justifications for the regional integration model as a strategy of development in the region. In the era of globalization, regionalism also provides a viable approach to integrating West Africa's largely small and fragmented economies into networked system.

Unlike in the early years of the integration process in West Africa, a broad consensus seems to have emerged around a certain number of key principles that should drive the process of regionalism in the region. Among these principles are the need for internal political stability, the need for harmonization and coordination of macroeconomic policies at the regional level, the need to improve the operational procedures in ECOWAS institutions, including the deployment of greater political will by Member States of the Organization.

One way ECOWAS has sought to boost the integration process has been to revise its Constitutive Treaty to reflect changing regional dynamics, and also to introduce a higher level of dynamism into its working methods and processes. For instance, the revised treaty, adopted in 1993, not only strengthened existing community institutions, but also created new ones, such as the West African Parliament, the Community Court of Justice, and the Economic and Social Council. Quite significantly, the revised treaty endowed ECOWAS with supranational status, by which Member States agreed to partial surrender of national sovereignty. Another important provision in the revised treaty relates to the introduction of financial autonomy for ECOWAS, through the imposition of the community levy. The broadening of the ECOWAS mandate also included active regional cooperation in the political and security sectors.

As we had argued elsewhere in this study, conflicts and political instability have been characteristic features of West Africa's political landscape over the past two decades. For example, the civil war which erupted in Liberia in 1989 could only be resolved in 2003, when democratic elections were held under international auspices. While Sierra Leone endured a brutal civil war from 1991 to 2002, Guinea-Bissau slipped into violence in 1994. Cote d'Ivoire, once a bastion of stability in an otherwise unstable region, caught the conflict virus in 2002. This crisis, which effectively spilt the country into two along ethnic lines, is still unravelling. Efforts to resolve the conflict through the democratic process has been protracted and uncertain. On its part, Guinea-Conakry is facing a rather difficult democratic transition whose outcome is also uncertain.

As for Nigeria, West Africa's most influential state, it has itself been slipping in and out of one crisis to another, the most notable perhaps being the conflict in the oil-rich Niger Delta region. This conflict has only just abated, thanks largely to a shaky presidential amnesty to insurgents and promises to address deep-seated grievances of people in the troubled region. Following yet another military putsch in Niger, the new military leaders are coming under intense international pressure to organize early elections and return the country to civilian democratic rule.

The West African political, economic, and strategic environment, therefore, presents both a challenge and an opportunity for regional integration. Being poor, economically and politically weak and crisis-prone, conventional wisdom would suggest that countries in the sub region would actively pursue integration, both as a way to enhance development but also as a means to addressing such regional challenges as poverty and conflict prevention and resolution. So far, progress at integrating the region has been slow and uncertain.

The reasons for this slow progress are not far-fetched. Unlike European integration which was constructed at the end of the Second World War, West Africa's integration is taking place in the midst of considerable regional upheavals and intra-state conflicts. ECOWAS response to the crisis of political succession currently unravelling in Cote d' Ivoire, a Member State, best illustrates the dilemma of regional integration in West Africa.

In the aftermath of the election dispute in Cote d' Ivoire, ECOWAS had threatened and cooperated with extra regional powers in deploying force to install Allasane Quattara, the widely acclaimed winner of the disputed presidential election. This kind of disposition, as well meaning as it is, is troubling because it reflects a failure of diplomacy. It is also instructive to note that, before the political crisis in Cote d'Ivoire, ECOWAS had successfully intervened militarily in Liberia and Sierra Leone to impose civil order and restore constitutional authority to power. When has force become a useful tool for regional integration? Again, unlike the European integration experience, there is no Marshall Plan of sorts to drive the regional integration project in West Africa. To be sure, China has been injecting substantial funds into West Africa lately, but these have been targeted at countries with proven natural resources deemed strategic to China's economic and developmental needs.

In addition to all these, there are also formidable structural, economic, institutional and political challenges hampering the integration process in West Africa. For example, the low levels of development and the limited possibilities for profitable intra-regional trade and exchange among ECOWAS Member States have not been particularly supportive of the integration process in West Africa. Most West African countries have suffered from severe macroeconomic disequilibria, foreign debt service burdens, over-valued currencies, lack of trade finance, and a narrow tax base. The protective import substitution strategies adopted by most countries since independence have resulted in a host of regulations restricting trade, such as licensing, administrative and foreign exchange allocation and sundry taxes. In general, therefore, the economic context has been unfavourable to the development of regional integration.

The ECOWAS integration scheme, built around inward-looking industrialization, means that the economic costs of participation for member states have been immediate and concrete (in the form of lower tariff revenues and greater import competition), while the economic benefits are long-term and uncertain. Often, these benefits are unevenly distributed among member states. The dominance of a few countries and the huge disparities in size among ECOWAS Member States has led to concerns about the distribution of benefits. Worse still, mechanisms to provide compensation to the less affluent members are poorly developed.

Furthermore, the dependence by ECOWAS Member States on their former colonial powers has tended to work against viable regional integration in West Africa. The enduring North-South Linkages, for example, Francophone and Anglophone links and the various Lome Conventions may have distracted commitment to the regional integration project. The poor state of regional infrastructure, notably transport and telecommunications, institutional weaknesses at national and regional levels, have all contributed to ECOWAS's shaky progress. The very nature of West Africa's weak states and strong opposition to the ceding or sharing of sovereignty with a supranational body has also undermined the integration process.

Politically, the parallel existence of the exclusive Francophone UEMOA has tended to undermine the integration process. The continued existence of UEMOA, even as ECOWAS is faltering, has led some critics from Anglophone West Africa to suggest that UEMOA is France's Trojan horse in ECOWAS, whose aim is to slow down the regional integration project. Until recently when France abandoned unilaterism in favour of a multi-lateral approach in its policy towards West Africa, its domineering and obtrusive postures in the region have been largely divisive and destabilizing to regional integration efforts.

It is impossible to exhaust the rather long list of obstacles militating against integration in West Africa. However, of all the negative factors, none has been more destabilizing, more impoverishing and more fatal to the integration process as conflict. As one of the world's poorest regions, the economic fortunes of West Africa have not been helped in any way by a succession of violent conflicts across the region since the end of the Cold War.

While the causal connections between security and development are difficult to establish, there is, at least at the general level, considerable evidence of a correlation between levels of insecurity and levels of development. For example, it is beyond dispute that the higher the level of development, the lower the likelihood of internal violent political conflict. The fact that developed countries have overwhelmingly been spared the ravages of war and violent conflict provides the most compelling empirical evidence that underdevelopment and insecurity interact in a negative mutually reinforcing cycle. Further evidence in this direction has been provided by the UNDP which, in its Human Development Report of 2002, indicated that since the early 1990s, 80 per cent of the world's poorest countries have suffered various degrees of violent conflict.[3]

Against this backdrop, the West African sub region, which is beset with a range of security and developmental challenges, has no option than to pursue the achievement of development and security complementarily. In other words, the overarching challenge for countries in the region is how to escape the conflict trap so that development and the creation of economic opportunities – the real business of ECOWAS – can commence in a sustainable fashion. What these countries need is to break the vicious cycle of conflict and poverty and promote a virtuous cycle of security and development.

The recognition of an intrinsic relationship between security and development does explain why, over the last three decades, ECOWAS has had to pay more attention to security issues, even as its core economic objectives remain largely unrealized. The dynamic evolution of ECOWAS from a regional vehicle for the economic transformation of West Africa to a regional security provider, therefore, represents a balancing of priorities and not a shift in priority. After all, the goals of security and development are complementary and mutually reinforcing. For countries in West Africa, the issue at stake is neither which of the two comes first, nor which is more important than the other. For these countries, the abiding lesson is that the one cannot be achieved at the expense of the other.

ECOWAS's balancing act is also consistent with the evolution of the concept of regionalism. In his conceptualization of the concept of 'new regionalism,' Bjorn Hettne, for example, has stressed the economic, political and security dimensions of regional integration, in which the political ambitions of creating territorial identity and regional coherence, political convergence and collective security are the primary goals driving a regional integration project.[4] The challenge for ECOWAS is to strike the right balance in its pursuit of security and development, not least because the difficulties in determining the causal connections between security and development can often lead to policy incoherence and misapplication of resources. Worse still, the goal of development – arguably ECOWAS's overarching priority – can easily be imperiled in the absence of security.

The central thesis of this study is that the gradual transformation of ECOWAS into a regional security provider is, in many ways, a reflection of the objective situation on the ground in West Africa in which poverty and insecurity sits side by side, feeding each other. As the five country Case Studies amply illustrate, conflicts in West Africa are the real "regional" challenge because:

(i)   They stem from causes that are common to all countries of the region;

(ii)   Their consequences extend well beyond their sources, creating regional externalities that affect neighbouring countries; and;

(iii)   Effective conflict prevention and resolution is beyond the capacity of any one state. The interdependence of security in West Africa, as the five Case Studies also

highlight, therefore, suggests a regional approach to security and conflict management.

Over all, the same logic driving West Africa's economic integration project, namely the comparative advantage from the pooling of resources in economic policy and management and also in the management of regional commons, such as infrastructures, transport and telecommunications, water resources and environmental challenges, is precisely the same reason for the adoption of a regional approach to conflict prevention and resolution in the region.

It may seem from the foregoing that the silver bullet that is needed to create a zone of peace in West Africa, so as to unlock the region's development potentials, involves merely striking the right balance between security and development. While we argue that both must be pursued in tandem, there are a range of factors that do mediate the interplay between security and development. In other words, there are key factors which, in their own right, can influence or determine security and development outcomes in any given region, including in West Africa.

One important way to reduce conflict risk, as we have argued elsewhere in this study, is to spur economic development, so as to reduce the incidence of poverty. The positive correlation between security and development obliges policy makers in the West Africa not to treat conflict primarily as a security issue, but rather as an important development issue. While poverty in itself does not cause conflict, the real problem is that people caught in extreme poverty and socio-political marginalization are especially vulnerable to conflict risks. In other words, poverty can make people more likely to be abused and manipulated for dysfunctional purposes by those who stand to profit from exploiting the poor's lack of opportunity choices, as is evident in the case of child soldiers in much of the recent intrastate wars in West Africa.

Similarly, poor countries are also more likely to become battlefields of proxy wars, mainly related to geopolitical contest among the great powers. While the end of the Cold War substantially diminished the spectre of proxy wars in West Africa, the outlines of a future conflict are already being drawn in the competition among the great powers over access to and control of the region's vast mineral riches. While this competition is still largely tactical rather than conflictual, this may not necessarily remain so in the future. Given the intensity of the competition over resources that are finite, there is sufficient reason to fear the so-called 'resource wars' may yet implode with far reaching consequences on the poor and fragile states of the sub region.

As crucial as economic growth and poverty reduction are in the security – development nexus, these may neither be sufficient to create a zone of peace nor guarantee sustainable development in West Africa. As Nicholas Sambanis has argued elsewhere in this study, economic development on its own may be insufficient to reduce the incidence of civil conflict in poor countries. Among the conflict-risk factors we have identified in this study is governance. We return to governance in this concluding section because, as the UNDP has argued, "governance matters for development."[5] Governance matters for development because institutions, rules and political processes play a big role in whether economies grow, whether children go to school, whether public goods are provided, including whether society enjoys peace or struggle through conflict.

Across West Africa, for example, the governance crisis is evident in widespread corruption, collapsing public infrastructures, political and economic exclusion, one party rule, life presidencies and secessionist threats. Several studies have pointed to Africa's stifling and closed political space, sectional and patrimonial politics as being largely responsible for much of the political violence and instability that have ravaged the West African sub region in the last two decades. As our five country Case Studies demonstrate, much of the crises in these countries are the direct results of years of political and economic marginalization of sections of the population. In other words, the privatization and criminalization of politics – in short, poor governance – is increasingly being held responsible for much of West Africa's crisis of insecurity and underdevelopment.

Given the African experience, it is self-evident that good governance furnishes a potent antidote to the patrimonialism and clientelism that infect politics and drive conflict across West Africa. This is so because good governance is an issue of democracy, accountability, rule of law, transparency and inclusivity. Good governance is also an economic issue because citizens are keen to see national resources allocated wisely and efficiently utilized for the common good. Thus, from the perspective of economics, good governance provides the assurance that economic decisions would be driven by considerations of efficiency and public good, rather than the satisfaction of private interests.

In regions such as West Africa, where states are weak and poverty is endemic, good governance can help foster capable states, which are able to provide security and support efficient public institutions to deliver vital services to citizens. As the Brookings Institution study by Suzan Rice and Stewart Patrick reveal, countries that are more successful at political governance also tend to be better providers of social welfare, including ability to provide for the security of citizens. This particular study, which sought to examine the phenomenon of state weakness, underscored the crucial role of governance in generating security and development outcomes in specific contexts.

However, precisely because it is in the nature of human beings to want to participate and have a say in debates and decisions that affect their lives, good governance may not be sufficient to satisfy this fundamental human need. People everywhere cherish their freedom in the same way they desire governance systems that are participatory, efficient and effective. Democratic governance alone offers the possibility that people can enjoy their freedom, while also benefiting from a governance system that is efficient and accountable to ordinary citizens. As Amartya Sen has argued, enjoying political freedom and participating in the decisions that shape one's life are not only fundamental rights, but part of human development.

From the foregoing, we see that governance for human development is much more than having efficient institutions and rules that promote development. Governance must entail protecting human rights and promoting wider participation in the institutions and processes that shape people's lives. In other words, governance for human development is not only concerned with efficient, equitable and fair processes, but also about participation and inclusivity. Governance for development is about democratic governance. It is for this reason that democratic governance is increasingly being seen as constituting a key element in the security – development nexus.

ECOWAS regional approach to security has been expressed through copious instruments, protocols and declarations of principles on a whole range of security and governance issues. These mechanisms and principles are intended to create a normative framework or rules of engagement for countries in West Africa. In relation to governance issues, the overall objective seems to be to promote political convergence around such issues as democracy, constitutionalism, rule of law and respect for human rights. A significant evidence of the gradual emergence of normative standards of political governance in West Africa relates to ECOWAS's zero tolerance approach to unconstitutional change of government in the region. In the past few years, any such attempt to supplant the constitutional order has attracted instant censure.

Furthermore, the revised treaty in Article 56 commits Member States of ECOWAS to the African Charter on Human and People's Rights and the Community Declaration of Political Principles. Article 56 of the revised treaty is significant because it represents an attempt to promote democracy and human rights as shared community values.

Given the extensiveness of ECOWAS security and governance mechanisms, including significant successes in the area of regional peacekeeping, could it then be said that the West African sub region is tending towards a security community? The evidence unfortunately, is no. Despite the acclaimed success of ECOWAS in the field of peace and security, it would appear rather premature to describe the West African sub region as a security community.

The West African sub region is still not a security community because, among others, wars and violent intrastate conflicts are still very much recurring features of the region's social and political landscape. As our five-country Case Studies illustrate, factions in some of the recent intrastate conflicts in West Africa had received substantial support from national governments in neighbouring countries. What this means is that the West African sub region is yet to delegitimize war as a means of resolving conflict, a key requirement identified by Karl Deutsch and his colleagues as a necessary condition for the building of a political or security community.

A 'security community,' as conceptualized by Deutsch, refers to a group of states among which war has become inconceivable, as the States share an understanding that force should not be used to resolve disputes among them. Empirically, Deutsch and his colleagues were analyzing developments in Western Europe after the Second World War, but their analysis of the building of economic and political communities point to the formidable challenges facing similar projects in a developing area as West Africa. In reality, it is not the absence of conflicts, but the ability and disposition to resolve them peacefully that is crucial to the success of security community building.

According to the mainstream approaches to regional integration, integration starts from economic and cultural cooperation and proceeds to political and security sectors only at the last stage, after there is confidence as well as shared values and material interests among the states creating a security community. While a plausible argument could be made that conditions in West Africa are different from those in Europe, West Africa is still grappling with various forms of conflicts, some existential while others are profoundly destabilizing. Given the regional dimensions of recent conflicts across West Africa, regional integration does have the potential to act as a peace promoter in the region, as it did for Western Europe after the end of the Second World War.

This is, however, where the comparison ends. In West Africa, a lack of political and social convergence, as epitomized in the several ethno-religious conflicts in the region, is clearly anathema to regionalism, whether in economic or security sectors. For instance, as our Case Studies illustrate, Nigeria has been particularly notorious for the periodic eruptions of deadly ethno-religious conflicts, whose consequences have been to polarize, rather than forge a common sense of nationhood. The civil war that has all but carved up Cote d'Ivoire along ethnic lines proves the fickleness of the state in West Africa. Before the debacle in Cote d'Ivoire, there were the cases of Liberia and Sierra Leone, both of which were triggered by ethno-sectarian antagonisms.

It is obvious that, at the very least, minimal security and stability are crucial as building blocks for regional cooperation in the construction of a security community. Domestic stability is critical because domestic violence can often generate tension among states in a geographical region largely because of spillover effects across national borders. As we have seen in our Country Case Studies, conflicts in West Africa easily generate regional externalities in the form of refugees, arms trafficking, mercenaries, and safe havens for rebel movements. All of these could stoke tension and mutual distrust among countries and imperil regional cooperation.

Now, because states are the building blocks of security communities, if the states themselves are unstable, it makes little sense to describe a group of such states as building or tending towards a security community. In any event, a viable security community requires, at the minimum, that states surrender or, at the least, delegate a part of their sovereignty to regional-level institutions. In practice such transfer of sovereignty can occur only if there is recognized sovereignty or political legitimacy at the national level in the first place. However, in much of the poor and weak states of West Africa, sovereignty is a hotly contested issue, as exemplified in ethnic conflicts and sundry insurgencies across the region. As our five country Case Study highlight, poor governance remains at the root of much of the conflicts in West Africa. The fact that governments of sovereign states in a conflict-prone region as West Africa might themselves be part of security problems within their territories therefore pose an obvious challenge for regional security integration.

At the regional level, countries of West Africa are too poor, too weak and too much divided among themselves to be able to construct a viable security community. Collectively, these countries lack the capacity to build and sustain common and capable cooperative frameworks, whether in economic (developmental) or in security matters, perhaps even more so in security matters. These countries are too dependent on outside powers as to be able to shape a distinct regional security agenda, including the capacity to deliver cooperative security outcomes.

West Africa's strategic relationship with the EU is symptomatic of this unequal and dependent security and economic relationship. Take the issue of security as an example. Many of the security challenges and strategic ambitions expressed in the European Security Strategy (ESS) – the framework governing EU-ECOWAS strategic relations – reflect European priorities, while marginalizing core security concerns of people of West Africa. For instance, the emphasis in the ESS on moral, political and governance issues, such as gender equality, good governance, terrorism, respect for human rights and migration reflect European security perspectives and provide proof that local priorities do not drive this unequal relationship.

The consolation for ECOWAS is that the emergence of a security community is not a necessary condition for a regional organization to play a role in the field of security. The United Nations has already given regional organizations such as ECOWAS the mandate to pursue peace, security and development, including the prevention or mitigation of conflict. According to Chapter VIII of the UN Charter: "nothing precludes the existence of regional arrangements or agencies for dealing with such matters relating to the maintenance of international peace and security as are appropriate for regional action, provided that such arrangements or agencies and their activities are consistent with the purposes and principles of the United Nations."[7]

Regional organizations are supposed to have an immediate interest in promoting peace and security since interstate and intrastate wars normally affect the region through spill over and destabilization, as have evidently been the case in West Africa's recent tragic history.

Regional security initiatives in West Africa are therefore a direct response to the regionalization of conflicts in the region. While security community points to a desirable goal within the context of the dynamic evolution of regionalism in West Africa, ECOWAS can get some satisfaction that it is at least making strong effort to promote security and development in the region. Its impressive compendium of normative security and governance frameworks may not, in themselves, be sufficient for the building of a West African security community, but these mechanisms may well provide the building blocks for more viable security architecture for the sub region.

Given the scope and complexity of the challenge confronting ECOWAS, what alternative futures are possible for the organization? In short, against the backdrop of the formidable structural, institutional and political factors slowing down the regional integration process, what might ECOWAS do to reinvent itself into an effective vehicle for the realization of its principal Charter goal, namely, the socio-economic transformation of West Africa and the achievement of a high living standard for community citizens? We make the case here that a compelling and urgent choice lies in developing a transparent, inclusive and accountable governance system that will ensure peace and security, and create and fertilize an environment for sustainable development and nation-building in individual countries.

The national context within which the regionalist process is taking place in West Africa presents a major challenge because most countries of the sub region are deeply divided, both as a result of flawed colonial policies and the persistence of patrimonial politics at the national level. The governance deficit and the social divisions it engenders also reproduce themselves at the regional level, where the political and cultural cleavages – legacies of colonial rule – necessarily create considerable mistrust among political elites who drive the regional integration project. This is why the challenge of national integration may be as important as the regional integration project itself. Indeed, as the EU success story does illustrate, viable, strong and modern states anchored on democratic principles are crucial to the success of security and developmental regionalism.

As Aboubakar Diaby-Quattara, ECOWAS pioneer Executive Secretary has argued, "the delicate problem confronting West Africa is how to create an integrated region from states, some of which have attained advanced levels of national disintegration, and have indeed ceased to exist as states."[8] This depressing assessment calls to question how countries of West Africa could integrate and create a zone of peace and prosperity when these same countries have yet to find the means to achieve social, cultural and political integration within their national territories?. Perhaps we should let Diaby-Quattara have the last words on this. According to him, "successful regional integration requires a zone where social calm and prosperity reign within the individual states, and peace among the states."[9] The evidence on the ground in West Africa suggest otherwise.

There are no easy answers, but a viable step could be

the construction of developmental states to replace the predatory, oppressive and dysfunctional states of West Africa, all of which have spectacularly failed to deliver security and development to their citizens. The developmental state which we propose would be one that is essentially democratic in orientation and conduct. It would be a state whose overarching priority would be the task of development underpinned by social equity in a stable and secure environment. Such a state will promote human security, facilitate the rapid process of capital accumulation and industrialization, while not compromising the goal of social welfare for the people. Regionalism may be deployed as a vehicle for this development process, but regionalism can play a facilitating role only when the states of West Africa are themselves fully integrated, cohesive, democratic, and equitably administered. As products of careful and deliberate process of social and political engineering, these states would be well placed to turn West Africa's cycle of poverty and conflict into a virtuous cycle of security and development.

Notes

1.   ECOWAS, "Regional Integration for Growth and Poverty Reduction in West Africa: Strategies and Plan of Action," ECOWAS and WAEMU, Abuja and Ouagadougou, December 2006, p.31.
2.   Ibid.
3.   United Nations, United Nations Development Programme, Human Development Report 2002: Deepening Democracy in a Fragmented World, Oxford University Press, Oxford, 2002.
4.   Bjorn Hettne, "Introduction," in Bjorn Hettne, and Inotai Andres, eds., The New Regionalism: Implications for Global Development and International Security, 1994.
5.   See UNDP, Human Development Report 2002, p.51.
6.   European Parliament, Directorate General for External Policies, "Options for the EU to Support the African Peace and Security Architecture," available online at:
http://www.chathamhouse.org.uk/files/11637_0508eu_africa.pdf
7.   United Nations, United Nations Charter, Chapter VIII, Article 52.1
8.   Aboubakar Diaby-Quattara, ECOWAS at Twenty, Regional Integration in West Africa: Proceedings of the Conference and Workshops commemorating ECOWAS's 20th Anniversary, Dakar, 29- 31 May 19995, p.34.
9.   Ibid.

BIBLIOGRAPHY

Abdullah, Ibrahim, and Ismail Rashid, "Rebel Movements", in Adekeye Adebajo, and Ismail Rashid, eds; West Africa's Security Challenges: Building Peace in a Troubled Region, Lynne Rienner, Boulder, 2004.

Adebajo, Adekeye, Building Peace in West Africa: Liberia, Sierra Leone, and Guinea-Bissau, Lynne Reinner, Boulder, 2002.

-        "Introduction," in Adekeye Adebajo, and Ismail Rashid, eds; West Africa's Security Challenges: Building Peace in a Troubled Region, Lynne Reinner, Boulder and London, 2004.

-        "Pax West Africana, Regional Security Mechanisms," in Adekeye Adebajo, and Ismail Rashid, eds; West Africa's Security Challenges: Building Peace in a Troubled Region, Lynne Reinner, Boulder and London, 2004.

Adedeji, Adebajo, "Economic Community of West African States: Ideals and Realities", Public Lecture Delivered at the Nigerian Institute of International Affairs, Lagos, Nigeria, 30 April, 1975.

-        "ECOWAS: A Retrospect Journey", in Adekeye Adebajo, and Ismail Rashid, eds; West Africa's Security Challenges: Building Peace in a Troubled Region, Lynne Reinner, Boulder and London, 2004.

-        "Problems and Prospects of Regional Cooperation in West Africa", in African Association for Public Administration and Management: Problems and Prospects of Regional Cooperation in African, English Press, Nairobi, Kenya, 1969.

Adedeji, Olu, "Mechanism for Conflict Management in West Africa: Politics of Harmonization", Paper delivered at the AFSTRAG Workshop on Conflict Management Mechanism in West Africa, Abuja, 21 – 23 May, 1997.

African Union, Constitutive Act of the African Union, Addis Ababa, July 2002.

-        Doc.AHG/Decl.5 (XXXVI), July 2000.
-        Non-Aggression and Common African Defence and Security Policy, Addis Ababa, Ethiopia, July 2004.

Agence France-Presse, November 28, 2002.

Ake, Claude, Democracy and Development, The Brookings Institution, Washington, D.C, 1996.

Annan, Kofi, In Larger Freedom: Towards Development, Security and Human Rights for All, Report of the Secretary-General of the United Nations, New York, September 2005.

Anyaso, Claudia, "Africom is Historic Step in U.S. – Africa Relationship", Address at U.S. Army Conference in Arlington, Virginia, U.S.A., 21 April, 2008, available online at America.gov/.../20080423140127wcyero, last accessed on 5 August, 2010.

Asante, S,K,B, Regionalism and Africa's Development, Macmillan Press, London, 1977.

-       " The Travails of Integration," in Adekeye Adebajo, and Ismail Rashid, eds; West African's Security Challenges: Building Peace in a Troubled Region, Lynne Rienner, Boulder and London, 2004.

Ate, Bassey, E, "The Presence of France as a Fundamental Problem for Nigeria", in Bassey E. Ate, and Bola Akinterinwa, eds; Nigeria and its immediate Neighbours: Constraints and Prospects of Sub-regional Security in the 1990s, NIIA, Lagos, Nigeria 1992.

Auty, Richard, Sustaining Development in Mineral Economies: The Resource Curse Thesis, Routledge, London, 1993.

Bach, Daniel, "Nigeria's Manifest Destiny in West Africa: Dominance without Power", Afrika, Spectrum, Hamburg, No.2, 2007.

-       "The Dilemmas of Regionalism" in Adekeye Adebajo, and Ismail Rashid, eds; West Africa's Security Challenges: Building Peace in a Troubled Region, Lynne Rienner, Boulder and London, 2004.

-"The Politics of West Africa Economic Cooperation: CEAO and ECOWAS", Journal of Modern African Studies, Vol.21, No.4, 1983.

Balassa, Bela, The Theory of Economic Integration, George Allen and Unwin, London, 1973.

Berschinski, Robert, G., "Africa's Dilemma: The Global War on Terrorism, Capacity Building, Humanitarianism and the Future of U.S. Security Policy in Africa", Strategic Studies Institute, U.S. Army War College, Carlisle, PA, available online at http://www.strategicStudesInstitute.army.mill, last accessed on 8 July, 2010.

Booth, Ken, "Introduction", in Ken Booth, ed.; New Thinking About Strategic and International Security, Harper, London, 1991.

Boley, G.E, Saigbe, Liberia: The Rise and Fall of the First Republic, St. Martin Press, New York, 1983.

Bryden, Allen, Boubacar N'Diaye, and Funmi Olonisakin, "Understanding the Challenges of Security Sector Governance in West Africa", in Allen Bryden, and Heiner Hanggi, eds; Security Governance in Post-Conflict Peace Building, Lit, VERLAG Munster, 2005.

Buur, Lars, Jensen, Steffen, and Stepputat Finn, eds; The Security Development Nexus, Expressions of Sovereignty and Securitization in Southern Africa, HSRC Press, Cape Town, South Africa, 2007.

Buzan, Barry, People, States and Fear, Lynne Rienner, Boulder, 1991.

Buzan, Barry, Ole Weaver, and Jaap De Wilde, Security: A New Framework for Analysis, Lynne Reinner, Boulder, 1988.

Chambas, Mohammed, Ibn, "Forward", in Adekeye Adebajo, and Ismail Rashid, eds; West Africa's Security Challenges: Building Peace in a Troubled Region, Lynne Rienner, Boulder and London, 2004.

Cilliers Jackie, "Human Security in Africa: A Conceptual Framework for Review", Monograph for the African human Security Initiative, available online at www.Africanreview.org, last accessed on 24 October 2010.

Chi-Bonnardee, Regine, The Atlas of Africa, The Free Press, New York, 1973.

Clapham, Christopher, Third World Politics: An Introduction, University of Wisconsin, Madison, 1985.

Collier, Paul, ed.; Breaking the Conflict Trap: Civil War and Development Policy, World Bank and Oxford University Press, Washington D.C., and Oxford, 2003.

Collier, Paul, "Doing Well out of War: An Economic Perspective", in Mats Berdal and David M. Mallone, eds; Greed and Grievance, Economic Agendas in Civil Wars, Lynne Rienner, Boulder, 2000.

Commission on Global Governance, Global Neighbourhood, A Report of the Commission on Global Governance, Oxford University Press, 1995.

Commission on Human Security, Human Security Now, New York, 2003.

Council on Foreign Relations, More than Humanitarianism: A Strategic U.S. Approach towards Africa, An Independent Task Force Report, No.56, Washington D.C., 2006.

Deutsch, Karl, et al, Political Community and the North Atlantic Area, Princeton University Press, Princeton, 1957.

Diaby-Quattara, Aboubakar, ECOWAS at Twenty, Regional Integration in West Africa: Proceedings of the Conference and Workshops Commemorating ECOWAS's 20th Anniversary, Dakar, 29-30 May 1995.

ECON Analysis, As, "Geopolitics, Energy Security and West Africa", ECON Report No.2004-063, Oslo, Norway, September 2004.

Economic Community of West African States, Annual Report 2001, ECOWAS Executive Secretariat, Abuja, Nigeria, 2001.

-       Conflict Prevention Framework, Regulation MSC/REG.1/01/08, ECOWAS Commission, Abuja, 2008.

-       Convention on Small Arms and Light Weapons, Their Ammunition and Other Related Materials, ECOWAS Executive Secretariat, Abuja, 2006

-       Declaration A/DCL.1/7/91 on Political Principles of the Economic Community of West African States, ECOWAS Executive Secretariat, Abuja, 6 July, 1991.

-       Protocol A/SPI/12/01 on Democracy and Good Governance Supplementary to the Protocol Relating to the Mechanism for Conflict Prevention, Management, Resolution, Peacekeeping and Security, ECOWAS Executive Secretariat, Abuja, December 2001.

-       Protocol Relating to the Mechanism for Conflict Prevention, Management, Resolution, Peacekeeping and Security, ECOWAS Executive Secretariat, Lome, Togo, 10 December, 1999.

-       Treaty of the Economic Community of West African States, ECOWAS Executive Secretariat, Lagos, Nigeria, July 1975.

-       Revised Treaty of ECOWAS, ECOWAS Executive Secretariat, Abuja, Nigeria, July 1993.

ECOWAS and WAEMU Commission, "Regional Integration for Growth and Poverty Reduction in West Africa, A Regional Strategic", Paper prepared by the WAEMA Commission and the ECOWAS Executive Secretariat, Abuja and Ouagadougou, December, 2006.

Ekeh, Peter, "Colonialism and the Two Publics in Africa", Comparative Studies in Society and History, Vol. 17, No.1, 1975.

Ero, Comfort, and Jonathan Temin, "Sources of Conflict in West Africa", in Chamdra Lekha Srinam, and Zoe Nielsen, eds; Exploring Sub-regional Conflict: Opportunities for Conflict Prevention, Lynne Rienner, Boulder, 2002.

Etzioni, Amitai, Political Unification: A comparative Study of Leaders and Forces, Oxford University Press, New York, 1964.

European Parliament, Directorate- General for External Policies, "Options for the EU to support the African Peace and Security Architecture", available online at http://www.chathamhouse.org.uk/files/11637_0508eu_af rica.pdf.

European Union Commission,The Single Market Review: Impact on Competition, Kogan Page, London, 1997.

Federal Republic of Nigeria, Report of the Presidential Transition Committee (Unpublished), Lagos, Nigeria, September 1983.

Fisher – Thompson, Jim, "China No Threat to the United States, U.S. Official says", U.S State Department Information Services, 28 July, 2005, available online at http:/usinfo.state.gov/eap/Archive/2005/July/29-550683.html, accessed 4 August, 2010.

Francis, David, J., "Linking Peace, Security and Developmental Regionalism: Regional Economic and Economic and Security Integration in Africa", Journal of Peace-Building and Development, Vol.2, No.3 2006.

Frank, Gunder, Andre, "Capitalism and Underdevelopment in Latin America: Historical Studies of Chile and Brazil", Monthly Press Review, New York, 1969.

Gambari, Ibrahim, A, Political and Comparative Dimensions of Regional Integration: The Case of ECOWAS, Humanities Press International, Inc, New Jersey, 1991.

Haas, Ernest, B, The Uniting of Europe: Political, Social and Economic Forces, Stanford University Press, 1958.

Hampson, Fen, Osler et al, Madness in the Multitude: Human Security and World Disorder, Oxford University Press, Oxford, 2003.

Hanggi, Heiner, "Approaching Peacebuilding from a Security Governance Perspective", in Allen Bryden, and Heiner Hanggi, eds; Security Governance in Post-Conflict Peace building, Lit VERLAG, Munster, 2005.

Hansen, Andrew, "The French Military in Africa", Council on Foreign Relations, available online at Cfr.org/French_military_in_africa.html, accessed on 2 August, 2010.

Hazelwood, Arthur, D, "Economic Integration: Lessons for African recovery and Development," in O. Teriba and P. Bugembe, eds; The Challenges of African Recovery and Development, Frank Cass, London, 1009.

Hegre, Harvard, et al, "Towards a Democratic Civil Peace? Democracy, Political Change, and Civil War, 1816 – 1992", American Political Science Review, Vol.95, No.1, 2001.

Hettne, Bjorn, and Inotai Andres, eds; The New Regionalism: Implications for Global Development, United Nations University/WIDER, Helsinki, 1994.

-       "Development, Security and World Order: A Regional Approach", in Sheila Page, ed, Regions and Development: Politics, Security and Economics, Frank Cass, London, 2000.

-       "The New Regionalism: A Prologue", in Bjorn Hettne, Andreas Inotai, and Osvaldo Sunkel, eds, National Perspectives on the New Regionalism in the North, Macmillan Press, Bassingstoke, 2000.

Herbst, Jeffrey, "War and the State in Africa", International Security, Vol. 14, No.4, Spring 1990.

Huntington, Samuel, P, The Clash of Civilization and the Remaking of World Order, Simon and Schuster, New York and London, 2002.

Hutchful, Eboe, and Kwesi Anning, "The Political Economy of Conflict", in Adekeye Adebajo, and Ismail Rashid, eds; West Africa's Security Challenges: Building Peace in a Troubled Region, Lynne Reinner, Boulder and London, 2004.

Ibrahim, Jibrin, "Toward a Nigerian Perspective on the French Problematic", in Bassey E. Ate, and Bola Akinterinwa, eds; Nigeria and its Immediate Neighbours, NIIA, Lagos, 1992.

Independent Commission on International Development Issues, North – South: A Programme for Survival, Pam Books, London, 1999.

Iroegbu, Senator, "ECOWAS Suspends Guinea, Niger", THISDAY ONLINE, 6 January, 2010.

International Crisis Group, "Liberia: Security Challenges", Africa Report, No.71, 3 November, 2003.

Jackson, Linda, "China's Diplomacy towards Africa: Drivers and Constraints", International Relations of the Asia – Pacific, Vol.9, 2009.

Jeune Afrique, 25 – 31 January, 1996.

Jonah, James, O,C, "The United Nations", in Adekeye Adebajo, and Ismail Rashid, eds; West Africa's Security Challenges: Building Peace in a Troubled Region, Lynne Rienner, Boulder and London, 2004.

Jonanovic, Miroslav, N., The Economics of International Integration, Edward Elgar Publishers, Cheltenham, UK, 2006.

Joseph, Richard, Democracy and Prebendal Politics in Nigeria, The Rise and Fall of the Second Republic, Cambridge University Press, Cambridge, 1987.

Kaplan, Robert, D., "The Coming Anarchy", Atlantic Monthly, Vol., 27, No.2, February 1992.

- "The Coming Anarchy: How Scarcity, Crime, Overpopulation, Tribalism, and Disease Are Rapidly Destroying the Social Fabric of our Planet", Atlantic Monthly, Vol.273, February 1994.

Karl, Terry, L, The Paradox of Plenty: Oil Boom and Petro States, University of California Press, Berkeley, 1997.

Kay, Sean, Global Security in the Twenty-First Century: The Quest for Power and the Search for Peace, Rowman and Littlefield Publishers Inc., New York, 2006.

Keen, David, "The Economic Functions of Violence in Civil Wars", Adelphi Paper, No. 320, Oxford University Press, Oxford, 1996.

Keili, Francis Langumba, "Small arms and light weapons transfer in West Africa," in Disarmament Forum, United Nations Institute for Disarmament Research, Geneva, No.4, 2008.

Klare, Michael, T, Resource Wars: The New Landscape of Global Conflict, Metropolitan/ Owl Books, London, 2001.

Krahamann, E, "Conceptualizing Security Governance", Cooperation and Conflict, Vol.38, Vol.1, 2003.

Krause, Keith, Towards a Practical Agenda of Human Security, Geneva Centre for the Democratic Control of Armed Forces (DCAP) Policy Paper, No. 26, DCAF, Geneva, 2007.

Kretzman, Steve, Oil, Security, War: The geopolitics of U.S. energy planning", Multinational Monitor, January/February, 2003.

Laakso, Liisa, "Beyond the Notion of Security Community: What Role for the African Regional Organization in Peace and Security?" United Nations University/WIDER Research Paper No.2005/52, August 2005.

Lesourne, Jacques, Governance of oil in Africa: Unfinished Business, IFRI, Paris and Brussels, 2009.

Levy, Jack, S, "Domestic Politics and War", Journal of Interdisciplinary History, No.18, 1998.

Lewis, Peter, M, "The Dysfunctional State of Nigeria", available online at http://216.109.125.130/Search/Cache?ei=UTF-8&P=development+%2 Challenges %...accessed on 21 August, 2010.

Lewis, John, P, "Overview: Development Promotion, A time for Re-grouping", In John P. Lewis, and V. Kallab, eds; Development Strategies Reconsidered, Transaction Books, Oxford, 1986.

Meagyer, Karl, and Earl Conteh-Morgan, Peacekeeping in Africa: ECOMOG in Liberia, McMillan and St. Martin Press, London and New York, 1998.

McNamara Robert, "Security in the Contemporary World," Address to the American Society of Newspaper Editors, Montreal, Canada, 18 May, 1966, available online at http://www.oldcolo.com/McNamara/mcnamara, text, last accessed 15 April, 2010.

Meagher, Kate, "New Regionalism or Loose Canon? Nigeria's role in informal economic networks and integration in West Africa," in Adekeye Adebajo , and Abdul Raufu Mustapha, eds; Gulliver's Troubles, Nigeria's Foreign Policy after the Cold War, UKZN Press, Scottsville, South Africa, 2008.

Medard, Jean-Francis, "Crisis, Change and Continuity ," in Adekeye Adebajo , and Abdul Raufu Mustapha, eds; Gulliver's Troubles, Nigeria's Foreign Policy after the Cold War, UKZN Press, Scottsville, South Africa, 2008.

Menkhaus, Ken, "Vicious Cycles and the Security – Development Nexus in Somalia, Conflict, Security and Development, Vol.2, No.4, August 2004.

Mitrany, David, A Working Peace System, Quadrangle Books, Chicago, 1966.

Morten Boas, and Helge Hveem, "Regionalism Compared: The African and Southeast Asian Experience", in Bjorn Hettne, Andras Inotai, and Osvaldo Sunkel, eds, Comparing Regionalism: Implications for Global Development, Macmillan Press, London, 2001.

Musah, Abdul-Fatau, "West Africa: Governance and Security in a changing Region", Africa Programme Working Paper Series, International Peace Institute, February 2009.

Nafzinger, Wayne, E, Economic Development, Cambridge University Press, Cambridge, 2006.

Nivet, Bastien, "Security by Proxy? The EU and (Sub) regional organization: The Case of ECOWAS", An ISS Occasional Paper, No. 63, March 2006.

Norwegian Institute of International Affairs, Norwegian Institute on Small Arms transfer, and United Nations Regional Centre for Peace and Disarmament in Africa, "The Making of a Moratorium on Light Weapons", Oslo and Lome, 2000.

Nye, Joseph, S, "Comparing Common Markets, A Revised Neo-Functionalist Model," International Organization, Vol. 24, No.4, Autumn 1970.

Okolo, Julius, Emeka, ECOWAS Regional Cooperation Regime", in German Yearbook of International Law, Vol.32, 1989.

Olayode, Kehinde, "Reinventing the African State: Issues and Challenges for Building a Developmental State", Paper presented at the 11th General Assembly of the Council for the Development of Social Science in Africa, Maputo, Mozambique, 6 – 19 December, 2005.

Oloyede, Iyabo, et al, "Nigeria: Oil Pollution, Community Dissatisfaction, and Threats to National Peace and Security", Occasional Papers Series, African Association of Political Science, Harare, Vol.4, No.3, 2000.

Olonisakin, Funmi, "Pan-African Approaches to Civilian Control and Democratic Governance", in Victor-Yves Ghebali, and Alexandre Lambert, eds; Democratic Governance of the Security Sector Beyond the OSCE Area: Regional Approaches in Africa and the Americas , LIT VERLAG GMBH & Co. Zurich and Berlin, 2007.

Omeje, Kenneth, ed., Extractive Economies and Conflicts in the Global South: Multi-Regional Perspective on Rentier Politics, Ashgate, Aldershot, UK, 2008.

Organization of African Unity, Declaration of the Assembly of Heads of State and Government of the OAU on the Political and Socio-economic Situation in Africa and Fundamental Changes taking place in the World, Addis Ababa, Ethiopia, July 2002.

Paris, Roland, "Human Security: Paradigms Shift or Hot Air", International Security, Vol.26, No.2, 2001.

Pinder, J, "Problems of European Integration", in G. Denton, ed., Economic Integration in Europe, Weidenfeld and Nicolson, London, 1969.

Power, Marcus, and Giles Mohan, "The geopolitics of China's engagement with African Development", Paper presented at the POLIS and BISA Supported Workshop on New Directions in International Relations and Africa, the Open University, 9 July, 2008.

Ravenhill, J, "The Future of regionalism in Africa", in R. I. Onwuka, and I.A. Sesay, eds, TheFuture of Regionalism in Africa, Macmillan Press, London, 1985.

Renninger, John, Towards Collective Self Regional: The Quest for Unity in West Africa, UNITAR, New York, 1977.

Reno, Williams, "War, Markets, and the Reconfiguration of West Africa's Weak States", Comparative Politics, Vol.29, No.4, July 1977.

-       Warlord politics and African States, Lynne Reinner, Boulder, 1999.

Richards, Paul, "Witches, Cannibals, and War in Liberia," Journal of African History, Vol. 42, January 2001.

Rice, Susan, and Stewart Patrick, "The Index of State Weakness in the Developing World", The Brookings Institution, Washington, D.C., 2008.

Rogue, Silvia, "Peacebuilding in Guinea-Bissau: A Critical Approach", Centre for Social Studies, University of Columbia, May 2009.

Rosenau, J, N, "Governance in a Globalizing World", in Held, D, and A. McGrew, eds; The Global Transformation Reader, Cambridge, 2000.

Ross, Michael, L, "The Political Economy of the Resource Curse", World Politics, No.51, No.2, 1999.

Rostow, W, W, The Stages of Growth: A non-communist Manifesto, Cambridge University Press, London, 1960.

Sarkozy, Nicholas, "Address to South African Parliament", Cape Town, South Africa, 28 February, 2008, available online at http://www.ambafrance-uk.org\President-Sarkozy-S-Speech-to-the-litmil, accessed 30 August, 2010.

Sasay, Amadu, "Can ECOWAS re-invent the Nationalist Dream?" in W. Alade Fawole, and Charles Ukeje, eds; The Crisis of the State and Regionalism in West Africa, CODESRIA, Dakar, Senegal, 2005.

Sawyer, Amos, "Governance and Democratization", in Adekeye Adebajo, and Ismail Rashid, eds; West African's Security Challenges: Building Peace in a Troubled Region, Lynne Rienner, Boulder, and London, 2004.

-        "Effective Immediately: Dictatorship in Liberia, 1980 – 1986, A Personal Perspective", Liberian Working Group, Bremen, Germany, 1987.

-        "Violent Conflicts and Governance Challenges in West Africa: The Case of the River Basin Area", Paper presented at Workshop in Political Theory and Policy Analysis, Indiana State University, 2003.

Sen, Amartyna, Development As Freedom, Anchor Books, London, 1999.

Shagari, Shehu, My Vision of Nigeria, Frank Cass, London, and Toronto, 1981.

Sheehan, Michael, International Security: An Analytical Survey, Lynne Rienner, Boulder, 1988.

Snow, Philip, "China and Africa: Consensus and Camouflage", Thomas W Robinson, and David Shamgaugh, eds; Chinese Foreign Policy, Theory and Practice, Clarendon Press, Oxford, 1994.

Soberbaum, Fredrick, "The Role of the Regional Factor in West Africa", in Bjorn Hettne, and AndrasInotai, eds; The New Regionalism and the Future of Security and Development,Vol.4 Macmillan Press in association with UNUWIDER, 2000.

Solana, Javier, A Secure Europe in a Better World: European Security Strategy, European Commission, Brussels, December 2003.

Srinam, Chandra, Lekha, and Zoe Nielsen, "Introduction: Why Examine Sub-regional Sources and Dynamics of Conflicts", in Chandra Lekha, and Zoe Nelson, eds; Exploring Sub-regional Conflict, Opportunities for Conflict Prevention, Lynne Rienner, Boulder, 2002.

Srinivasan, Sharath, "A Rising 'Great Power' embraces Africa", in Adekeye Adebajo, and Abdul Raufu Mustapha, eds; Gulliver's Troubles: Nigeria's Foreign Policy after the Cold War, UKZN Press, Scottsville, South Africa, 2008.

Steward, Francis, "Development and Security", Conflict, Security and Development, Vol.4, No.3, December, 2004.

Stockwell, Edward, G, and K, A, Laidlaw, Third World Development, Problems and Prospects, Nelson-Hall, Chicago, 1981.

Stiglitz, Joseph, in Pedro-Pablo Kuczyuski, and John Williamson, eds, After the Washington Consensus, Restarting Growth in Latin America, IIE, Washington DC, 2003.

Taylor, Charles, "The West Wants to Suffocate Liberia", West Africa Magazine, No.4251, 6 – 12 November, 2000.

Theobold, Robin, "Patrimonialism", World Politics, Vol. 34, 1992.

Tschirgi, Necla, "The Security – Politics – Development Nexus: The Lessons of State Building in Sub-Saharan African", Paper prepared for the European Report for Development Workshop, Florence, Italy, 16 – 17 April, 2009.

Ukeje, Charles, "From Economic Cooperation to Collective Security: ECOWAS and the Changing Imperative of Sub-Regionalism in West Africa," in W. Alade Fawole, and Charles Ukeje, eds; The Crisis of the State and Regionalism in West Africa, CODESRIA, Dakar, Senegal, 2005.

United Nations, United Nations Human Development Report 2002, Deepening Democracy in a Fragmented World, Oxford University Press, Oxford and New York, 2002.

-        The Causes of Conflict and the Promotion of Durable Peace and Sustainable Development in Africa," Report of the Secretary-General, UNDOC.S/1998/318, 13 April, 1998.
-        General Assembly Resolution 60/1, 2005.

-        Human Development Report 1994, Oxford University Press, Oxford and New York, 1994.

-        Concept and Measurement of Human Development, Human Development Report, Oxford University Press, Oxford and New York, 1990.

-        Poverty reduction and good Governance, Report of the Committee for Development Policy on the Sixth Session, 29 March – 2 April, 2004, New York, 2004.

-      2005 World Summit Outcome Document, A/60/L.1 20 September, 2005, available online at http://www.un.org, accessed on 22 April, 2010.

-      Security Council Resolution 1625, 2005.

University of British Columbia, Human Security Centre, The Human Security Report 2005: War and Peace in the 21st Century, Oxford University Press, Oxford, 2005.

Viner, Jacob, The Customs Union Issue, Carnegie Endowment for International Peace, New York, 1950.

Whiteman, Kaye, and Douglas Yates, "France, Britain, and the United States", in Adekeye Adebajo, and Ismail Rashid, eds; West Africa's Security Challenges: Building Peace in a Troubled Region, Lynne, Rienner, Boulder and London, 2004.

Yongjian, Jin, "China's Economic Development: New Opportunities for the Sino-African Relations", Speech delivered at African Institute of South African Seminar, 17 May, 2005, available online at http://39.China-embassy.org\eng\znjc/+196028/litmil, last accessed on 4 July 2010.

Anglophone, **9, 33, 41, 63, 64, 74, 79, 80, 97, 107, 181, 183, 274, 382, 383**

Bakassi Boys, **290**

Bary Buzan, **116, 174**

Bela Belassa, **48**

Biafra, **74**

Bjorn Hettne, 15, 109, 386, 402, 414, 419, 424

Burkina Faso, **23, 43, 45, 73, 271, 286, 297, 305, 314, 316, 318, 327**

Cape Verde, **21, 41, 42, 43, 44, 103, 110**

CEAO, **12, 73, 74, 75, 76, 77, 78, 79, 80, 110, 112, 209, 407**

CFA, **12, 63, 90**

Chad, **45, 103, 189, 195, 207, 213, 278**

Chad Basin Authority, **103**

Charles de Gaulle, **187**

Charles Taylor, **133, 245, 284, 290, 297, 298, 299, 300, 301, 305, 316, 368**

China, **9, 97, 184, 220, 221, 222, 223, 224, 225, 226, 227, 228, 229, 230,** **231, 232, 233, 234, 235, 236, 254, 255, 260, 261, 380, 412, 415, 421, 423, 427**

Claude Ake, **161, 178**

Claudia Anyaso, **217, 259**

Cold War, **20, 112, 115, 149, 153, 154, 174, 188, 211, 221, 223, 225, 237, 251, 253, 256, 266, 281, 282, 283, 284, 285, 286, 288, 291, 348, 353, 354, 383, 389, 418, 424**

Colonialism

   colonial rule, 9, 411

Cote d'Ivoire, **14, 23, 42, 43, 66, 67, 73, 96, 189, 195, 196, 241, 244, 268, 283, 290, 297, 311, 313, 314, 316, 317, 318, 327, 348, 356, 378, 380, 395**

Daniel Patrick Moynihan, 154

David J. Francis, **16**

David Mitrany, 15, 38, 56

Delta, **153, 244, 246, 268, 275, 321, 322, 323, 378**

ECA, **12, 68**

ABOUT THE AUTHOR

Dr. Gbara Awanen has extensive experience in diplomacy, public policy, security and strategic risk assessment, following a long and illustrious career in Nigeria's Foreign Service. His last diplomatic posting was as Head of the Political Section of the Embassy of Nigeria, Washington DC, from 2014 to 2017. He had previously served at the High Commission of Nigeria, London, and the Permanent Mission of Nigeria to the United Nations Office at Geneva, Switzerland. Between 2003 and 2005, he was Speechwriter and Director of Strategic Communication to the First Lady of the Federal Republic of Nigeria.

Dr. Awanen earned his doctorate degree in International Relations from the Geneva School of Diplomacy and International Relations, Geneva, Switzerland, after graduating with the Bachelor of Arts degree in Mass Communication from the University of Nigeria, Nsukka. An alumnus of the National Institute of Policy and Strategic Studies (NIPSS), Nigeria's premier public policy think tank, the author also holds the Senior Managers in Government Certificate of the Harvard Kennedy School of Government, Harvard Kennedy School's premier Executive Programme in Public Leadership.